I0212426

DON CHERUBIN FALLS IN LOVE WITH DONNA BLANCA.

THE BACHELOR OF SALAMANCA

BY

ALAIN RENÉ LE SAGE

TRANSLATED BY

JAMES TOWNSEND

WILDSIDE PRESS

PRESS

CONTENTS.

PART THE FIRST.

V

CONTENTS.   vii

PART THE THIRD.

CHAPTER PAGE

XII. Of the journey which the three cavaliers made to the Castle of Villardesaz—They disguise themselves as pilgrims to get into the Castle—In what manner they were received—Singular conversation, with a domestic of Donna Francisca's—Surprise of the latter...... 152

XIII. Our three travellers sup with Donna Francisca and Donna Ismenia—Don Cherubin converses privately with his sister—She marries her first lover, Don Gregorio—Donna Ismenia also marries Don Manoel de Pedrilla—Don Cherubin and Don Manoel retire to the Castle of Clevillente, and set out with their wives for Alcaraz—Agreement which they made...... 158

XIV. Singular farce at which Don Cherubin was present—Serious reflection on his fortune, and on that of his sister—Don Manoel and he are robbed by one of their servants—They take another—Who he was—Surprise of Don Cherubin and his friend when they recognize him...... 162

XV. Tragical history of Don Carlos and Donna Sophia...... 166

PART THE FOURTH.

I. Don Cherubin de la Ronda, fifteen months after his marriage, becomes the most amorous of husbands—Don Gabriel carries off his wife—He pursues her ravisher in vain—He gives up the pursuit, and resolves to go to Mexico...... 170

II. Don Cherubin de la Ronda sails from Cadiz and arrives at Vera Cruz, where he hires mules to proceed by land to Mexico—Of the curious conversation which he had on the first day of his journey with his muleteer, and of the stories which Tobias relates—He conceives great expectations... 176

III. Of the meeting which Don Cherubin had with a friar of the Order of St. Francis, on entering the town of Xalapa—Consequence of this meeting—He sups with the Superior of the monastery—Description of the monks whom he meets with there—After supper he plays, wins, and retires at midnight from the monastery...... 182

IV. Of Don Cherubin's arrival at Mexico, and in what place he went to lodge—He is charmed with his host's wife, notwithstanding her blackness...... 186

THE

BACHELOR OF SALAMANCA.

PART THE FIRST.

CHAPTER I.

I owe my birth to Don Roberto de la Ronda, a native of the
environs of Malaga, but settled in the province of Leon; where
he became secretary to Don Sebastian de Cespedez, Corregidor
of Salamanca, by whom he was afterwards made Alcade of Molorido, a large borough in the neighborhood of that city. My
father, in virtue of his office, assumed the title of Don; and,
happily for him, no one thought proper to contest his right to
that distinction. As he had always been a man of pleasure and
extremely generous, he had amassed so little wealth, that on
being snatched from his family by a premature death, his
widow and three children were left with but a bare subsistence. I was at this time with my elder brother, Don Cæsar,
at the University of Salamanca, where I know not how we
should have been able to continue our studies, but for the
assistance of the Corregidor, who very generously contributed
to our support, and omitted nothing which might tend to our
comfort. He was very fond of us; and whenever we went to
visit him, never failed to assure us that he regarded us as his

I

own children. We might, indeed, be really so ; though this is a supposition I am not much inclined to, notwithstanding my mother had, it is true, the reputation of being a little inclined to coquet.

Unfortunately, our protector died before we were out of college; so that, finding ourselves reduced to our patrimony, which was very inadequate to the supply of our wants, we were obliged to abandon ourselves to the protection of Providence. Don Cæsar, feeling an inclination for the pursuit of arms, joined a regiment of cavalry, which the government about this time despatched to Milan. For my own part, profiting by the friendship of an old relation, a doctor of the University, I accepted a lodging, which he offered me gratuitously, together with a seat at his table. My mother, thus divested of the charge of all but Donna Francisca, my sister, who was not yet seven years old, was, consequently, left in a state of tolerable competency.

So great was the progress I made at college, that nothing was spoken of there but Don Cherubin de la Ronda. I shone particularly in philosophy, by the extraordinary talent I evinced in disputation. In effect I labored so successfully, that I had speedily the honor of obtaining a Bachelor's degree.

Shortly after, my old doctor, who began to be tired of the expense of having me for a boarder (for the good man was a little avaricious), addressed me in the following terms :—" My friend, Don Cherubin, you are now of an age to think of an establishment for yourself, and capable of procuring yourself a livelihood by undertaking the office of a preceptor ; it is, in my opinion, the best course you can adopt. You have only to go to Madrid, where you will easily find some respectable house, from which, after having completed the education of your charge, you may retire with a pension for life, or at least a benefice. You are a young man of talent, and have an air of wisdom ; you were born for the office of a preceptor."

Having seen at Salamanca two or three tutors, who appeared content with their situation, I took it into my head that their employment must be extremely agreeable. The old doctor, therefore, found little difficulty in prevailing on me. I told him that I was ready to set out ; and, after thanking him for his kindness, I departed for the capital by the Muleteer's road, carrying with me a trunk containing my effects, that is to say, a small quantity of linen, my Bachelor's habit, and a few pistoles, with which the old man, notwithstanding his avarice, had managed to supply me.

Arrived at Madrid, I took up my residence at an hotel, where the necessaries of the table were decently furnished, and where many respectable persons were lodged. With these I speedily became acquainted, and among the rest, cultivated a particular friendship with the Rector of Leganez, whom an affair of importance had brought to Madrid. He told me in confidence the object of his journey, and I in return made him acquainted with the motive of my own.

As soon as he heard that I was desirous of becoming a tutor, he indulged in a distortion of features, which I could never since think of without laughter. " I am really sorry for you, Signior Bachelor," said he. " What is it you are about to do ? What a life are you going to enter upon ! Are you aware of the obligations under which it will lay you ;—that it will condemn you to sacrifice your liberty, your pleasures, and your best years, to a laborious, obscure, and tedious occupation ? You must take charge of a child, who, however well born he may be, will, notwithstanding, not be free from faults. You must apply yourself incessantly to the task of forming his mind to science, and his heart to virtue. You will have to combat his caprices, to conquer his idleness, and to correct his ill-humors. You will not be quit," continued he, " for all the trouble which your pupil will cause you. You will frequently be obliged to submit to unkind treatment from his parents, and be sometimes exposed to mortifications the most humiliating. Think not, therefore, that the situation of a preceptor is one full of pleasure : it is rather a kind of servitude, to qualify one's self for which, it is requisite, as in order to become a monk, to be something either more or less than man.

" You may," added the Rector of Leganez, " rely upon me in this matter ; I have exercised the office you are desirous of undertaking. Next to that of a bishop's almoner, it is the most miserable I can conceive : I know well what it is. I educated the son of an Alcade of the court. It is true I did not entirely lose my labor, because my benefice is the fruit of it ; but I protest to you that it cost me very dear. I spent eight years in a state of slavery, worse than that of the Christians in Barbary. My pupil, who of all the children in the world was perhaps the worst calculated for receiving a superior education, joined to a natural stupidity a perfect aversion for everything like order and propriety, so that to instruct him I had to toil myself to death, and found after all that I had scattered my seed upon a barren sand. I should not, however, have lost my patience, had the Alcade, less blinded by paternal love, done justice to his son; but not being willing to believe him so stupid as he really was, he laid all the blame of his deficiencies on me. He reproached me with the inutility of my lessons; and what rendered me the more sensible of this injustice was, that he expressed himself in terms by no means the most delicate.

"I was thus," continued the Rector, "condemned to suffer equally from the father and the son, in different ways; I had also in the domestics, tyrants of my repose, vigilant spies, and inferiors, ever ready to gratify themselves by treating me with disrespect."—"What a wretched house!" exclaimed I; "in my opinion you are extremely fortunate in not having been forced to leave it without any remuneration for your services." —"You are very much in the right," said he, "and you will also please to take notice, that there are nearly a thousand crowns due to me for my salary, which my friend, the Alcade, has not the least notion of paying me, or rather which he conceives he has amply paid me, by obtaining me a country benefice."—"And your pupil," said I, "is he not grateful for the pains which you have taken with him? Are you not on terms of friendship when you meet?"—"I never see him," replied the Rector; "scarcely had he entered upon the world ere he forgot both his Latin and his tutor."

Such was the style in which the Rector essayed to vanquish my desire of becoming a tutor. Sensible, however, as was his discourse, it made no more impression on me than the arguments addressed to a young girl, to prevent her from taking a husband. He perceived it, and judging, very properly, that it would only be losing time to attempt turning me from my purpose, he thus pursued the subject: "I perceive very plainly that it is in vain to combat your resolution. You are determined on undertaking the office of a preceptor! Well and good. Since, however, I am not blessed with eloquence sufficient to make you change your mind, I will at least entreat you to remember the advice I am about to give you. Keep the strictest guard over yourself while in a house in which there are women: the devil is fond of tempting tutors; and if the instrument he employs be possessed of ever so little beauty, they seldom fail to yield to the temptation."

I promised the Rector of Leganez to comply implicitly with his advice, the fair sex being, in fact, a dangerous rock for me; for I was already but too sensible that I had received from nature a temperament, with which my virtue would find it no easy matter to contend.

CHAPTER II.

THE Rector of Leganez, seeing me determined to take upon myself the office of a pedagogue, introduced me to the Reverend Father Thomas, of Villareal, a friar of the order of Mercy, who had a very peculiar talent for discovering houses in which preceptors were wanting. This good father speedily pointed out one to me, or rather he conducted me himself to the house of Signior Isidore Montanos, a rich citizen of Madrid, who, in consequence of the good character which his Reverence gave of me, engaged me, at the rate of fifty pistoles a year. Montanos had been a merchant, and had retired from commerce, to divest himself of its rust and enjoy a life of greater tranquillity. He had two sons, the eldest of whom was sixteen, whose air did not much prepossess me in their favor. The eldest stammered, and the youngest was lame. I put some questions to them, in order to enable me to judge of their intellects, and could perceive by their answers that it would depend wholly upon themselves to profit by my instructions.

My first care in this house was to observe with attention every person in it, from the master down to the meanest lackey; and I resolved to conduct myself so, that no defect in me should be apparent; an undertaking scarcely less difficult than that of becoming really free from any. I soon became acquainted with their characters, and this knowledge was attended with some uneasiness. Signior Isidore was a man of weak mind, who affected to be a wit, and was ever amusing himself by putting off some stale jest. Proud of the possession of ten thousand ducats a year, he strutted along, his cheeks inflamed

6

with pride, and with an air which marked a conviction of his own superiority: for the rest, he was morose, clownish, brutal, and capricious. The sons, on the other hand, were badly enough disposed. Though time had not yet made them men, they were rendered so by their passions; nature appeared to have given them, if I may use the expression, a dispensation of years, in order to become vicious. They had a favorite attendant, a kind of *valet-de-chambre*, who possessed their confidence, and by whose private services their irregularities were facilitated; so, at least, I conceived; and my reasons for thinking it appeared so strong, that I could not avoid mentioning my suspicions to their father.

I expected, on giving him this information, that he would be sensible of its importance, and that he would immediately take fire, as any other father would have done in his place. But I greatly deceived myself; instead of being at all moved, he laughed in my face, saying: " Go, go, Signior Bachelor, let them go on in their own way; they will get tired of it in time, as I have. I was," he continued, "a mettlesome spark in my youth, and made all the fathers and mothers in my neighborhood tremble. I do not expect that my children should be better than myself; I do not give you fifty pistoles a year to make saints for me. Do you teach them history and the Latin language, and make them men of the world; that is all I ask of you."

When I found that Montanos had no delicacy as to the morals of his sons, I forbore to trouble myself by watching their conduct; and, confining myself within the bounds prescribed, contented myself with performing my other duties. I caused my pupils to translate the Latin authors into Castilian, and to turn the works of good Spanish writers into Latin. I read to them the wars of Grenada and other histories, and accompanied my reading with instructive reflections. Likewise, whenever anything escaped them contrary to the dictates of good breeding or of charity, I did not fail to reprove them. But it was in vain that I remonstrated with them; all my advice was rendered ineffectual by the conversation of their father. Whenever he was in a good humor, he used to boast before them of the libertinism of his youth. It appeared as if he really described his debaucheries in order to induce them to follow his example. There are parents of this description, who throw off all restraint before their children, and who are themselves the means of turning them from the paths of virtue.

After all, if Signior Isidore had been free from this defect, we should notwithstanding have been unable to live long together. I might, indeed, have put up with many others which he had, excepting his ill-humor. When he gave way to this, a circumstance which occurred but too often, he was perfectly insupportable. On such occasions he did not hesitate to use the harshest and most disobliging language. He was even so unjust as to reproach me for the natural defects of his sons. "Why do you not," he would ask me, "teach my eldest son (this was the stammerer) to speak plain? What is the reason that the youngest (this was the lame one) carries himself so badly? Why is one of them so pale? Why are the other's clothes so full of stains and dust?"

It was thus he used to address me. How was it possible to listen with patience to reproaches of this kind? One morning, no longer able to contain myself, I quitted the house of Signior Montanos, never more to return to it; after telling him that I could not accommodate myself to a man who wished that the tutor of his children should be, at the same time, their doctor, their dancing master, and their *valet de chambre*.

CHAPTER III.

I WENT the same day to visit the friar of the order of
Mercy, who by no means blamed me for having quitted the
service of Signior Isidore. On the contrary, he told me that
he was sorry for having been the means of placing me in so
bad a house. " Return hither in two or three days, Signior
Bachelor," added he. " I shall, perhaps, by that time have
been able to find you a more eligible place."

In effect, he informed me on my return that he had some news
for me. " A member of the Council of Castile," said he, " is
in want of a tutor for his only son. You may go and present
yourself in my name to this magistrate; I have spoken of you
to him, and I think that you will suit each other very well. I
have only to warn you that he is possessed of a plentiful portion
of pride, as these gentry usually are: with the exception of
that, he is amiable and well-disposed, as far as I can learn. I
hope that you will be better pleased with him than with Signior
Montanos."

I repaired immediately to the residence of the Councillor,
whom I found on the point of stepping into his carriage to attend the Council. I approached him with the greatest respect,
and informed him that I was the Bachelor of whom Father
Thomas, of Villareal, had spoken to him. " You have chosen
your time very badly," replied he, with a grave, dry air; " I
cannot give you audience at present: return at six o'clock in
the evening."

Finding an hour appointed for my audience, I did not fail

9

to attend my great man before the time prescribed. I was announced, but was allowed to remain full two hours in the anteroom, after which I was ushered into a closet where the Councillor was seated in an arm-chair. I made him a reverence so profound, that I was in danger of falling on my face. He returned my salute by a slight inclination of the head, and pointing to a low stool, which very much resembled that on which a prisoner sits at the time of his trial, he motioned me to be seated.

I never in my life saw a personage of more proud deportment. He cast on me a penetrating glance, and, as if determined to scrutinize me thoroughly, addressed me in these words: "Were you born a gentleman?"—"I did not think," replied I, "that it was necessary to be so in order to become a tutor."—"I grant you," replied he, "that it is not absolutely necessary; but, besides that he is none the worse for it, it appears to me that a dogma has more force from the mouth of a man of gentle blood, than from that of a plebeian."

The respect due to a member of the Council of Castile prevented me from bursting into the fit of laughter, into which these last words had nearly thrown me, so ridiculous did they appear. "However," replied the Councillor, "though you be not noble, I have no objection to waive that consideration, provided that you have all the other good qualities which I expect in a man whom I shall constitute preceptor of my son, who will probably one day fill my place."

I asked the Councillor of what qualities he deemed it requisite this preceptor should be possessed? To which he replied: "I desire a person who shall be a great man, a man of learning, a religious man, and a man of the world, at the same time. He must unite all the talents, he must possess all sciences, divine and human, from the catechism to mystical philosophy, and from heraldry to algebra. Such is the master I am desirous of obtaining; and as it is just and proper to render happy the lot of a person of so much merit, I will give him a seat at my table, with fifty pistoles annually. This is not all," added he; "for when my son's education shall be completed, I can easily procure him a benefice, or, at least, will reward him with a small pension for life." I admired the generosity of this magistrate, and being perfectly satisfied in my own mind that I was not the pedagogue of whom he had formed so perfect an idea, I rose from my stool, and said: "Farewell, my lord; may you meet with the man you seek: but to be candid with you, I believe he will be as hard to find as Cicero's Orator."

CHAPTER IV.

FATHER THOMAS PLACES THE BACHELOR AT THE HOUSE OF THE
MARQUIS OF BUENDIA—CHARACTER OF THE PUPIL HE HAS TO
INSTRUCT—HE LEAVES THE HOUSE—THE REASON.

I GAVE an account of this conversation to Father Thomas,
and we both laughed a great deal at the expense of the
Councillor, whom we set down as an original. " I cannot be
at ease," said the monk, " since I have failed to provide for you.
The more I see of you, the more I esteem you. I will again
exert myself, and it shall go hard, but I will secure you in one
of those houses where tutors are well off in all weathers."

In effect, a few days after, imagining that he had made my
fortune, he came to my lodging and said with an appearance
of satisfaction which heightened the merit of the service : " At
last, my dear Bachelor, I have an excellent place to offer you.
The Marquis of Buendia, one of the principal lords of the court,
is willing to confide to your care the education of his son, in
consequence of the picture I have drawn of you. Call on me
to-morrow morning, and I will take you to him. You will meet
with one of the most polished of noblemen. You will be
charmed with your reception, and I doubt not that you will be
perfectly happy in his house."

On the following morning Father Thomas conducted me to
the levee of the Marquis : and that nobleman received me with
a gracious air, telling me that he was convinced of my merit,
since the reverend father, who was his friend, had chosen me
to be near the person of the young Marquis, his son. " As to
your salary," said the Marquis, " I shall pay you one hundred
pistoles a year, and you shall not leave me without a recompense equal to your exertions, and proportioned to my
gratitude."

I had my trunk removed the same day to the house of the Marquis, where I found an apartment furnished expressly for me. I saw my pupil;—he was a child of seven years old, beautiful as the day, and of the mildest manners. He was as yet in the hands of women, but he was immediately given up to me, and a *valet-de-chambre* and a lackey were appointed to attend us. As children are generally born with some propensities which it is necessary to restrain, I employed myself in ascertaining those of my pupil. I could, however, discover none that were bad, such care had been taken by the women who had the charge of his early infancy, not to suffer in him the growth of any vicious inclination. They had even taught him to read and write, so that he was already able to form his letters.

I procured him an accidence, and began to instruct him in the principles of the Latin language, and mixed with my lessons some light fables, proper to open his mind at the same time that they afforded amusement. These he imbibed with surprising facility, and when he repeated them to his father, acquitted himself with so good a grace that the Marquis shed tears of joy. It is certain that much was to be expected from this young nobleman. I was delighted with his happy disposition, and proud beforehand of the honor which I was to derive from his education.

I was so well contented with my situation, that I could not refrain from going to see the friar of the order of Mercy, to impart to him the satisfaction I felt. " My reverend father," said I, with an air which informed him at once of the motive of my visit, " I come full of gratitude, to return you the thanks which are your due. You have placed me in a house where I am beloved, considered, respected. I have for a pupil the most gentle creature in the world, in whom it is impossible to perceive any defect ; he is not a child, but an angel."

At these words, Father Thomas, embracing me with joy, exclaimed : " How happy do you make me by the information that you are so well satisfied with your pupil."—" Nor am I less so," rejoined I briskly, " with his father. The Marquis of Buendia is an amiable nobleman. What politeness I I am absolutely embarrassed with his attentions. Far from having any of those inequalities of temper, or those moments of caprice, in which people of rank make their superiority felt, he never speaks to me but to say something obliging. He has even, in my presence, charged his domestics to attend to my orders, if on any occasion I should require anything from them."— "Once more," said the friar, "you delight me. You will, doubtless, make your fortune in the house of this nobleman."

I now viewed my situation as so completely happy, that I heartily wished the Rector of Leganez, who was no longer in Madrid, could be witness of it. "By his account," said I, "there is no tutor who is not wretched; I find myself, notwithstanding, in circumstances worthy of envy."

My felicity was undisturbed during an entire year. Though I did not touch a single penny of my salary, I had my mind perfectly at ease on that subject. "Whenever I may be in want of money," said I, "Don Gabriel de Pompano, our steward, will supply me. I need only speak two words to him, and he will immediately tell me out as many pieces as I desire."

Confident on this point, I let six months more pass over without troubling myself; but at length my want of a few pistoles became so pressing, that I could no longer refrain from applying to Don Gabriel Pompano. "I beg of you," said I, "to give me thirty pistoles on account of my salary."—"Signior Bachelor," said he, affecting an air of chagrin, "you take me at a moment when I am quite unprepared; and I am extremely sorry for it. Be assured that I would give you a hundred pistoles, instead of thirty, if I had the funds; but I protest to you that I have not ten crowns in my chest."—"This," said I, "is the steward's usual cant. If you be desirous of obliging me, you will not refuse me what I ask. There are more than a hundred and fifty pistoles due to me; and I am in extreme want of money: let me entreat you to reflect a little on my situation." Useless prayer! Vain were all my arguments; vain was it even to entreat Don Gabriel to assist me even with ten pistoles; the barbarian was inexorable: a steward's heart is flint.

My clothes were, however, beginning to be extremely shabby, a circumstance which gave me considerable uneasiness. One day I took the dancing master aside, and asked him if his visits were well paid. "Not too well," said he; "I do not know the color of the Marquis's money, though I come here three times a week regularly. You are, I presume, much in the same

case?"—"You have hit it," said I, " and unfortunately I have
not the same resources as you: you have twenty scholars; and
if ten out of them do not pay, you will at least obtain from the
other ten enough to support your table and to keep up your
equipage. I am, as you see, more to be pitied than yourself."

After having made several other attempts to soften the barbarous Pompano, I came to the resolution of making known my
wants to the Marquis. It was not without a great deal of pain
that I brought myself to do so; necessity, however, at length
compelled me to dispense with further ceremony. I represented
to his lordship the straits to which I found myself reduced, and
the ineffectual efforts I had made to procure relief from Pompano. The Marquis was, or, to speak more justly, appeared to
be, in a great rage with the steward, said "that he would rate
him soundly, and that he would take care I should be paid
regularly every quarter."

Who would not have supposed that I was on the point of
touching at least fifty doubloons? My cause was not, however,
in the least advanced; whether Pompano and his master were
hard run for cash, or, as is most probable, they laid their heads
together to treat me in the same way as the rest of their creditors.

I was in a case of too much extremity not to make some violent effort to extricate myself. I therefore, for the fourth time,
employed Father Thomas, who pitying my misfortune, introduced me to the house of a Contador;* but previously to
leaving the Marquis's house, I addressed him a letter, in which
I respectfully represented to him that, not being rich enough to
continue in his service without remuneration, I was under the
necessity of seeking another house than his; a proceeding I
entreated him not to take amiss. This was requisite, for whatever cause a common person may have to complain of a man
of quality, it is notwithstanding necessary to give him fair
words.

---

* A money broker, or person appointed by authority to settle accounts.

CHAPTER V.

I PASSED from one extreme to the other. If the Contador
had not all the politeness of the Marquis of Buendia, he was,
on the other hand, much better supplied with cash. Oh, the
charming abode ! Nothing was to be heard there from morning
to night but the rattling of silver and gold. How were my ears
enchanted with the melodious sound !

The Contador was a man who came at once to the point. He
wished to know what was my salary in the house of the Marquis of Buendia. " That nobleman," said I, " promised me a
hundred pistoles a year ; but he has not been very exact to his
word." The Contador smiled at these last words, and said,
" Very well ! I promise you—I—a hundred and fifty pistoles,
which shall be paid you without fail, and which you may even,
if you please, receive in advance." At the same time, calling
his cashier, " Raposo," said he, " pay the Bachelor immediately a hundred pistoles, and take care whenever he may want
money from you, not to refuse him."

These words completely confounded me. " How the deuce
is this ? " said I to myself. " A Marquis and a Contador are
two very different species of men. One fails to pay that which
he is indebted ; and the other does not wait till he owes money
before he pays it." As soon as the cashier had delivered me
the money, I sent for a tailor, of whom I ordered a complete
suit, and paid him twenty pistoles in advance, in order to be in
the Contador fashion.

Seeing myself all at once possessed of money, I recovered the

good-humor, which the Marquis and his steward had, in some
degree, deprived me of ; and began with a good heart to discharge the duties of my employment. My new pupil was not
far advanced. Although he was ten years of age, he had not
yet learned to read ; I was his first master. "Signior Bachelor," said his father, " I give up my son to your care, and confide entirely in you for his improvement. I have no inclination
to make him a divine ; a small tincture of Latin will, therefore,
suffice. Teach him what is called good manners, and procure
an able arithmetician to instruct him in all kind of calculations.
Be this your care."

I set myself to work to accomplish the views of the Contador,
and to lick the young cub, to which he desired I should impart
a form. I had no small trouble in teaching this hopeful youth
the letters of the alphabet. He had no more inclination for
learning than the disciple of the Rector of Leganez. I, however, took such extraordinary pains that I had the happiness of
succeeding in enabling him to read, tolerably well, all kinds of
Spanish books. When I communicated to his mother the information of this attainment, she was transported with joy.
Although she tenderly loved her son, she was by no means
blind to his imperfections ; and, regarding the success of
my lessons as an absolute prodigy, ascribed to me all the
honor of it : it obtained me both her esteem and her friendship.

Insensibly, Portia (so was the lady named) began to admire
me, and took so much pleasure in my company, that every day,
after the siesta,* she sent for me into her apartment, under
pretence of seeing her son, whom I, on those occasions, carried
to visit her. She was a woman of about five and thirty at most ;
extremely witty, but so reserved, that perhaps I deceive myself
in supposing that she indulged any particular inclination for me.
I could not, however, help giving way to such a conjecture ; and
the reader may judge by what I am about to relate, whether or
not I was a coxcomb for thinking so.

However amiable Portia appeared in my eyes, and though
she regarded me in such a manner as to give very good reason
to suspect that she had some design upon me, I evinced no
kind of sensibility to the marks of favor she bestowed. My

* The afternoon nap in which the Spaniards usually indulge.

2

attention was entirely engaged by her servant Nise, whose inclination corresponding with my own, rendered me perfectly indifferent to the advances of the mistress. I was by no means proof against her keen and coquettish air, notwithstanding the stock of morality and virtue which I had laid in at the university. After a few amorous glances on both sides, our intrigue was perfectly established.

In addition to many other qualifications which she possessed, Nise had an uncommon share of ingenuity in contriving secret interviews with her lovers; and this was an art particularly useful in a house where the greatest management was necessary to avoid the resentment of a gallant, whom she was desirous of quitting for me, or to whom, at least, she was resolved on giving a partner. This slighted gallant was the *valet-de-chambre* of my pupil. Nise, who had not perhaps found in his homage a sufficient gratification of her vanity, aspired to the honor of making a conquest of the tutor.

Be this as it may, triumphant over my rival without even being aware that I had one, I went on in the quiet enjoyment of my happiness, which was not, however, long concealed from him. He obtained some intimation of the stolen interviews which I had with his princess, and determined, in revenge, to effect the ruin of us both. He was silent at first, having nothing more against us than suspicions, which, however well founded, could prove nothing; he therefore proceeded with caution. He won over to his party all the lackeys in the house; and these gentry, commonly the enemies of tutors, lent themselves without much difficulty to his projects. Thus, surrounded with spies, Nise and I could not, with all our ingenuity, avoid being surprised in a *tête-à-tête*.

This adventure caused a horrible outcry in the house. All the servants made themselves remarkably merry at my expense. The Contador himself, contrary to the custom of most of his class, who are very little concerned about scenes of this kind occurring in their houses, took up the affair as a point of honor, and flew into a most violent passion. The lady, still more incensed than her husband, declared it an unpardonable offence. "How," exclaimed she, "a man whom I thought possessed of sentiment and taste, to degrade himself by an intrigue with a servant!" The result was, that the catastrophe fell upon me. Portia, who was fond of her Abigail, or who had

THE BACHELOR IS SURPRISED IN A TÊTE-À-TÊTE.

perhaps confided in her secrecy on former occasions, contented herself with scolding her; and for my own part, I was ignominiously dismissed as a seducer, for not having manifested nobler sentiments.

CHAPTER VI.

WHAT HAPPENED TO THE BACHELOR ON QUITTING THE HOUSE
OF THE CONTADOR—HIS REFLECTIONS ON HIS CONDUCT—HE
IS INTRODUCED BY HIS HOST INTO THE HOUSE OF A WIDOW
—CHARACTER OF THE LADY—DON CHERUBIN BECOMES HER
STEWARD—REGARD WHICH THE WIDOW CONCEIVES FOR HIM
—INTERVIEW WITH THE DAME RODRIGUEZ—THE SUBJECT OF
THE INTERVIEW, AND WHAT WAS THE RESULT OF IT.

I WAS not inclined, on leaving the house of the broker, to
visit the friar of the order of Mercy, who would doubtless have
reproached me, very justly, for the conduct which had caused
my dismissal; and who perhaps, viewing me only as a miserable wretch whom he ought to abandon, would have scrupled
to interest himself any further in my service. I did not even
dare to return to my hotel, where I imagined that my story
was known; for, when a man has been guilty of an indiscretion, it is common to suppose the whole world acquainted
with it. I therefore retired into an obscure quarter, where,
as I was not without money, I continued about a fortnight,
deliberating what course I should pursue.

I called to mind more than once the advice of the Rector of
Leganez, with bitter repentance for having neglected it; and,
reflecting on my weakness, could not think of Nise without
feeling myself ready to expire with shame. "Fool!" exclaimed
I to myself, "was it to make love to waiting women that thou
becamest a tutor? Instead of carrying scandal from house to
house, renounce at once an employment which thou dischargest
so ill; or, if thou wilt still continue in it, reform thy manners,
and endeavor to obtain those virtues which are requisite for
properly filling it." In short, I repented heartily of my fault;

20

and, by promising myself to grow wiser, began to entertain the
hope of really becoming so.

About this time, my new host, having conceived a friendship for me, was anxious to render me a service. "Signior
Bachelor," said he one day, "I am desirous of procuring you
a good place, by fixing you in the house of a woman of quality,
who is bringing up her grandson under her own eye." This
word, widow, made me tremble. "May there not be some new
precipice in this?" I reflected to myself. "May not the
fiend be desirous of again spreading a net for my feet?" I,
however, consoled myself with the reflection that the lady in
question was a grandmother, a circumstance which implied an
age calculated to throw a rein on any illicit inclinations. I
therefore told my host that I should feel very much obliged to
him for this favor.

"I promise you I will do it," said he. "Doubt not that I
will effect your business. I have been servant to this lady, and
my word will go a great way with her; I will this day propose
you as a tutor for the young gentleman." He was as good as
his word; and so loud was he in my praise, that the widow
was impatient to see me. When I presented myself, my
appearance was found prepossessing, and I was immediately
engaged.

The name of the widow was Donna Luisa de Padilla. Her
husband, who had been a general officer, was killed in the low
countries, fighting against the French. For a grandmother, I
found her well enough, without however perceiving anything
dangerous in her charms. She had in immediate attendance
upon her person (perhaps out of policy) two ancient waiting
women, whose decrepitude served in some degree to give their
mistress an air of youth. One of these, who was called Dame
Rodriguez, was in the entire confidence of her mistress, and
had obtained over her the most perfect ascendency. I was
secretly rejoiced, and thanked heaven that, instead of these
antiquated confidantes, Donna Luisa had not a pair of bloom-
ing young maids, whose allurements might once more have put
my chastity in danger.

Established in my new post, everything went on smoothly at
first. I became very fond of my scholar, who, joining docility
to an excellent genius, acquired most rapidly the elements of
the Latin language, though he was not yet eight years of age.

In less than six months he made such progress as completely surpassed my expectations, and procured me several presents. Donna Luisa desired my acceptance of a gold watch, and shortly after sent me a large package of very fine linen, with some of the finest cloth of Segovia, to make an entire suit. But all these gifts, which I considered as the result of her gratitude, proceeded from another motive, as the reader will presently understand.

While engaged one morning with my pupil, I was informed that Donna Luisa demanded to see me. I flew immediately to her apartment, where I found her with her two tire-women, who were exerting all their abilities to patch up her decaying charms. She was in a dishabille, sufficiently immodest to be alluring, if it had not at the same time displayed wherewith to counteract the temptation.

Having no farther business with her women, she motioned them to retire, and drawing me near her with a mysterious air, "Sit down there," said she, "and attend to what I am about to say; I have some intentions in your favor, which I am happy in being able to make you acquainted with. I do not look upon you as one who is fit for nothing but to employ himself in the education of children: I think you qualified for far other matters. I have resolved, in fine, to commit to you the charge of my affairs. My present steward, Francisco Forteza, begins to grow old. I design to dismiss him with a pension, and to put you in his place, which you will fill better than he; though, at the same time, it is not my intention that, in accepting this new employment, you should relinquish that of preceptor to my grandson. You may easily perform the duties of both places at the same time."

I represented to the lady that, never having exercised the business of a steward, I feared I should not be able to acquit myself so as to afford her satisfaction. "You are mistaken," said she, "nothing is easier: I have no lawsuits; I owe nobody a Marved; you have nothing to do but to receive my rents and superintend the expenditure of my housekeeping. You need only," continued she, "come every morning to my apartment; we will set ourselves to work for an hour or two, and you will very speedily become acquainted with the routine of your duty." I assured her I was perfectly ready to do whatever she desired, and so took my leave, though not without remarking that my fair widow's eyes were sparkling, and her cheeks on fire.

I had too much experience, or, rather, I had too good an opinion of myself, not to interpret these symptoms to my own advantage. I suspected the good lady of having taken a fancy to me, and my suspicions were speedily converted into certainty. I, one morning shortly after, received a visit in my apartment from Dame Rodriguez. She saluted me with an air of gaiety, exclaiming, "Heaven preserve you, Signior Bachelor! What will you give me for a piece of good news, of which I am the bearer?"—"Heyday!" said I, "what have you, so very good, to acquaint me with?"—"That you are," replied she, "the most fortunate of tutors, past, present, or to come. You have inspired my mistress with a passion for you, and she has permitted me to make known to you this important secret. But what!" continued she, perceiving that I was not much interested in the happiness she announced to me, "you receive this news with perfect indifference! How many men would be happy to be in your place! If my mistress be past the bloom of youth, she is not, thank God, arrived at that dreary period of life, in which the company of our sex ceases to be desirable to men."

"Oh!" it is not for that, Madam Rodriguez," replied I; "I must be out of my senses if I thought otherwise than yourself on that subject. Yes, Donna Luisa has indeed abundance of charms; she is at most but in the commencement of their autumn. Nevertheless, I must avow, that however highly I am honored by her regard, I cannot profit by it. Affairs of gallantry are by no means consistent in men of my description. Although I am not yet in orders," added I, with a hypocritical air, "it is sufficient that I wear the habit of an ecclesiastic."

"What an idea have you dared to express," exclaimed Rodriguez, hastily interrupting me; "what a horrible injustice have you done my mistress! Could she be capable of indulging in an illicit intrigue, whom the very shadow of crime inspires with terror? If, unable to resist, she yield to her love for you, think not that she is inclined to gratify it at the expense of her virtue. Shall I tell you?—she has resolved to marry you."

I was a little startled at these last words. "Sage and discreet Rodriguez," said I, "even though your lady be inclined to honor me with her hand, will not her relations exert themselves to prevent such a marriage? "—" Donna Luisa," replied the old lady, " is mistress of her own actions. Besides, I presume you are of a noble family; and she proposes to be married so privately, that nobody will know anything about it." Finding that my widow was really foolish enough to resolve on carrying the thing so far, I thought it was not necessary that I should be foolish enough to oppose her. I desired Rodriguez to thank her mistress for her good intentions, and to assure her that I did not mean to be ungrateful for them. After giving the old lady time to repeat my message to her mistress, I hastened to confirm her report in person. " Madam," said I, throwing myself on my knees before my enamoured widow, " is it possible that you can have honored with your regard a man so wholly unworthy of possessing you? I cannot think of it without trembling for the reality."—" Do not yourself blame me," said she, " for what I am inclined to do for your advantage. When I close my eyes on what is most reprehensible in my design, is it for you to open them? Profit by my weakness instead of condemning it. What Rodriguez has informed you is the truth: you have pleased me, and our destinies shall speedily be joined in marriage, if you have a just sense of my kindness."—" Ah! madam," cried I, embracing with transport one of her withered hands, " do you think that a man of sentiment can repay with ingratitude the enviable lot you are disposed to confer upon me? Be assured that my sense of obligation will be equal to the excess of my happiness."

I accompanied these words with an air and manner the most seducing. I took upon myself the character of a passionate lover; but if there was art in this, there was, notwithstanding, a great deal of nature. I felt myself so penetrated with her kindness, that I began to view her faded beauties with a more favorable eye.

CHAPTER VII.

HOW DON CHERUBIN, ON THE POINT OF BECOMING THE HUSBAND
OF DONNA LUISA, LOST ON A SUDDEN THE HOPE OF EVER BEING
SO—HE IS CARRIED OFF BY FORCE—HIS TERROR AT FINDING
HIMSELF IN THE HANDS OF BRAVOES—DESCRIPTION OF HIS
SUPPER AND COMPANY.

DONNA LUISA, delighted at finding me so disposed, hastened
privately to forward the preparation for our nuptials; but, on
the evening before the day which had been fixed for their cele-
bration, an accident happened which effectually separated us.

As I was returning home, and just on the point of entering
the house, four *valientes*, with the most tremendous mustachios
that ever were seen in Spain, darted on me, and forced me into
a coach, in which were two others of their fraternity. They
carried me to the extremity of one of the suburbs, caused me to
alight at a house of no very brilliant appearance, and introduced me into a hall which resembled an arsenal. Nothing was
to be seen but halberds, swords, cutlasses, guns, and pistols.
At another time, I should have been pleased with the sight of
so singular a place; but I was too much engaged in reflecting
upon the peril in which I conceived myself, with a parcel of as-
sassins, the very sight of whom made my blood freeze in my
veins. One of these bullies, remarking my embarrassment,
began to laugh, and, in order to dissipate my alarm, addressed
me in these words: " Signior Bachelor, fear nothing; you are
here in good company. You are with some honest persons,
who make a profession of preserving good order in society, and
maintaining the quiet of families. It is we who are in reality
the ministers of justice. An ordinary judge contents himself
with adhering strictly to the laws, whereas we sometimes make
up their deficiency. The laws, for instance, do not forbid a

widow of quality to marry a man inferior to herself.   It is, notwithstanding, a degrading conduct, for which reason we do not
suffer it ; and it is to prevent the just regret which the family
of Donna Luisa de Padilla must necessarily feel, if you should
become that lady's husband, that we have taken you into cus-
tody ; a course which we have adopted at the request of one of
her nephews, who has promised us a hundred pistoles to effect
your separation.

"It is for you to choose," continued the bravo.   "If you refuse to remove from this widow and from Madrid, our directions
are to kill you; but we are allowed to spare your life, and even
to let you off without a drubbing, provided you will abandon
this business with a good grace.   You have but to choose."
—"What do you call choosing?" retorted I eagerly ; "do you
think me sufficiently mad to hesitate for a moment, under such
circumstances, about quitting Madrid, and all the ladies in the
world ?   I wish I was already far enough from it."—"I believe
you," replied the bravo, with a malignant sneer; "and upon
that footing we are perfectly agreed.   You shall sup, and pass
the rest of the night with us at table, and at the break of day
two of my comrades will conduct you as far as Leganez, from
whence you will be able to go to Toledo, at which place I advise you to reside.   It is a fine town, where there are a great
number of the nobility.   You will have your choice of tutors'
places."

On this, I informed these gentlemen (so great was my impatience to be out of their clutches) that, if they would allow
me to go and lodge at an inn, I promised, on pain of falling
again into their hands, to set out for Madrid before the first
dawn of Aurora.

This proposal excited the most immoderate laughter among
the bravoes.   "You grow tired of us then, Signior Bachelor,"
said one of them, "by what I can perceive.   But have a little
patience : it is necessary to accommodate one's self to the time.
You will have much better cheer with us than you could at the
inn ; and, among those who will bear you company at supper,
there will perhaps be some who may render the repast agreeable
to you."   I was obliged therefore to make a virtue of necessity,
since it was impossible to escape.   I affected to appear reso-
lute, and even to laugh with these bravoes, whose good-humor

gradually excited mine, or at least divested me of some portion of my fear.

Supper being ready, we passed into a saloon, where there was a sideboard set out with glasses and bottles, and a large table covered with all sorts of viands. We sat down with three ladies, who had arrived, and who, they told me, were the wives of three of these gentlemen ; which story, I suffered them to believe, passed current with me, though these women had an air too free and familiar to admit of even so good an opinion being formed of them.

They were in a gay dishabille, which did not hide from the view that which, without the last degree of effrontery, could not be exposed to sight. For the rest, they might pass for three tolerably pretty girls. There was one among them whom they called La Gitanilla,* doubtless because she was of the Bohemian race. I never saw a creature, with a countenance so keen and expressive : her eyes were of dazzling brilliancy, and the vivacity of her mind equalled that of her eyes. It is true that she had an intemperance of tongue, which sometimes carried her too far ; but this would have been amply compensated by the abundance of *bon mots* and pleasant sallies which escaped her, if these sallies and *bon mots* had not encroached a little upon delicacy. In fine, while listening to her, I admired her, and could not help thinking, that a waiting maid of this kind in a house would have been a terrible stumbling-stone for me.

Signior Bachelor began to be pleased with his company. Inspired by the glances of La Gitanilla, and the wine which he was every moment obliged to drink, in answering to the healths with which he was assailed from all quarters, he insensibly forgot with what kind of people he was getting drunk. We continued at table till the approach of day ; then having taken leave of the bravoes and their nymphs, I quitted the town with two of the former, and took the route to Toledo.

* The gipsy.

CHAPTER VIII.

OF DON CHERUBIN'S ARRIVAL AT TOLEDO, AND OF THE FIRST
EDUCATION WHICH HE UNDERTOOK—BAD CHARACTER OF HIS
PUPIL, WHO TAKES A DISLIKE TO HIM—HOW HE COMES TO BE
DISMISSED.

On arriving at Leganez, one of my companions said: "So, there, Signior Bachelor, in accompanying you thus far, we have executed our orders: do you, on your part, remember to keep your word with us. Be not again seen in Madrid, for, as you have been before informed, if you venture to set foot in it you are a dead man."—"Gentlemen," said I, "you may boldly assure all the nephews and grand-nephews of Donna Luisa that you have forever separated me from her." On this my algua-zils wished me a good journey, and we parted with mutual civilities of salutation.

Our separation delivered me from a cruel fright. I had felt apprehensive that the bravoes, in bidding me adieu, would have done me the favor of emptying my pockets. As soon, therefore, as they were out of sight I pulled out my watch, and kissing it, as a mother would kiss a beloved child just escaped from shipwreck, " My dear watch," cried I, apostrophizing it, "you have escaped an imminent peril. I thought, I must con-fess, that we should not have arrived together in Toledo, and that you were going to take the road back to Madrid."

I had, in fact, reason to be surprised that they had not robbed me, for these rogues in general are no better than Bohemians. Besides my watch, I had a purse full of doubloons, which, in quality of steward to Donna Luisa, I had received the evening before, from a person who was in her debt, so that they would have gained more by robbing me than they did by forcing me out of Madrid.

I did not like to pass through Leganez without calling on my friend the rector. I anticipated a great deal of pleasure in giving him an account of my late adventure, and in passing a few days with him. But I was deceived, for I did not meet with my good priest, who, being one of those who admire residence no more than a bishop, was absent from home at the time. I was told that he was gone to Cuença, and that it was not known when he would return.

I continued my route as far as Mosioles, where I had the good fortune to meet with a muleteer of Toledo, who was returning thither with his mule. I hired him, and pursued my journey. We were joined near Illescas by an ecclesiastic, who, coming after us on a good horse, hastened to overtake us, that he might have the benefit of our company. We saluted each other politely, and entered into conversation. My desire to know who he was made me take the liberty of asking him. "I am," replied he, "one of the sixty canons of the church, commonly called the holy see of Toledo."

At these words I was inspired with a most profound respect for my companion, having heard that a canonship of this church was worth two Italian bishoprics. Finding, therefore, that I had the honor of being with a man possessed of so important a benefice, I took a lower tone with him, and began to measure my expressions. I do not know whether he remarked it, but he did not appear more vain or more haughty than before. He inquired in his turn who I was? I replied that I was a Bachelor of Salamanca; that I was coming from the court, where I had been educating a young nobleman, and that I was going to Toledo to seek a new engagement. "You will easily obtain it," replied the canon, "being, as you appear, a young man of merit."

We did not cease conversing during our journey; and when, having arrived at Toledo, it became necessary to part, he extended his hand to me. "I shall not bid you adieu, Signior Bachelor," said he. "I am called the licentiate Don Prosper. Come and see me; I am interested in your welfare. I will begin to-morrow to make exertions for discovering some house where your services may be wanted, in which you will find yourself comfortable." I thanked the canon for his kindness in interesting himself about me, and went to lodge at an inn, the merits of which had been much extolled by the muleteer.

Four days after, having supplied myself with a fresh stock of linen, and got a new suit of clothes, I went to see the canon. "I have done your business," said he. "Don Jerom de Polan, a knight of Calatrava, and my intimate friend, is in want of a clever man to complete the education of his only son, the young Don Luis. I have this place at my disposal; will you accept it?" I assured the licentiate that I desired nothing better, and he immediately conducted me to the house of Don Jerom de Polan. As soon as this gentleman saw Don Prosper, he ran to him with open arms, and such demonstrations of friendship, as gave me to understand that they lived on terms of the utmost intimacy. The canon, after having received and returned half a dozen embraces, presented me to Don Jerom, saying: "I understand that Don Luis is without a tutor; I bring you one, for whom I can answer. He is a learned Bachelor of Salamanca, who is returning from Madrid, where he has been educating a young nobleman." Don Jerom, while the canon was thus addressing him, regarded me with attention; and it appeared to me (without vanity be it said) that I passed well through this ocular examination. It was what I had reason to suppose from the thanks which he gave Don Prosper, for having procured him a person who carried in his appearance his own recommendation. He conducted me to his wife's apartment, where that lady was sitting with her son, in whom I thought I perceived an air of stubbornness, and a servant maid, who did not cause me any uneasiness, though she was under twenty years of age. All these persons examined me thoroughly, and I dare venture to say that my looks prepossessed them in my favor.

Thus then was I established in this house, where, being looked on as a master recommended by the licentiate Prosper, I enjoyed during a fortnight all the pleasure that a tutorship is susceptible of. I was treated with attention by Don Jerom and his lady, respected by the domestics, and, I thought, loved by my pupil; but him, I was not yet fully acquainted with. He had a *valet-de-chambre*, who, having conceived a regard for me, said to me one day: "Signior Bachelor, I find you such a civil gentleman, that I cannot avoid informing you of something which it is essential you should know. You have a very bad subject to deal with, in your scholar. Don Luis is a liar, and possesses a malignant, slanderous disposition. He has an especial aversion to his tutors; he cannot endure them, and there is no stratagem that he will not resort to, to get rid of them. The two last he had were persons of distinguished merit; nevertheless, he managed his matters so well, that they were dismissed."—"By what I can perceive," said I, "the father and mother idolize their son."—"Yes," replied he, " he is a spoiled child ; you will find it a difficult matter to obtain any control over him."—" I will do my best for that purpose," said I ; " and if, after all, I cannot accomplish it, I will go and seek elsewhere a pupil more worthy of my attention."

That I might have nothing to reproach myself with, I began to fulfil my essential duties with an assiduity which approached to slavery. I left nothing undone which could contribute to make me loved, and at the same time feared, by my good little man. Although he was twelve years old, and had had three or four masters, he was scarcely competent to the simplest exercises. I was eternally talking to him, and laboring to secure his attention. I endeavored, as much as possible, to prevent his faults, or, if he had been guilty of any, I punished him without passion, or pardoned him without weakness.

Nevertheless, with all this management, and in spite of all my address, I experienced the truth of what the valet had said. Don Luis conceived an aversion for me, and his hate increasing in proportion as I evinced zeal for his improvement, determined on procuring my dismissal. In order to succeed in this, he complained of me privately to his parents : he accused me of being severe and unreasonable, turned me into ridicule, and declared that, if he were not to be delivered from his tyrant, he would never make any progress in his studies. To this menace he added a few crocodile tears, and in short played his part so well, that his parents, touched with his pretended grief, took his part, and turned his tutor out of doors. It is thus that fathers and mothers, through weakness for their children, will sometimes dismiss an honest man, who has, perhaps, discharged his duty but too well.

To add to my grief, on leaving this house I went to call on the licentiate Don Prosper. I wished to represent to him the bad qualities of the young Don Luis, and detail the manœuvre he had employed to get me out of the house ; but the canon, who appeared to have been prejudiced by Don Jerom, instead of pitying me, heard me with coldness, and turned his back upon me, after telling me drily, "that he would take care to recommend no more tutors, at least without being previously well acquainted with them."

CHAPTER IX.

I HAD formed an acquaintance with a little Biscayan licentiate, who like myself exercised the profession of a tutor, and
who was also, at this time, without employment. His face was
not disagreeable, but his person was so very small that he
might have been taken for a dwarf. To make amends, he had
a considerable share of wit and lively humor. He thought
pleasantly, expressed himself equally so, and his expressions
were rendered still more striking by his provincial accent.

I liked particularly to hear him when he was in a passion;
and to put him in one, it was only necessary to speak before
him of fathers and mothers. This subject never failed to rouse
him. "Parents," he would say emphatically, "are almost all
ungrateful. Listen to the father of a family :—'I am content,'
he will say, 'with my son's tutor, and I design to procure him
a solid establishment : but there is no hurry ; it will be time
enough to think of that when my son shall be out of his hands.'
Is not this the same," Carambola would add, "as if he said, 'I
will not yet do good to an honest man, who is at the present
moment rendering me service, who has already merited my
bounties ; I will think about his fortune when he will no longer
be before my eyes, when I shall have nothing more to remind
me of him'?"

Such were the amusing tirades with which the Biscayan re-

32

galed me from time to time, and of which I failed not to take
advantage. Meeting him one evening on the promenade, he
came up to me with an air of great gaiety. " What is the
matter with you ? " said I ; " by your joyous air, one would suppose that you had discovered some admirable employment."—
" There is something in that," said he. " I have, in fact, discovered a place which suited me most admirably ; but, unfortunately, they did not find me suited to the place."—" I do not
comprehend you," said I ; " speak more clearly."—" You must
know, then," replied he, " that having yesterday learned, from
public report, that a lady was in want of a tutor to begin the
education of her son, who is not more than five years old, I
went this morning to offer her my services, which were rejected. I was told that I was too little."—" How then," interrupted I, laughing, " to get into this lady's house is it necessary
to be six feet high ? "—" Yes," replied Carambola ; " the lady
wishes for a young man of fine figure, and desires, besides, that
he should be very young ; for, though I am but three and
thirty, I was too old for her."

I redoubled my laughter at this, and judged that the lady in
question must be some silly creature. When I expressed this
opinion to the licentiate, he replied with a serious air : " No,
no, she is a woman of very good sense ; a prude, who knows
how to conciliate her taste for pleasure with her regard for her
reputation, and would have a lover in the tutor of her son."—
" What is her name ? " I asked. " She assumes," said he,
" the title of Marchioness. Her husband is a captain in Lombardy. That is all I know about her. For the rest, I can
assure you that she is a fine woman, and appears to have a
great deal of wit. Are you not curious to see her ? "—" You
have inspired me with a wish," replied I, " and I have a mind
to go and present myself to-morrow to this said Marchioness."
—" I exhort you to do so," cried he ; " and I am persuaded
that you are the preceptor whom she wants."

I did not fail to call the following day on the captain's lady,
to whom I caused myself to be announced by the title of
Bachelor of Salamanca. An old female attendant, who bore
some resemblance to Rodriguez, introduced me into a closet,
where her mistress was occupied in reading. She suspended her
study at the sight of me, and inquired my business. " Madam,"
replied I, " I have been informed that you are in want of a

3

tutor for your son, and I take the liberty of offering myself to fill that situation, if my services be agreeable to you." The lady, at these words, fixed her eyes steadfastly upon me; nor was I less attentively considered by the waiting woman, and I could perceive that my figure had found in them two favorable judges: I appeared in their eyes quite a different man from Carambola.

"How old are you, Signior Bachelor?" asked the lady. As I remembered that the licentiate had been thought too old at thirty-three, I boldly replied that I was but twenty-two years of age, though, in fact, I had already completed twenty-six. "So much the better," said the Marchioness; "I wish for a tutor who is young. I have that particular fancy. But do not deceive me," continued she; "are you a young man of sober habits? for, I assure you, I could by no means endure a libertine who would be going out every day to seek amusements in the town. I desire a sedate man, and one who will bring up my son under my own eye."

"I am, then, exactly the man, madam," said I. "Although I am of an age in which the passions are on fire, my reason, aided by the profitable studies I have pursued, keeps a rein over them, so that I fear nothing from their sallies. Independent of that, I have no acquaintance in Toledo, particularly female acquaintance; thus, bounding my pleasure to the education of your son, I shall devote myself to nothing but the cultivation of that young plant, if you will entrust me with the care of it."

"I shall be very well satisfied with you," replied the captain's lady, "if you pursue so sensible a conduct. I, therefore, choose you to instruct and govern my son. With regard to your salary," she added, "be under no uneasiness: I shall regulate that in proportion to your zeal and your services." She delivered these words with an air so modest and reserved, that, in spite of my vanity, I could not suffer myself to be prejudiced against her virtue, nor flatter myself with the hope of attracting her attention.

To perform the part of a faithful historian, I must confess that I was struck with the charms of the Marchioness, who was not yet five and thirty years of age. Her beauty appeared to me ravishing. I felt, without knowing why, a secret joy at being engaged in this house, to which I proceeded with all ex-

pedition to remove my effects. I met the little licentiate in the
street, where he was induced by curiosity to wait for me.
" Well, my friend," said he, " how has the Marchioness received you ? "—" She could not have done so better," replied
I, " and I have to inform you that I am preceptor to her son."

At these words Carambola began laughing. " I was not
wrong," cried he, " in supposing that your youth and person
would have their proper effect. What a deal of pleasure you
will have with this lady ! "—" Oh ! softly there, Master Licentiate," interrupted I, penetrating his thought ; " do not judge
so uncharitably of her. For my own part, I believe her to be
virtuous ; at least, she shows a fair outside. Why tax with
hypocrisy an air of so much prudence ? If we must not trust
to fair appearances altogether, neither ought we to condemn
them."—" You are right," said he ; " I may be deceived, but I
would lay a wager that I am not."

I returned some hours after, with my effects, to the house of
the Marchioness, and took possession of an apartment prepared
for my scholar and myself. I requested to see the child, and
he was brought to me by the old woman whom I had before
seen, and who acted as his governess. I thought him very
handsome. He was in leading-strings, and could but just lisp.
What a pupil for a Bachelor of Salamanca ! A proud pedagogue
in my place would have refused to debase himself so much as
to teach the letters of the alphabet ; but I looked on the matter
in another point of view, and, as Aristotle took credit to himself for being the first instructor of Alexander, so I made it my
glory to be so to a young marquis.

I entered into conversation with the old governess, whose
name was Sephora. " Signior Bachelor," said she, " I am very
glad that your person has pleased my lady. Nothing less than
a man like yourself could have met her approbation, such is the
delicacy of her taste. There have been here twenty tutors to
present themselves, all of whom have been rejected, though
there were among them some very agreeable persons. You will
not regret," she continued, " having come into this house.
The Marchioness is rich and generous. In a word, your fortune is made, provided you pay my mistress a great deal of attention, and yield with a blind complaisance to her opinions.
It is her weakness, I must tell you: profit by it, and, above all
things, accommodate yourself, if you can, to her foible of being

passionately fond of books of knight-errantry. Shall you be capable of entering into these sentiments ? "—" Without doubt," replied I; "it will be by no means difficult to flatter her infatuation, for I am myself extremely fond of books of that description."—"In that case," said she, "you will charm her : that you may rely on."

In truth I had discovered, in the very first conversation I had with the Marchioness, that she had her memory stuffed with rags and tatters of romances. She spoke to me of nothing but Roland the Amorous, the Knight of the Sun, Amadis of Gaul, Amadis of Greece, and, above all, of the incomparable knight, Don Quixote de la Mancha, and of a number of other works of the same kind, which formed her whole delight, and constituted the contents of her library. Although I was not exactly of her mind about these extravagant productions, I pretended to be so, and set these romances above all the books in the world. Perhaps, indeed, I was myself the dupe, and the lady only affected to have her head turned with these kind of books in order to gain her ends. However this may be, if she had confined her folly to the pleasure of reading these nothings, I should always have had complaisance enough to flatter her in defiance of good sense; but she carried it still further.

"Signior Bachelor," said she, as I entered her apartment one day while she was reading Don Belianis of Greece, "I am enchanted with what I have been reading. How well do Don Belianis and Florisbella understand the art of love ! What delicacy in their sentiments ! How touching are their expressions. I am still all in a tremor."

"I have no doubt of it, madam," said I; "nothing can be better calculated to rouse the feelings. I am like yourself ; I find myself enchanted when I read some passages in certain books of chivalry ; they throw my mind into a disorder, a kind of rapture."—"What do I hear ? " interrupted the Marchioness with an air of emotion. "Is it possible that I have met with a man as sensible as myself to the pleasures of romances, and that that man should be you? I am so much the more delighted, as I now hope to have a lover who will devote himself to me, and serve me in the quality of a knight-errant. I made choice of you, my dear Bachelor. Let us become, you the hero, and I the heroine of chivalry. Take me for your mistress, and I will love you as my knight. Let us sigh for each other: let us burn with a flame as ardent as that which consumed the Prince of Greece and his mistress."

She accompanied her discourse with demonstrations so enticing, that poor Don Cherubin, who had already found the lady but too amiable, became most desperately in love with her. Instead of shunning this infatuated woman, I had the weakness to lend myself to all these fooleries. Adieu my reason! Behold the Bachelor of Salamanca changed into a knight-errant. The Marchioness and I began to talk in the style of the heroes of romance. I assumed the character of the Knight of the Sun, and she that of the Princess of Lindabrides. We had, every day, conversations supported in the elevated strain; but it happened unfortunately, sometimes, that the heroine became a little too tender, and the hero too fond.

Whilst I was thus living with the Marchioness, like Reginald in the palace of Armida, I heard a piece of news which dispelled my enchantment: I was told that Captain Torbellino, the husband of my princess, was on the point of arriving from Lombardy, and it was intimated to me at the same time that he was a man of violent and jealous temper. To avoid all discussion, and not being (although a knight-errant) at all fond of duelling, I took the wise resolution of removing to a distance from Toledo; a proceeding the more judicious, as there was an old servant in the house completely devoted to his master, whose reports might, very probably, have exposed me to become a victim to his resentment.

CHAPTER X.

I SET out privately from Toledo one morning with a muleteer
who was going to Cuença, one of the most celebrated towns in
Spain. A few days after my arrival, the master of the inn
where I lodged, told me that he knew an old priest, who undertook to procure situations for tutors, on consideration of a certain sum, which he exacted in return for his services; and this
sum was to be more or less considerable, according to the
value of the place.

I made myself acquainted with the priest's address, and, calling on him, demanded if he knew of any tutor's place vacant.
He answered that there were several; and when I told him
that I was a Bachelor of Salamanca, he cried: "That is your
eulogy in a single word; I need know nothing more about you.
I will present you to Signior Diego Cintillo, the richest and most
famous jeweller in Cuença. He is in search of a sensible and
well-conducted man, under whose care he wishes to place a
nephew of his, to whom he is guardian. I think that you will
suit him exactly."

The old priest took me immediately to call on Signior Cintillo, to whom, though he knew nothing of me, he undertook to
be responsible for me, and who directly received me into his
house, on the footing of fifty pistoles a year salary, an offer
which I deemed it prudent to accept, until something better
should offer. The jeweller was a man who affected a great
deal of devotion. He had always a rosary in his hand, passed
a great portion of the day in church, and reconciled with all
that the business of an usurer, which he exercised so secretly
that nobody in the town was ignorant of it.

In order to please this personage, I took care to put on a

pious exterior, which agreed most admirably with his own
hypocrisy. He called his nephew, a youth of about eighteen,
and presenting him to me, said : " Here is the scholar I have
to place under your care : he already knows how to read and
write; he even understands a little Latin. Instruct him in
philosophy, and, above all things, direct him to the love of
virtue, for that is the matter of most importance."

My new scholar was named Chrysostom. He had such a
muddy conception, that I could not help telling his uncle that
I did not find in my scholar the slightest inclination to profit
by my precepts, and, in fact, that I wholly despaired of making
him a philosopher. " Be not discouraged," replied he ; " I
know very well that my nephew is a dull subject. I shall,
therefore, not be so unjust as to complain of you, if you should
be unable to render him learned.

" Between ourselves," continued he, " I have it in view to
make a friar of Chrysostom. I think him born for the frock."
Here I interrupted the jeweller. " Ah ! Signior Diego," said
I, " be very careful not to force the inclination of your nephew :
the number of bad friars already in existence does not want
augmenting."—" What are you saying ? " cried Cintillo, with an
air of astonishment. " God forbid that I should constrain the
inclinations of Chrysostom, and make him a recluse in spite of
himself. Do me more justice ; I desire only his good. Not
thinking him formed for the world, I should be happy that he
would embrace the monastic life of his own accord. Assist me,
I entreat you, to turn his mind that way. I double your salary,
in the hope of engaging you to second my intentions. Let us
unite to persuade him to this course, which is in reality the
best. How happy should I be to behold my nephew living
piously in a monastery ! "

The good jeweller had not told me all. Besides the pleasure
he promised himself, in having a new St. Chrysostom in his
family, he was not sorry to see a nephew devote himself to
religion, to whose property he by that means became heir. I
now entered into his views, being paid for doing so, and took
upon myself the office of a preacher. I began to declaim
against the world, and to extol to my pupil the sweetness of a
monastic life. Cintillo, on his side, was eternally preaching to
him the same thing ; till at length the poor boy, stunned with
our sermons, which he stupidly believed to the very letter, com-

menced his novitiate, in about ten months, at the Convent of the Fathers of St. Dominic, where, persevering in his fervor, his uncle had the satisfaction of seeing him profess, and of becoming heir to all his fortune. The good Signior Diego, having then no further need of me, paid me my salary; which I had very well earned, for I had been every day to see Chrysostom during his novitiate, in order to confirm him in his laudable sentiments. Thus Cintillo and I parted, perfectly satisfied with each other.

Shortly after, I quitted Cuença, in consequence of a piece of information which was given me, and which, I conceive, I ought not to pass over in silence. One day that I was walking along the street, wrapped up in meditation, I found myself tapped gently on the shoulder, and, on turning my head, perceived a man whom I recognized as one of the two bravoes who had conducted me from Madrid to Leganez. I trembled at the sight of this bird of ill omen, and exclaimed: " How now, Signior Bully! am I again so unfortunate as to have you at my heels? have I not persevered in banishing myself, agreeably to my promise? "—" Pardon me," replied he, laughing; " you are a man of your word, and we have no longer anything to do with each other; I can even assure you that you may return to Madrid, if you think proper."

" I understand you," said I; " Donna Luisa is dead, I suppose? "—" No," replied the bravo, " she is still alive, and you may renew your acquaintance with her, if your heart be so inclined. We shall not prevent you. I will tell you the reason; it is that our company has separated, on account of a dispute which arose between two of us about La Gitanilla, that little brunette whom you supped with one night, and whom you thought so pretty. They fought together, to decide which of the two should have the sole possession of her, and they had the misfortune to be both run through the body. This event has caused a general separation, and each of us retired whither he pleased."

I was very much delighted with this news, and I did not fail shortly to put myself on the road to Madrid; having so much the more desire to see this town, as it had been forbidden me, on pain of death, ever to set foot in it again.

CHAPTER XI.

I HAD scarcely arrived in Madrid ere I met by accident with my ancient host, Martin Cinquillo, he who had placed me in the service of Donna Luisa de Padilla. We easily recognized each other. "Signior Bachelor," said he, with an air of astonishment, "is it possible that I behold you once more, safe and sound, after the adventure which happened to you? I thought, I confess, that the bravoes who carried you away had taken your life, and Donna Luisa actually considers you among the dead. What pleasure it will give her to hear that you are still alive! Call on me to-morrow," added he, "and I will apprise you how she has received this piece of information."

Curious to know in what manner this lady would be affected by my return to Madrid, I failed not on the following day to call at Cinquillo's house, where I found Dame Rodriguez waiting my arrival. As soon as this good lady saw me, she embraced me with tears in her eyes, exclaiming: "Welcome back, Don Cherubin. Alas! both my mistress and myself had given up the hope of ever seeing you again. We imagined that the family of Padilla, irritated against you, had had the cruelty to sacrifice you to their resentment. How afflicted have we been in this opinion! What tears has Donna Luisa shed for your sake! Judge by the grief she has felt at your absence, how great must be her joy at your return. I come to assure you of it on her part, and to convince you that she is disposed to render your fortune agreeable and happy.

" It is not," pursued Rodriguez, " that she still entertains the design of marrying you. Thank heaven, her eyes are opened to the folly of such a marriage, and the ridicule to which it would expose her. In a word, she has entirely given up the idea ; but she would, out of friendship, put you in the way of making a fortune, by placing you in the house of the Duke de Uzeda, her relation, and the favorite of the king. She flatters herself with having sufficient interest to get you received among this minister's secretaries. You are sensible of the importance of such a post ; and I doubt not that you will be happy to fill it, at least if it be not your intention to consecrate yourself to the service of the church."—" No, no ! " replied I, " I have no such intention. I feel that I have virtue enough to be a secretary, but not of having enough to make a good priest."—" That being the case," said Rodriguez, " lay aside your present dress and adopt that of a layman."—" That is what I can promise to do," replied I, " without the slightest hesitation ; for I am beginning to tire of the office of preceptor, which I conceive one that no respectable man ought to hold but as a matter of necessity." I therefore laid aside my ecclesiastical habit, and speedily entered into the office of the prime minister ; a single word from Donna Luisa to her niece, Donna Maria de Padilla, Duchess de Uzeda, having been sufficient to obtain me the appointment.

As soon as I was installed in my new post, I expressed to Dame Rodriguez my desire of seeing her mistress, in order to return her thanks ; but she informed me that Donna Luisa would dispense with this piece of attention. " After what has passed between you," said she, " she deems it prudent to forbid you her presence, lest she should again expose you to any unpleasant treatment. She wishes to protect you without seeing you ; a conduct which will not expose her to the censure of her relations : you ought to give her credit for her prudence."—" To that," said I, " my dear Rodriguez, I have nothing to reply ; and since I am not allowed personally to return thanks to Donna Luisa, do you, at least, assure her that I am penetrated with the most lively gratitude for her kindness." At bottom I was not much grieved that my protectress refused

to see me ; for if I had been established on the footing of paying her visits, I might very probably have found myself shortly
engaged in an affair with a new set of bravoes, who would perhaps have treated me worse than their predecessors.

As I wrote a tolerably good hand, having learned to write at
Salamanca, I was employed in my office in making fair copies
of all kinds of despatches. I became acquainted with the
clerks, and had even the honor of attracting the particular
friendship of Don Juan de Salzedo, principal secretary to the
Duke de Uzeda. This Don Juan was not deficient of sense,
but he had the defect of being rather too fond of Latin, and
of eternally quoting, on all occasions, passages from Horace,
Ovid, etc. Whenever we met he accosted me with some Latin
sentence, and to accommodate myself to his foible, I always
replied in the same language. By this method I completely
won his esteem ; a convincing proof that in order to please it
is only necessary to comply with the humor of our companions.
" Don Cherubin," said he one day, " I have a regard for you,
and whenever I shall find occasion to give you proof of it, I
will seize on it *lubenti animo.*" Fortune ordained that the
occasion should speedily present itself ; but it is necessary to
detail the circumstances which gave rise to it.

One evening, at a grand ball given by the Duchess de Uzeda,
at her palace in the great square, where the bull-fights are
exhibited, it happened that I was of the party. There were
present a great number of noblemen, and also of the most handsome ladies of the court. It might have been supposed that a
selection had been made of the most amiable persons in the
kingdom, to form so charming an assembly.

Before the commencement of the ball, the ladies shared in-
differently the admiration of the men ; but no sooner had the
company witnessed the dancing of Donna Isabella de Sandoval,
the only daughter of the Duke de Uzeda, than she engrossed
the attention of all. Every one admired the gracefulness of her
manner, her noble and majestic air, the lightness of her step,
the symmetry of her person, and the fineness of her ear. Thus,
no sooner had she finished the dance, than the hall resounded
with applause. " She is inimitable," said a marquis. " Why
have we not such a dancer in our theatres ? I would take her
under my protection, cost what it would."—" I would entreat
her to ruin me," said a count. " I would beg of her the pref-

erence," said a duke. In a word, the whole company was enchanted with this new Terpsichore, nor was I the least delighted of the number.

It may easily be supposed that so rich and noble an heiress was not likely to want admirers. Among those who aspired to the honor of espousing Donna Isabella, no one had better reason to flatter himself with hopes of success than Don Juan Telles Giron, Count de Urenna, the only son of the Duke de Ossuna and certainly the most worthy of preference. This young nobleman fulfilled the duties of Gentleman of the King's Bedchamber for his father, who was then at Naples, of which he was governor.

While the lovers of the Duke de Uzeda's daughter were essaying, by their attentions, to recommend themselves to notice, that minister sent for the Count, and thus addressed him: " Don Juan, you are aware of the strict friendship which exists between your father and myself, and the interest I take in all that concerns the welfare of your house; I have requested this interview in order to represent that you ought to profit by the opportunity presented you, while fortune is in a good humor. The Duke de Ossuna has more enemies than ever: they are laboring incessantly to effect his ruin, and it is to be feared that they may succeed in their purpose. While his credit is yet good, you ought to think of establishing yourself; you are of an age to marry, and even to enter upon important employments. It is now twelve months," continued he, " since your father wrote to me, requesting that I would seek a wife for you." I answered him, "that I had already fixed on one; but, as nothing has since passed on the subject between us, I am ignorant whether he be still in the same mind."—" Do not fail," added he, "to recount to him what I have said to you, and to assure him, that if he desire a daughter-in-law at my hand, I have it in contemplation to give him one rich enough, handsome enough, and noble enough to deserve such a father-in-law as himself."

At this discourse, the Count, rightly judging that Isabella was the daughter-in-law alluded to, manifested such lively joy, as afforded considerable satisfaction to the Duke de Uzeda. Without, however, appearing to notice it, he continued: " Send immediately a despatch to Naples, and the answer of the Viceroy will decide the affair of your marriage." The Count, to evince the impatience he felt to become his son-in-law, immediately took leave of his Excellency, telling him "that he would forthwith write to his father," and went directly to Don Juan de Salzedo, whom he esteemed as an ancient servitor of his house, and without whose counsel he never did anything of importance. After acquainting him with the conversation he had just had with his Excellency, he said: "I know not whom I can send to Naples; I shall want a sensible and confidential person, who may make known to my father a thousand things which I dare not venture to commit to writing."

Salzedo, recollecting me, and considering it an opportunity of throwing a good windfall in my way, proposed me as a person well qualified to execute the commission; on which the Count, being content to avail himself of my services, expressed a desire to see me. In a private conference which I had with him, he instructed me in all that he was desirous his father should be informed of; after which, having received from this young nobleman two packets, one for the Duke, and the other for the Duchess de Ossuna, with a purse containing two hundred pistoles, I prepared to set out for Italy; but before my departure, I went to take leave of the secretary Salzedo, who said, affectionately embracing me, "Go, my dear Don Cherubin; I am delighted that you are about to take this voyage; it will produce you a good allowance of pistoles *et lavina videlis littora.*" I then set out from Madrid; and, following close upon a courier whom the Count had despatched to Naples, arrived nearly as soon as he.

CHAPTER XII.

THE Duke de Ossuna had been three years Viceroy of the
kingdom of Naples, after having governed Sicily four. I
alighted at the royal palace in which he resided, and caused
myself to be announced to his Excellency as a courier despatched by his son the Count de Urenna. The Viceroy was
at that moment in his closet, into which he caused me to be introduced. I presented him the packet with which I had been
entrusted. After reading the contents, " These," said he, " are
despatches of a most agreeable nature, and not the less so for
being presented by a secretary of the Duke de Uzeda himself.
But tell me, I entreat you, is the daughter of this minister
possessed of all the merit which my son attributes to her ? I
place no very great reliance on the portraits which lovers draw
of their mistresses."—" My lord," replied I, " in whatever colors
your son may have painted Isabella de Sandoval, the copy cannot fail to be inferior to the original. In a word, however
great an idea you may form of this lady's charms, your imagination cannot carry you above the truth. Picture to yourself
a creature of fifteen, who joins to a beauty the most perfect,
a sprightly wit and solid judgment ;—this idea will but include a
part of the transcendent qualities of Isabella. It is true that
she has not the serious disposition and the gravity by which
the Spanish ladies are generally distinguished; but this imper-
fection (which is only one in Spain) will meet with toleration
from your Excellency."—" You are right," replied the Duke,

smiling; "Spaniard though I am, I prefer a lively disposition to a grave one."

In this part of our conversation, the Duchess, who had been informed of the arrival of a courier despatched by Don Juan Telles, entered the closet, full of impatience to learn some news of her dear son. "Madam," said her husband, "a most advantageous offer is held out for the Count de Urenna; the Duke de Uzeda offers to make him his son-in-law, in preference to all the great noblemen who seek the alliance of his only daughter Isabella." I then delivered to the Vice-Queen her packet, which contained only a repetition of the same things which had been detailed in the other. As soon as they had read it, they began to deliberate, not whether they should consent to the marriage, but what steps they were to take on the occasion. They resolved on sending me back to Madrid on the following morning, to testify to the Duke and Duchess de Uzeda the impatience they felt for the alliance of the houses of Giron and Sandoval: it was likewise determined that they should write to the Duke de Lerma and to Donna Isabella.

They spent the day in preparing their despatches; and as Don Juan had written to his father that I could instruct him on several points necessary for him to know, I had in the evening an interview with his Excellency, longer than the preceding. "Give me," said he, "a faithful account of all that the Count, my son, has desired you to inform me. You are about, I suppose, to speak of the last letter I wrote to the king; you will tell me, perhaps, that it disgusted the greater part of the grandees."—"Exactly so, my lord," replied I; "it is there I would begin. In proposing to render places vendible in Spain, you have raised the council against you, which, being principally composed of grandees interested in rejecting, was of course very little inclined to approve of such a measure. What is most to be regretted," added I, "is that these grandees do not content themselves with merely opposing the sale of places; they indulge in murmurs, and, by means of secret contrivances, endeavor to propagate the opinion that you are an enemy to the nation. They are even seconded by the Neapolitan noblemen, who, in concert with them, are continually writing letters to the Court, calculated to render you suspected."

The Duke de Ossuna at this passage could not refrain from interrupting me. "These," cried he, with a sigh, "these are

the faithful subjects, who are always declaring that they are
ready to spill their blood and to sacrifice their property for the
good of their sovereign. If the king were to sell those places
which he now bestows gratuitously, what family in the kingdom
would lose more than my own? I sacrifice to the profit of the
monarch my relations and my friends ; I have only his interest
in view, and yet of this they make a crime. Such is the recompense of those servants whose fidelity is greatest.

" Continue," pursued he ; " I am very well content with the
choice my son has made, in appointing you to instruct me as to
what is passing at Court to my prejudice. You acquit yourself
of the task perfectly to my satisfaction—continue therefore.
What further injustice do they do me ? "—" The most alarming," replied I, " and the most touching that can be done to a
faithful subject of King Philip; it is said that you have formed
the ambitious project of rendering yourself King of Naples."
The Duke at this accusation shut his eyes, shrugged up his
shoulders, and asked me who could possibly be the enemy
capable of accusing him of so culpable a design.   " The Count
de Benevento," said I, " and some other grandees spread this
report, which your armaments, or, to speak more properly, your
glorious actions, and the services you have rendered, appear to
justify. There are those points in your administration, of
which they are jealous, which will, they say, be sufficient to
form matter for a process against you."—" I am in the wrong,"
again interrupted his Excellency; " I am in the wrong. I
ought to have followed the examples of former viceroys of
Naples and Sicily: I ought to have suffered both kingdoms to
be ravaged by the Turks; to have enriched myself at the expense of the king and his subjects, and then have returned to
Court, there to be thanked for my judicious government. Oh,
unhappy monarchy ! " added he, lifting up his eyes to heaven,
" must, then, those who serve thee with the greatest ardor, and
who seek only to augment thy glory, be stigmatized as thine
enemies ! "

After this apostrophe, full of bitterness, the Duke put other
questions to me. " Tell me," said he, " who are the grandees
who are at present most in confidence with the Prince of Spain ? "
I mentioned to him several, and did not omit Don Gaspard de
Guzman de Olivarez. " It is this last," said I, " who appears
to be most in favor. It is true, if one may believe the report

of Madrid, that he takes a sure method of gaining the friendship of the young Philip."—"What method is that?" inquired the Duke. "It is," said I, "the application of that which procures success to all enterprises—money. It is said that the Count de Olivarez, who has an immense fortune, employs a great part of it in procuring for the young prince those pleasures which the avarice of the king denies him. Perhaps," added I, "the report is correct; at least I know that the Prince of Spain, when engaged in the pleasures of the chase, often finds superb collations, prepared by the care and at the expense of Don Gaspard."—"Ay!" said the Viceroy, shaking his head, "Olivarez is well acquainted with the means of supplanting the Duke de Lerma and his son. I hope that my prediction may prove false; but if it should so happen, they will have only themselves to thank for it. Why do they suffer near the person of the heir of the Crown a courtier so polished and so subtle, who is seizing, before their eyes, the helm of government?"

When the Duke de Ossuna had exhausted all the questions he wished to ask me, he delivered me his despatches, saying: "Go and repose yourself, and to-morrow morning set out on your return to Spain; but before you go, pay a visit to my treasurer; I have given him some directions concerning you." This was the first thing I did the next morning. The treasurer put into my hands, on the part of his Excellency, a bill of exchange for three thousand crowns, payable at sight. Besides this present, I received another, which was brought me from the Vice-Queen by one of her gentlemen-ushers: it was a gold chain of exquisite workmanship, and which was worth at least two hundred pistoles. I set out from Naples with all these riches, and resumed the route to Madrid, where I had the happiness of arriving without encountering any accident.

4

CHAPTER XIII.

DON JUAN DE TELLES MARRIES THE DAUGHTER OF THE DUKE
DE UZEDA——CONSEQUENCE OF THIS MARRIAGE——OF THE NEW
COURSE TAKEN BY DON CHERUBIN.

The first thing I did was to render an account of my expedition to Don Juan Telles, who embraced me with joy as soon as he had read his father's letter. This young nobleman, to convince me how well he was satisfied with me, or, more properly, with the news which I brought him, rewarded me with a purse in which were two hundred doubloons.

He immediately went to communicate to the Duke de Uzeda the despatches of the Viceroy, and, two days after, his marriage with Donna Isabella was made public. Preparations were made with a magnificence suitable to the dignity of the parties; and the Duke de Uzeda testified as much impatience for the completion of it, as had been manifested by the Duke de Ossuna. The relations and friends of the houses of Giron and Sandoval celebrated it with the most lively demonstrations of joy, and certainly Hymen could never have united two persons more fit for each other.

No sooner were the rejoicings finished than the Viceroy wrote to the Duke de Uzeda that, to arrive at the entire completion of his wishes, he had only one to be fulfilled, which was that of having his dear daughter-in-law near him; that he begged him to send her to see Italy, and, in particular, the city of Naples, and finally, that to render this journey the more agreeable to the young bride, he wished that her husband should accompany her, if such were the pleasure of his Majesty. The son of the Cardinal de Lerma entered into the sentiments of the Duke de Ossuna, and obtained permission from his Majesty to send his daughter to Naples, together with the

Count de Urenna. The preparations for their departure were speedily made, the Viceroy having expressly forbidden his son to have a numerous and splendid suite. They shortly set out for Barcelona, where two vessels, sent by the Duke de Ossuna, waited to convey them to Genoa, from whence Don Octavio de Aragon was, with eight galleys, to conduct them to Naples.

It is very seldom that a beggar becomes rich without suffering himself to grow giddy with the contemplation of his wealth. I was not proof against this weakness. When I came to count my cash, and saw that I had before me nearly two thousand pistoles, I took a dislike to my post of secretary. It appeared to me that a young man who possessed so much money ought to lead a life, free, independent, and above all inactive, such as is generally indulged in by the honest people of Spain. " Since," said I, "I can live like a gentleman and act the gallant in the world, I should be a great fool to remain in the offices of ministers, where one must consume the day in labor. It is far more agreeable to have nothing to do but to walk about and amuse one's self with one's friends." It was thus that, yielding to the inclination by which I found myself impelled, I suffered myself to be drawn into libertinism, without my philosophy being able to save me. On the contrary, I would listen to none of its remonstrances, and when I bade adieu to the Secretary Salzedo, all that he could say to induce me to retain my post in the office, though full of sense and ornamented with Latin, was thrown away. I hired a handsome apartment in a furnished hotel, and had made two rich suits of clothes, in which I walked out alternately to show myself at Court and on the Prado.

CHAPTER XIV.

DON CHERUBIN MEETS WITH THE LITTLE LICENTIATE CARAMBOLA
—OF HIS INTERVIEW WITH HIM—PLEASANT ADVENTURE WHICH
HAPPENS TO THE LICENTIATE—WHAT WAS THE CONSEQUENCE
OF IT.

ONE day, being on the public walk, where I amused myself
with ogling the ladies, I observed the little Biscayan licentiate
whom I had left at Toledo. He did not at first know me in my
new dress. However, I called to him, and he came over and
embraced me. " I am delighted," said I, " my dear friend,
that fortune has again brought us together." Instead of making me any reply, Carambola set his eyes wide open, and began
attentively to review me from head to foot. Then bursting into
a loud fit of laughter—" Here is a metamorphosis," exclaimed
he. " You in the dress of a cavalier ! Who has induced you
to quit the cassock for the sword ? I am strongly inclined to
think that it has been that handsome marchioness at whose
house you were tutor in Toledo ; it is she, apparently, who has
robbed the church of the Bachelor Don Cherubin." I informed
him that he was mistaken. " You are then," said he, " amusing
yourself with some rich widow who shares with you the contents
of her purse. Tell me the truth : have you not met here with
some piece of good fortune of this description ? "
"If you will listen to me a moment," said I, " I will satisfy
your curiosity." As soon as he gave me leave to speak, I related to him what had occurred to me since our separation. I
then requested him to inform me, in his turn, what he was then
doing in Madrid. " Still the business of teaching," said he ;
" I am unfit for any other. I am condemned to the tutorship,
or, to speak more justly, to the galleys for my life. While you

were at the Marquis de Torbellino's, and passing your time very
agreeably, I found myself on the *pavé* without money, or at
least on the point of wanting it; I therefore abandoned Toledo
as a town which was becoming every day more disgusting to me.
I arrived at Madrid, where I found the means of getting into
the house of a rich citizen, who was a widower and who had a
son of about twelve years of age.   This citizen was seldom at
home; he always went out to dine and sup, a circumstance
which by no means tended to improve our ordinary at home.
A woman of about five-and-forty, who had the management of
his house, provided our meals.

"Oh, the abominable cook!   Sometimes she put too much
salt into her ragoûts, and at other times an equal superabun-
dance of pepper, cloves, or saffron.   It was useless for me to
complain; the old devil had the malice never to mend her hand.
I even thought that she did it purposely to disgust me with the
house and oblige me to quit it, having taken an aversion to me
—I know not for what reason, unless that, in my behavior to
her, I had somewhat the air of a Cato.

"For my own part, out of spite to this old sorceress, I persisted in remaining in the house, where I should probably have
been still, but for an accident, such as perhaps never happened
to any preceptor before.   One day that I had received about
twenty pistoles, I went into a tennis court, which, indeed, I
could seldom keep out of while I had a crown remaining.   Fortune, who is generally rather averse to me, was on this occasion
favorable.   I won ten doubloons, which were no sooner in my
pocket than I took it into my head to go and give a supper to
two ladies with whom I had become acquainted, and who lived
in the Sun Gate.   I went to visit them with this laudable intention, after having bespoken a very respectable supper at a
tavern.

"I was received by these ladies with the more good will, as I
was in the habit of regaling them when I favored them with
my visits.   We began to converse with great gaiety, and as
soon as the supper which I had ordered arrived, we sat down
to table.   I expected to have plenty of amusement for my
money, but on a sudden the door opened, and in a visitor who
suddenly entered, I recognized the citizen whose son I was educating.   When he perceived me his surprise was not less than
my own.   We remained for a moment mute with astonishment,

and looked at each other as if we doubted the evidence of our own senses. But the confusion into which we were thrown lasted not long; we recovered ourselves immediately, and, getting over the shame of meeting in such a place, burst into such immoderate fits of laughter that the ladies took us for two very intimate friends who had accidentally met together in their company.

"'By what I can perceive,' said one of the nymphs, 'you are acquainted with each other!'—'We ought, indeed, to be well acquainted,' replied the citizen; 'we see each other every day; we dine together sometimes, and we sleep under the same roof: it was only wanting to us to have friends in common—we have now nothing more to wish for.' The air of raillery with which he uttered these words put me in the humor for jesting likewise, an inclination in which I indulged at all hazards, determined to outface the citizen, if he should take me to task about our rencounter. But, instead of evincing the least discontent on the subject, he sat down with us at table, saying with an unembarrassed air, that he did not suppose he should make too many in the company. In fact, he was in so good a humor that he appeared to me extremely agreeable. He drank my health, and showed me a thousand little attentions. Insensibly, I forgot that I was with the father of my pupil, and we drank together most jovially.

"When it was time to retire, we took leave of the ladies and returned home. When we had arrived there, the citizen, addressing me, said: 'Signior Licentiate, I have no quarrel with you for going to visit the ladies at whose house we met to-night, but be careful, I pray you, not to take my son there.'"

Carambola could not help laughing at these last words, and his laughter was accompanied by my own. "This was," said I, "an admirable father, and the house an excellent one for a tutor."—"I quitted it notwithstanding," said Carambola, "for the honor of my character: I did not think it consistent that a vicious licentiate should remain in a house where he was known. I am now in another place. I am bringing up the natural son of a member of the Council of the Indies; and I am in hopes that his education will be more useful to me than that of a legitimate child."—"I wish," rejoined I, "that you may not be flattering yourself with a vain hope; but you have told me a hundred times, one must not reckon too much on the gratitude of parents."—"That is but too true," replied the little licentiate. "However, those whom I have to deal with at present appear so generous, that I cannot avoid placing great confidence in them."

CHAPTER XV.

OUR conversation was interrupted by the arrival of a gentleman with whom I had formed an acquaintance, and who, at
this moment, joined me on the promenade. "I bid you not
adieu," said the Biscayan; "we shall see each other again."
He then retired, leaving me in the company of my new friend,
who was named Don Manoel de Pedrilla. He was a gentleman of the town of Alcaraz on the confines of New Castile,
about my own age, and of an agreeable person. The desire of
seeing the Court had brought him to Madrid. He lodged in
the same hotel with myself; we used to dine at the same table,
and go every day together to the public walks and places of
amusement. In a word, we became so attached to each other
that we were inseparable.

One morning, as we were sitting together in his apartment,
there entered a little footboy who delivered him a letter. Don
Manoel read it, and then said to the bearer: "My child, you
may assure your mistress that I will not fail to be there."
Then, addressing me—"Don Cherubin," said he, "I am to
sup this evening at the house of two ladies, where I am at
liberty to introduce a friend: are you inclined to accompany
me thither?" I accepted the invitation, telling Don Manoel
with a smile, that I thanked him for the preference he had
given me. "You ought so," said he, smiling in his turn;
"the favor I propose you is well deserving of thanks. Know
that you are to sup with two ladies who are highly amiable and

56

interesting : their manners are dignified ; they are two women of quality, who live together at their common cost, and in the French fashion. Their house is open to men of honor, who are admitted to play and sup there."—"And they requite themselves, doubtless," said I, laughing, "with the profits of the game."—"Of that I know nothing," replied he. "Perhaps they may have lovers who supply them secretly with the means of supporting their expenditure ; but there is no appearance of any such thing : nothing is to be seen about them which can render their virtue liable to suspicion."

I asked the names of these ladies. "One," said he, "is called Ismenia, and the other, Basilisa. They give themselves out as widows of two gentlemen of Grenada, and by their own account have come to Madrid merely out of curiosity."—"To which of them," said I, "has your heart surrendered itself ? "—
"I am in love with Donna Ismenia," said Don Manoel, "and by what I can judge, I sigh not for one who is ungrateful ; but I am not loved as I would be : she is but half kind to me."—
"I am impatient to see Ismenia," said I, "as also her companion."—"You will see," returned he, "two persons with whom you will be much obliged to me for making you acquainted."

In the evening Don Manoel conducted me to the ladies, who resided in a tolerably handsome and well-furnished house. "Ladies," said he, presenting me, "I hope that you will not be displeased at my having brought with me one of my most particular friends, a gentleman from the province of Leon, and a young man of merit." The ladies replied, "That my appearance would justify whatever he could say in my favor," and honored me with a most gracious reception.

I shall not draw a portrait of these ladies ; I shall only say that I was struck with their beauty, and that after a quarter of an hour's conversation, I found myself equally pleased with both of them, though they were in character extremely different. Ismenia was serious, and Basilisa remarkably lively. The former conversed with as much dignity as elegance, and said nothing inconsiderately ; the other hazarded everything, but almost always successfully. Don Manoel perceived that I took considerable pleasure in listening to them. "Signior Don Cherubin," said he, "I think you are not displeased with me for bringing you hither ? "

At the name of Don Cherubin, Basilisa looked at me attentively, and asked in what part of Spain I was born. I replied, "In the province of Leon,—why do you ask that question?" The lady appeared troubled at my answer. "It is not without reason," said she, "that I ask you, for I am acquainted with some persons of Salamanca. Were you born in that town?"—"No," replied I, "but in the neighborhood of it. I first saw the light in Molorido, a considerable borough, of which my father was alcade."—"What was his name?" asked Basilisa. "Don Roberto de la Ronda," I replied. "Ah, my brother," cried the lady, rising to embrace me, "my dear Don Cherubin, it is you! Is it possible that fortune this day restores you to your sister Francisca? for it is she whom you have met here, under the name of Basilisa."

The force of blood was no less powerful on my side. I was so delighted at having recovered my sister that I enfolded her in my arms with such warmth, as for a time to prevent her utterance. On her part, penetrated with my sensibility, she in her turn became mute, so that it was long before we could express ourselves otherwise than by tears. Ismenia and Don Manoel were much affected, and overwhelmed us with embraces.

After so many endearments we again placed ourselves at table, and began to converse as gaily as before. The conversation was not, however, always general: from time to time Basilisa, whom I shall in future call Donna Francisca, questioned me in a low tone of voice about the family, and while we conversed thus, Don Manoel entertained himself with Ismenia in the same way. The night was far advanced when we took leave of these ladies. "Don Cherubin," said my sister, "you will come to-morrow to dinner. I am dying with impatience to hear your adventures, and you cannot have less to be acquainted with mine."

END OF THE FIRST PART.

PART THE SECOND.

CHAPTER I.

DON CHERUBIN DE LA RONDA GOES TO DINE WITH HIS SISTER—
THEY RELATE TO EACH OTHER WHAT HAS OCCURRED SINCE THEIR
SEPARATION—HISTORY AND GALLANTRIES OF DONNA FRANCISCA.

On my return to my hotel I tried in vain to obtain a few hours' sleep; my spirits were in such a state of agitation that I could not close my eyes.

I was not a little curious to learn my sister's adventures, though I doubted not that I should get but a mutilated account. For her part, being no less anxious than myself for an opportunity to converse with me, she was as little able to rest; so that when I called on her, at the earliest moment I thought I could with propriety, I found her dressed and waiting for me in her apartment. " Come, brother," said she, " come and satisfy my curiosity, and I will afterwards gratify yours. Well, what have you been doing since you quitted the University of Salamanca ? "—" My dear sister," said I, " I shall very speedily comply with your desire." I then gave her a faithful account of my adventures. When I had concluded, Donna Francisca complimented me on the present state of my fortune. She then proceeded to recount her own history in the following terms :—

" After the death of our father, Don Roberto de la Ronda, or, rather, after that of the Corregidor of Salamanca, you and Don Cæsar, as you know, each embraced your different mode of life, and I remained with my mother, whom the narrowness of our circumstances prevented from giving me a superior education. She took this so much to heart, that it caused her death. Fortunately, Donna Melancia, my godmother, and Don Balthasar de Faranella, her husband, were no sooner informed of this, than they came to seek me at Molorido, and, as they had no children of their own, conveyed me to Salamanca, with the design of bringing me up in their own house. I found in my godmother and her husband a second father and mother, who, every day giving me fresh marks of tenderness, allowed me to feel very little of the inconvenience of being an orphan.

"Although I was at that time scarcely ten years old, I was so advanced for my age, that I attracted the attention of one of our neighbors, a young gentleman named Don Ferdinand de Gamboa. He called on us frequently in company with his father, who lived on terms of such intimate friendship with Don Balthasar, that they were almost always together. Under favor of this union, Don Ferdinand was at liberty to see and speak to me whenever he pleased. As he was only two or three years older than myself, it was not deemed necessary to keep any watch over us in our little interviews. We, however, deserved very well that they should be looked to, and they, doubtless, would soon have been so, but that Don Ferdinand was on a sudden snatched from me. His father carried him away to Court, in order to place him in the Spanish Guards, in which he had just obtained him an ensigncy through the interest of his friends. I was for two or three days very much afflicted at the loss of my lover, but at last consoled myself, as it was very natural to a girl of my age.

"Shortly after the departure of the young Gamboa, I gave birth to a new passion. Don Balthasar, although he was fifty and some odd years of age, conceived an affection for me, to which I at first, though unconsciously, corresponded, receiving his caresses as the innocent marks of friendship from a godfather ; for so I called him. This old sinner would infallibly have seduced me, had not my godmother fortunately penetrated his design, and averted it by sending me promptly to a convent in Carthagena, of which the Abbess was her relation. After having escaped these two imminent dangers, I entered into the convent, as into an asylum in which, in all likelihood, I must be sheltered from the shafts of love. But this deity, fond of his prey, had resolved to pursue me everywhere ; and I believe no asylum is to be found which is inaccessible to his power.

"The Lady Abbess, to whom Donna Melancia had most

strongly recommended me, became very fond of me. She placed me in the number of the boarders and young nuns who formed her court, and among whom were several of the most perfect beauty. All these girls emulated each other in striving to divert her by the exertion of their talents. Those who had good voices joined in concert with such as could play on musical instruments; and those who could dance contributed also to the amusement of the Abbess; who, environed with her elegant damsels, appeared like Diana surrounded by her nymphs. I beheld with envy the efforts of these girls to please, and wished I could unite in myself all their different talents, in order to be agreeable to the superior. Although I had the principles of dancing, and did not want for a good voice, yet I was but an uninstructed creature, or at least I was not sufficiently clever to contribute to the amusement of our Abbess, who, seeing my good inclination, had me taught to dance and sing by two excellent masters.

"So great was my talent for these two qualifications, that they had very little difficulty in rendering me a proficient. In less than a year I became the best singer and dancer in the convent. I also learned to play extremely well upon the lute, so that I became by degrees a most admirable and accomplished person. All the ladies of Carthagena who came to our parties overwhelmed me with compliments, and did not fail to give the Abbess her share, on the advantage of having a young girl of so much merit under her protection. The Abbess herself took credit for my talents, which she looked upon in some degree as her own work. However, instead of applauding herself for the accomplishments she had bestowed on me, she ought rather to have reproached herself; and, indeed, it was not long ere she had reason to repent it. One of her nephews, of whom she was extremely fond, who was called Don Gregorio de Clevillente, came to Carthagena for the purpose of passing a fortnight with her, as he was in the habit of doing once a year. This gentleman was young, beautiful, and extremely well formed. He supped every evening in the parlor, with his aunt and the favorite boarders, in which number I had the honor of being included. The most sprightly among us joined in lively discourse to divert Don Gregorio; after supper, all who were qualified assembled to form a concert, and the amusement always finished with dancing.

"I remarked the first day that Clevillente, delighted at seeing so many handsome girls together, suffered his eyes to range among them without being able to decide to which he should give the preference. If he were affected by the soft voice of one, he was presently after enraptured at the graceful dancing of another: he was as much embarrassed as a sultan about to throw the handkerchief. He was, however, fixed at last, and became enamoured of my face, in prejudice of others more worthy than myself. Of this he made me sensible on the second day, by the glances with which he favored me, for, in fact, he appeared to have eyes for none but your sister.

"I did not at first appear to be sensible of this, nor make any reply to his looks ; but the devil lost nothing by that. From the moment I was aware of having secured a lover in Don Gregorio, I felt an inclination for him, though I had formerly looked on him with impunity. What delight would it have afforded him could he have read in my face what was passing in my heart ! But I so well concealed my growing affection that he had not the least suspicion of it. On the contrary, imagining that I had paid no regard to his attentions, he resolved on making me a formal declaration of his sentiments ; and thus it was that he put his design in execution.

"He imparted the secret of his attachment to a young valet in his service who was a youth of great dexterity. 'Brabonel,' then continued he, ' can you contrive to convey a billet secretly to Donna Francisca ? '—'Why not ? ' said Brabonel ; 'I have done things much more difficult than that. I have formed an acquaintance with a portress of this convent, and I can easily induce her to perform this little service for you. Only give me your letter, and leave the rest to me.'

"Brabonel had not exaggerated in boasting of his influence with the portress, for, in effect, she said to me the same day, slipping into my hand a billet from Clevillente : ' Here, beautiful Francisca, read this paper ; you will find in it something which will please you.' I asked her what it was ; but instead of answering me, she withdrew with a precipitancy which induced me to think that this good portress was a little too obliging.

"I found in this letter of Don Gregorio's a most lively declaration of love, and the most earnest solicitations from that cavalier to allow him to speak to me in private. I ought, I confess, immediately to have carried this letter to the Abbess; but this was what I did not do, and what I had, besides, no inclination to do : a girl of thirteen has not quite so much prudence. More flattered with the conquest of a lover who was not unpleasing to me, than angry at his audacity, I resolved to dissemble, and see whether he would persist in loving me, or rather in wishing to seduce me ; for he had no other intention. He again employed the agency of the portress, who, not content with bringing me billets, had the address to prevail on me to answer them and to contrive an interview between us, in which Don Gregorio told me that he was resolved to marry me, but that, in order to be able to do so, he must carry me off, as his aunt would not, he was confident, give her consent to our union.

" He had little difficulty in prevailing on me, and, imagining that I was following a husband, I quietly suffered myself to be conducted, disguised in man's apparel, to the castle of Clevillente ; where, during two months, my seducer paid me the greatest attention. After this he relaxed, and at length became perfectly indifferent. I reminded him that he had promised to marry me, and pressed him to keep his word ; but he only put me off with evasions. This disgusted me, and, piqued at his want of faith, I began to despise him. From contempt I passed to hatred, and being once arrived at that, I speedily determined to leave the perjurer ; a resolution I courageously executed. One day when he was gone hunting in the direction of Alicant, I made my escape in my male attire, and walked towards Origuela, where I arrived that evening. I entered an inn kept by a good widow, who, judging by my air that I must be the son of some person of distinction who was running about the country, said to me : ' My pretty young gentleman, what brings you to Origuela ? '—' I am come,' replied I, ' to seek for a place. I served at Murcia, in quality of page, a lady with whom I was not content ; I have left her, and am determined to travel from town to town until I shall have found a new mistress, or some gentleman of distinction who will take me into his service.'

" ' A youth of your figure,' said the daughter of the hostess, joining in the conversation, ' will not be long in this town without being provided for agreeably.' I replied to this gracious compliment by a bow, and I perceived that the person who had made it regarded me with the most particular attention. I also

observed that she was a young woman, probably from five and
twenty to thirty years of age, tolerably pretty, and possessed of
a good figure; observations which a young cavalier in my place
would perhaps have made with more pleasure than I did.

"Finding myself fatigued with having walked all day, I requested a room, that I might go to bed. 'Juanilla,' said the
hostess to her daughter, 'take this little chicken to the closet
which looks out on the garden; there is a good bed in it.'
Juanilla immediately conducted me thither. 'Signior Page,'
said she, 'you will be here as comfortable as a prince. When
any person of importance comes to lodge at our house, it is in
this room we put him to sleep.'

"The better to imitate a cavalier under similar circumstances,
I thought it requisite to act the gallant, and say a great many
sweet things. This, however, I did with a great deal of
caution, for fear of raising a flame which I should be incapable
of extinguishing. But, with whatever circumspection I endeavored to address her, all the flattering words that escaped me
were so many arrows which pierced her heart. As she was retiring I embraced her, and this embrace completely intoxicated
her senses. She, however, escaped rapidly out of the room, like
a girl who is agitated by emotions too tender, and who is fear-
ful of yielding to their influence.

"I was well pleased with her retreat; and, laying myself
down immediately after, in a few minutes sleep had taken entire possession of my senses. I awoke about the middle of the
night; and, hearing something stirring in my room, asked who
was there. Immediately a low soft voice replied: 'Sweet page,
who can enjoy the repose of which you deprive others, wake
and learn your victory. You have inflamed Juanilla, who must
die with grief and despair if you refuse her your heart and
hand.' I pretended, in order to amuse her, that I was sensible
of her regard, thinking that I should get rid of her by a few
tender speeches; but she approached my bed, and made such
advances that it would not have been possible to continue the
deception much longer. 'My dear Juanilla,' said I, 'why can
I not seal your love with the seal of Hymen! You are the person in the world for whom I should have the greatest fancy, if
heaven had made me a man, instead of causing me to be born
a girl like yourself.'

"If the shades of night had not concealed her from my view,

I am sure I should have seen her change color at these words;
and when she could no longer doubt my sincerity, I believe
she was a little sorry for being undeceived. Taking the affair,
however, like a girl of spirit, she began to laugh at her error,
and submitted with a good grace to necessity. 'By my faith,'
said she, ' I am more lucky than wise, and it must be admitted
that I have had a most fortunate escape. When I think of my
weakness, I tremble at the idea of a danger which was but
imaginary.'

" Seeing in what way Juanilla was inclined to treat the subject, I followed her example; and after we had both exhausted
ourselves in pleasantries on our adventure, we vowed an eternal friendship for each other. To engage me to recount to her
my affairs, she made me the confidante of her own; and I had
full cause to believe from her recital that she had not always
met with young girls in those who wore male attire. The
frankness of Juanilla excited my own. I gave her a faithful
detail of my elopement, and informed her why I had separated
myself from my seducer. She praised me for having had the
resolution to withdraw myself from this base and perfidious be-
trayer: she, however, persuaded me to lay aside my disguise;
'in order,' said she, with a smile, 'that no other girls may
be deceived by it.'

" 'I have no other intention,' said I, 'than to enter into the
service of some lady of quality; and I shall be in a situation to
supply myself with female attire as soon as I shall have sold a
large diamond which I got from Don Gregorio.'—'Keep your
diamond,' said Juanilla, 'and let me follow an idea which has
just come into my head. I am known and, I dare assert,
esteemed by a rich and virtuous lady who has been living at
Origuela since the death of her husband, who was governor of
Majorca. I will but just mention you to her, and I doubt not
that she will receive you immediately.'

" I gave permission to Juanilla to act as she pleased; and the
next day she told me that she had spoken to the Countess
Saint Agni. ' In consequence of the representation I gave of
you,' said she, 'this lady has expressed her readiness to take
you into her service. It is true, indeed, that I made her the
confidante of your misfortune; but pardon me for this indiscretion; by doing so, I have but the more effectually served you.
The Countess is the best lady I ever knew. A young girl who

5

has been betrayed appears to her an object rather of pity than contempt. In a word, she compassionates your misfortune, and imputes your fault only to the traitor who has been the cause of it.

" ' You now, therefore, belong to the Countess Saint Agni,' continued the daughter of my hostess. 'Go and call on her in about an hour; she wishes to see you in your page's dress, after which she will give you other habiliments.' I thanked Juanilla for the service she had rendered me, and, getting directions to the house of the Countess, I immediately set out to present myself."

CHAPTER II.

" You may well conceive, my dear brother," said Francisca,
" that I could not, without blushing, offer myself to the view of
a lady who had been made acquainted with my history. Nay
more! I was exceedingly troubled; and though naturally bold
enough, did not approach the Countess without trembling.
She perceived my disorder, and penetrating the cause of it,
'Compose yourself,' said she, after sending out of the room a
woman who was with her; 'Juanilla has told me everything,
and I pity you. If your youth, your shame, and your repentance cannot render your fault excusable, they at least secure
you my compassion.'

" At these words I threw myself at the feet of the Countess,
and only replied by a torrent of tears which I found it impossible to restrain. My tears produced an admirable effect, the
lady was much affected; and raising me kindly, 'Console yourself, my child,' said she; 'it is useless to afflict yourself now.
Rather come to a firm resolution of being in future on your
guard against the arts of men; you cannot be too careful to
avoid them."

" She said many other things of the same kind to inspire me
with a love of virtue. Then wishing to know who I was, and
to hear me converse, she questioned me about my parents.
As I am not of a birth which I need be ashamed of, I did not
pass myself off for anything more than I was, and I replied
with sincerity to all her questions. Whatever may be our birth,

we ought not to blush at it : virtue is not dependent upon
rank.

" The Countess appeared perfectly satisfied with my answers.
' Francisca,' said she, after a long conversation, ' I am happy
that fortune has led you to apply to me ; I conceive an affection for you, and would stand in the place of a mother to you.'
I returned all the thanks which so generous a lady deserved,
and hastening to profit by her bounty, entered into her house,
less on the footing of a waiting woman, than as a young girl
whom she esteemed, and of whom she was desirous of taking
particular care.

" I immediately began to contemplate thoroughly the character of my mistress.   Oh, what amiable qualities did this study
lead me to the discovery of !   I found her mild, amiable,
affable, gentle, and even-tempered : she was prudent, virtuous,
and even devout, without affecting to appear so.   A mistress
of such a character is too amiable not to be adored by all about
her ; the Countess was, therefore, the idol of her servants.   For
my own part, I was so charmed with her, that I thought I could
never exert myself sufficiently to please her.   I am not naturally awkward, and I contrived to pay my court to her so well,
that in a short time I gained her confidence, or at least shared
it with Damiana, an old waiting woman who had been twenty
years in her service.

" You will observe, if you please, that the Countess Saint
Agni was then at the completion of her ninth lustrum.   She
had passed for a beauty in her youth, and was even still handsome ; but her charms began to yield to the power of time.   I
was much surprised one morning to hear her sighing mournfully
at her toilet, and to remark that her eyes were filled with tears.
I took the liberty of asking her, respectfully, if any secret uneasiness troubled her repose.   I pressed her to tell me what
was the matter with her ; and my requests were so strongly
urged, that she was unable to resist them.   ' Yes, my dear
Francisca,' said she, looking sorrowfully upon me ; ' yes, I am
the victim of a grief, the force of which is increased by my
being obliged to confine it to my own breast.'

" ' Do not rest there, madam,' said I, perceiving she had done
speaking ; ' open to me your whole heart.   Do not conceal
from me the subject of your sorrows ; I already participate in
them, though without knowing what they are, and you will find

consolation in confiding them to me.'—' I dare not reveal them
to you,' said she ; ' they are ridiculous to think of, and I cannot
without confusion make you the confidante of them.'—' You
must, however, tell me, my dear mistress,' said I, throwing myself on my knees ; ' I cannot live without knowing them.
Ought you to leave me in ignorance of them ?—me who am
entirely devoted to you ? I entreat you no longer to make a
mystery of what afflicts you. If I cannot console you, at least
let me participate in your grief.'

"I evinced so great an interest in the situation in which I
beheld the Countess, that I at last extracted from her the
secret. ' My child,' said she, ' I can no longer hold out against
your zeal and friendship ; I must acquaint you with my weakness. Learn, then, the cause of my affliction. I am sensible to
the loss of my charms : I find them falling, one by one, in ruin, in
spite of all the assistance I can derive from art for their preservation. This it is which afflicts me. What do I say ? it
plunges me into a melancholy which sometimes arrives at such
a height, that I am afraid of losing my reason. You are astonished at this,' said she, observing that I really was surprised to
hear her talk in this way, ' but it is a weakness over which, with
all the aid of my reason, I cannot obtain the victory.'

" ' Allow me to represent to you, madam,' said I, ' that you
do not really witness what you think you do. Why, too ready
to torment yourself, do you imagine that you are not what you
have always been ? View yourself with more favorable eyes,
or rather believe the report of mine. They will inform you
that time has not yet destroyed your charms, and that you are
still in possession of all your beauty.' At these words, which
for a moment suspended her grief, the Countess replied with a
smile : ' You are a flatterer, Francisca ; my glass is more sincere than you ; it announces to me every day some change in
my person, and my eyes cannot deny its testimony.'

"After the Countess Saint Agni had reposed in me this
singular confidence, she was no longer under any restraint before me ; and giving free vent to her complaints, I had the
same scene every morning at the toilet. I often spoke on the
subject with Damiana, who could not refrain from laughing.
' If my lady,' said she, ' were a woman of gallantry, I could
pardon her for her grief. An old coquette has indulged in
such habitude of having lovers, that she must be quite in de-

spair when she finds herself no longer able to attract them.   But
my mistress has always shunned gallantry.   It is her interest
in her own proper person that renders her so sensible to the
outrages of age.   One must be very fond of one's self to grow
old with such a bad grace.'

"The Countess Saint Agni had but this one fault, and of
that, unfortunately, we could not hope that she would ever
divest herself.   On the contrary, finding herself every day less
lovely as she advanced in her career, at the end of two or three
years she appeared to herself so changed that she no longer
dared to look in her glass.   'Francisca,' she exclaimed one
morning, as in absolute despair, 'my dear Francisca, I am perfectly decrepid : it is no longer possible to look in my face
without horror; I can no longer show myself in the world.   I
must hide myself in the recesses of a cloister : I had rather be
shut up there for the rest of my life than exhibit an object so
frightful.'

"It was in vain that Damiana and myself tried every method
to restore her spirits, and induce her to consider her face with
more indulgence (and, in fact, although old, she had the remains of beauty, from which a coquette, in her place, would
not have failed to derive some advantage); it was impossible
to alter her design of going into a convent.   Previous to executing her resolution, she asked if I would be willing to follow
her.   'If you doubt it, madam,' said I, 'you will do me great
injustice.   The convent, it is true, viewed in itself, does not
much please me; but it will become an agreeable residence to
me, if I am to be there in your company.'   The lady was so
pleased with this answer that she embraced me, and declared
that my attachment to her formed her only consolation.

"My mistress, therefore, buried herself in a convent, and
Damiana and I shut ourselves up with her.   We might have
lived there with a great deal more comfort, but that, during
six entire months, we were under the necessity of constantly
exhorting the lady to sustain with greater fortitude the decay
of her charms.   She would no longer hear any reason on the
subject.   Happily heaven interfered.   Madam Saint Agni returned by degrees to herself, and triumphed insensibly over
her weakness.   What a change !   This woman, who had been
so proud of her beauty, became insensible to the loss of it, and
quite detached from the world.

" The good widow was only two years in her retreat. She fell sick and died there, after having made a will, in which her attendants were not forgotten. She left a thousand pistoles to each of us, to enable us to live decently, without being again obliged to go to service. Our own inclinations came some-what near the intentions of the Countess. Damiana shortly made me the following proposition : 'I am weary,' said she, ' of having a mistress; I would take my turn in playing the part of a lady in the world. Follow my example, my love. Let us not separate; let us unite our fortunes : let us go and establish ourselves in some large town of Spain, and there, giving ourselves out for women of quality, we shall make good acquaintance, and live very agreeably.' If I had had experi-ence, I should have revolted against such a proposal ; I should have penetrated the views of Damiana, and have left her, as a jilt who had a design of ruining me. But seeing nothing but what was perfectly innocent in that which she had suggested, I readily joined my destiny with hers. We held a council as to what steps we should pursue, and the result was as follows.

CHAPTER III.

"WE fixed on Seville for our place of residence, Damiana
having assured me that Andalusia was the most pleasant part
of all Spain ; and determined to proceed thither by sea as soon
as we should be put in possession of our legacies.

"Accordingly, as soon as they were paid us, we went to
Carthagena and embarked on board a ship which was about to
sail for Malaga. We were a little incommoded by being at
sea ; but, as we had a favorable wind all the way, we soon
arrived at Malaga, where, having remained a few days, we set
out for Seville by land, and arrived there without sustaining
the slightest accident.

"We hired a house near the Exchange, which we had properly
furnished, and took into our service a cook and a lackey, who,
being strangers to us, could give no information as to who we
were. 'Aunt,' said I to Damiana (for it had been arranged
that I should pass for her niece), 'I think we are beginning
upon too high a scale. Shall we always be able to maintain
the figure which you are desirous of making ? '—' Hold your
tongue, niece,' replied she ; 'why need you trouble yourself ?
Leave to me the care of managing our expenses, and you will
find that we shall never be under the necessity of reforming
our housekeeping. It is more likely that we may augment it
in the end.'

"My good aunt, in talking to me thus, had views which she
hoped to be able to accomplish without communicating them
to me. She flattered herself that we should make some useful
acquaintance in a town, into the harbor of which come the

fleets and galleons from the West Indies loaded with Spanish dollars, with plates of gold and with bars of silver; she calculated that I should gain the heart of some rich merchant, and that we should not fail to enrich ourselves with his spoils. It was upon this notable expectation that she founded the duration of our brilliant mode of living.

"Damiana, as you may perceive, relied a great deal upon my beauty and address. The result showed that she was not mistaken. A Mexican, being one day at the Church of San Salvador, whither I went every morning to hear Mass, was struck with the elegance of my figure, and still more with two large black eyes which I turned towards him now and then as if by accident. He gave me to understand by his looks that I had charmed him. Even though I had failed to notice this myself, it could not have escaped my aunt, who was closely on the watch in this matter and took notice of everything. Both, then, had made the observation; and we doubted not that this gallant from the new world would shortly endeavor to introduce himself at home.

"We were not deceived in our conjecture. He wrote to my aunt, requesting to be allowed the favor of an interview with her; which permission she granted. He had a long conversation with her, in which, after having declared his love for me, he proposed to marry me and to take me to Mexico, where he stated that he possessed immense wealth. Damiana replied that she would mention to me the honor he was desirous of conferring on me, and in three days return him my positive answer.

"My aunt having informed me of this conversation, asked me if I felt any curiosity to see the country of Montezuma. 'No, truly,' replied I; 'to consent to taking such a voyage as this, it would be necessary to view my new lover with the same eyes as I did Don Gregorio; and that is what I am very far from doing. I will tell you more: I feel an aversion for the Indian without knowing why. There is about him an air of gloom which prejudices me against him,'—'Let us say no more about him, then,' rejoined Damiana; 'I have no more inclination than yourself to go to the Indies. When the Mexican shall return for his promised answer, I will give him his dismissal.'

"He did not fail to come at the appointed time. She

informed him that our inclinations did not correspond with his own, and requested him never more to set foot in the house. He did not appear much mortified by this compliment, and it might have been supposed, from the air with which he retired, that he did not take the refusal he had met with much to heart; but we were deceived. The more vexed in reality, in proportion as he had taken pains to conceal it, instead of resolving to forget me, he contemplated only the means of obtaining me in spite of myself, and, in order to effect this, he had recourse to the expedient of Romulus; that is to say, he resolved to carry me off by force. You shall hear directly what was the success of his project.

"One evening, having been walking with Damiana in the royal garden, near which we resided, just as we had left it to return home, I found myself seized by three men, who endeavored to force me into a carriage which was waiting. The screams which were uttered by my aunt and myself before they could effect their purpose, prevented them from succeeding. They attracted the attention of the two young cavaliers who happened to be near, and who, seeing the violence which was offered me, did not hesitate in affording their succor. They immediately drew their swords, and attacked my ravishers with such impetuosity, that they, despairing of being able to retain their prey, abandoned me and took to flight.

"My deliverers did not do things by halves: they conducted us home, where Damiana and I returned them all the thanks which their services demanded. We gave them an invitation to supper, which they willingly accepted. During the repast, we talked of nothing but the late adventure. One of the cavaliers asked me if I knew who could have been the author of the attempt? I replied that I suspected the Mexican of having formed it, out of revenge for my having refused his hand. 'That is enough,' said the other cavalier; 'in less than three days we shall be informed of the whole. I am the son of Don Indico de Mayrenna, Corregidor of this town. There are alguazils coming every morning to my father's; I will commission one of them to examine into the business. It is not enough,' continued he, 'to have prevented the execution of this enterprise, we must punish the audacious wretch by whom it was conceived. This is what I undertake to do, and you may trust the performance of it entirely to me.'

" He pronounced these last words in the style of a man whose heart is beginning to be inflamed, and his companion appeared no less ardent than himself in assisting my revenge.

" The son of the Corregidor was named Don Josef, and his friend was Don Felix de Mendoza. They were both equally lively and elegant in appearance. I expected every moment some sudden and violent declaration of love ; however, they contented themselves for that evening with ogling me ; which they did in a manner to make me sensible that I had caught both their hearts at a single cast of my net. They repeated their assurances on retiring, that they would use every exertion to procure me satisfaction for the Mexican's insolence.

" As soon as they had left us, I asked Damiana what she thought of these two young gentlemen. ' I fear', added I, ' that they will make me pay dear for the service they have rendered us.'—' That is what I apprehend,' replied Damiana. ' They are both struck with your charms, or I know nothing about such matters. They would not sigh for one who would be ungrateful : that is embarrassing.'—' We may deceive ourselves, my good aunt,' said I, ' and we are perhaps taking the alarm unnecessarily.'

" The next day we heard nothing of our deliverers, they being engaged in looking after the Indian, of whom they were extremely happy to have some intelligence to give me at their next visit. But, on the following day, the son of the Corregidor came to me in haste. ' Madam,' said he, ' you are revenged. The audacious man who essayed to carry you off is in prison, as also the three wretches who dared to lay their hands upon you. Their process is about to be commenced, and you will soon see with how much zeal I have served you.' I told him that it was impossible to be more grateful than I was for what he had done for me, and that I hoped an occasion would speedily present itself of giving him proof of it. ' The occasion already presents itself,' replied he. ' Sympathize in the sentiments with which you have inspired me, and I shall be repaid with interest.'

" This discourse was but the commencement of a great deal more of the same kind, which he addressed to me, accompanied with the most lively demonstrations of tenderness. Scarcely was he out of the house, ere his friend Don Felix came to supply his place, and entertain me with a repetition of all that I

had just heard. By his own account, never was man more enamoured. He told me that he would only live to consecrate
every moment to my service. It must be confessed that Don
Felix possessed an eloquence more seducing than Don Josef,
and that he had a better face and figure ; nevertheless he made
no more impression on me than the other, so difficult had it
become to please me.

" Although I held out no hopes to either of these cavaliers, I
received them graciously as visitors, the obligations they had
conferred not leaving me at liberty to do otherwise. These
rivals, therefore, began to contest my heart by the most diligent
attentions, without any apparent injury to the friendship by
which they were united ; but by degrees they became cool to
each other, and their jealousy at length gave birth to a hatred
which terminated in a duel, in which Don Josef lost his life, and
Don Felix was dangerously wounded. The Corregidor, having
learned the cause of this combat, arrested both aunt and niece,
and, in the first impulse of his anger, shut them up, as two
wretched adventurers, in the asylum for female penitents.

" However, two days after, reflecting that I had been guilty
of no other crime than that of pleasing two cavaliers too much,
his equity prevailed over his resentment, and he set us at liberty,
but with orders to go immediately out of Seville. We could have
consoled ourselves if, on getting out of prison, we had found at
home the effects which we had left there ; but they had been
pillaged and carried off by our domestics, so that all that remained to us were sixty pistoles and my diamond, with which
we left Seville, and were conducted by a muleteer to Cordova,
along the banks of the Guadalquivir.

CHAPTER IV.

OF THE NEW CONQUESTS WHICH DONNA FRANCISCA MADE AT COR-
DOVA—SHE BECOMES UNFAITHFUL TO HER FIRST LOVER, AND
FOLLOWS A PRETENDED VALET OF THE COMMANDANT'S TO
GRENADA.

" As we could make but a very moderate figure at Cordova,
being so low in our affairs, we took a furnished lodging, and
began to live with a great deal of circumspection. We went
out in the morning to church, and passed the rest of the day at
home, without seeking to make any acquaintance. Damiana
imagined that so retired a life would be noticed, and be the
means of procuring us some useful visit. This expectation was
justified by the event.

" An old woman named Camilla, tolerably well dressed, came
to see us one day. 'Ladies,' said she, 'you will not object to
a neighbor, who judges by your appearance that you are persons
of respectability, coming to evince her desire of forming a little
knot of friendship with you.' We answered politely, that she
did us both an honor and a pleasure. We then entered into a
conversation, which turned principally on the manners of Cordova. 'There is not a town in the world,' said she, 'where
gallantry is more in fashion. The men here are gallant even
in their old age; and withal, generous even to prodigality.'
She then related us several stories of girls who were strangers
having made a fortune there, to which we paid an attention
which enabled her to judge that we found them extremely interesting. But if she perceived that we had swallowed the bait,
we, on the other hand, perceived that she had all the manners
of one who is in the habit of conducting intrigues.

" We were not wrong in our opinion of her. She was a
maker of clandestine marriages, and one who was particularly
expert in uniting graybeards with minors, and superannuated

77

widows with young men: that was her peculiar fort. The second time she called on us, she offered her talents and services to my aunt, telling her, in private, that she had something in view for me extremely advantageous. ' It is,' said she, ' the love of the Commander of Montereal, of the house of Fonseca. He is not, indeed, young, but, with the exception of that, you have seldom seen a more agreeable nobleman ; never, at least, one who knew better how to make himself beloved. Besides, I assure you that he lives in a style of great magnificence, and has a considerable fortune ; since, without mentioning his other property, his Commandery brings him in ten thousand crowns a year.'

" This offer of a heart by no means displeased my aunt, who, desiring nothing better than to assist in plucking a bird of so rich a feather, entered without ceremony into the views of Madam Camilla, and this hopeful pair took upon them the charge, one, of representing to me the charms of the Commander and the other, of disposing me to regard him with a favorable eye.

" The first time I saw this old nobleman was at church, where I was with Damiana, who, considering attentively all the cavaliers by whom we were surrounded, singled out one whom she judged to be the Commander. She made me remark him ; and I joined in opinion that it was he, by the care he took to cast on me some tender looks, of which I suffered not one to escape me, though I affected to avoid them all. I examined, by stealth, this nobleman, who being studiously dressed and ornamented, still appeared young, I thought, though he was more than sixty years of age.

" ' What do you think of the Commander ? ' said my aunt, when we returned home. ' For my own part, I do not think him too old to deserve the regard of a lady. Besides that his figure is still good, there is an air of neatness in him which should supply the place of youth. What say you, my fair Francisca ? Does he not appear to you deserving of some complaisance ? '—' Yes, indeed,' said I, ' he appears to me still an accomplished man ; but we do not know whether the man we speak of be really the Commander of Montereal.'—' That we shall very shortly be informed of,' replied my aunt. ' Our old neighbor will come to see us to-day. She will inform us if we have been mistaken.'

" In effect, the very same day Madam Camilla came to visit us. She told us that the Commander in question had been in church, and had seen me; and we perceived by the description she gave of him, that we were not wrong. 'This nobleman,' said she, ' is already quite enraptured with Donna Francisca. What a noble air she has ! said he to me; how majestic ! If the beauty of her face do but correspond, she is a person whom I should love all my life. He then,' she added, ' urged me most strongly to procure him the pleasure of an interview with her. This I promised him, and I am to bring him here this evening.'

" At these words, Damiana, imagining herself already in possession of the revenues of the Commandery of Montereal, could not refrain from giving vent to her joy, and to conceal nothing from you, I did not fail to partake in it; for which I was the more pardonable, as we were beginning to be assailed by poverty. Though, to confess the truth, being constantly exhorted by my false aunt to put my beauty to profit, it was impossible that I could avoid becoming a coquette.

" I therefore prepared to receive the visit of the Commander. I passed several hours at my toilet, consulting my glass, and still more Damiana, who affected, having herself formerly indulged in gallantries, to have discovered what description of looks would insure a conquest. But I can assure you that I occupied myself with very unnecessary cares, for to effect the conquest I meditated, or rather to preserve it, I had only to show myself such as I was by nature : my youth was sufficient to inflame a man of this old nobleman's character. As soon as he saw me without my veil he imagined that he beheld the heavens opened. He testified an extreme surprise; he seemed as if he had never seen anything so beautiful. ' Ah ! Camilla,' cried he with enthusiasm, addressing his conductress, ' you have not set too high a value on these charms. What do I say? You have undervalued the charms of the divine Francisca rather than exaggerated them. She is, indeed, lovely. What happiness can equal that of possessing her ? '

" As my ears were well accustomed to flattery, I listened coolly to the noble Commander, who, rightly judging that something of a more interesting nature would be necessary in order to arrive at his ends, continued in these terms, apostrophizing Damiana : ' Madam, I implore your protection. Let me entreat you to employ all the power you have over your niece to engage her to permit my attentions. I will attach myself wholly to her, and change the aspect of her fortune, which does not appear to me at present to be equal to her merit.'

" Here he paused in expectation of my reply, but I left it to my aunt to answer for me. I did not only remain silent, but affected to be bashful and embarrassed, which had by no means a bad effect. Damiana undertook to answer, and acquitted herself like a woman of talent. If she thanked the Commander for the favorable sentiments he expressed for me, she gave him also to understand that I merited them : she boasted to him of my education and my talents, and related such a pretty romance about the conduct which I had always pursued, that this old nobleman was induced to consider me the very best acquaintance that he could ever make.

" By way of commencing under fortunate auspices, he made us quit our furnished apartment to occupy a lodging which he caused to be hired and handsomely furnished at an hotel. He also gave us servants, of whom he undertook to defray the expense. Besides this, he overloaded us with presents, so that in a short time we found our circumstances tolerably respectable. You may well imagine that I did not repay with ingratitude a proceeding so gallant and so generous, but you would never guess what was the nature of the recompense.

" At the first private interview I had with him, I was given to understand what was to be my behavior. 'Charming Francisca,' said he, ' I am not ignorant that it would be a folly for a man of my age to expect to inspire you with love. I do justice to myself ; I only expect from you esteem and friendship. Notwithstanding, I must tell you, such is the passion I have for you, that I should expire with jealousy if I were to see a rival beloved.

" ' I discover to you the bottom of my heart,' added he, ' and perhaps yours will revolt against the sacrifice which I have to ask from you, and which will perhaps appear to you absolute tyranny.'—' What, then, is this sacrifice ? ' said I ; ' it must be impossible if I refuse it to you. What is the nature of it? Speak boldly.'—'It is,' replied the Commander, 'to confine your conquests to myself, and, in order to accommodate yourself to my delicacy, to listen to no other lover than myself. Do you feel yourself capable of so much complaisance to a man who has nothing but his tender sentiments to merit it from you?'

"I affected to laugh at this discourse, though at bottom what this old gentleman required of me was not exactly to my taste; then affecting reserve—'What then,' said I, 'Signior Commander, is this the terrible effort which you expect from my gratitude as the price of your kindness to me? Ah! be assured that I could without pain sacrifice to you all the men in the world, so indifferent are they all to me.' My old lord appeared ready to die with pleasure at hearing me pronounce these words. He kissed my hands with rapture, and told me that I was born to form the happiness of his life.

"Well! I promised him to listen to nobody but himself, and I performed my promise faithfully. I resolved to keep my word with him as far as it should be possible, and as a proof of what I say, from the moment of our conversation I was particularly careful to do nothing at which he could take umbrage. When at church, instead of throwing my eyes, as formerly, on all the cavaliers who surrounded me, I took particular care to cover up my face in such a way as completely to defeat their curiosity. If the master of the house brought home, as was his custom, some of his friends to supper, far from endeavoring to attract them by coquettish glances, I turned my eyes from them with an assiduity for which the Commander knew not how sufficiently to thank me. I was sure to receive from him some rich present the very next day.

"I thus formed, with little inconvenience to myself, the felicity of my ancient lover, who, on his side, omitted nothing to perfect my own, when at length love interfered, to destroy the quiet of our innocent union. The Commander was induced to take into his service a tall young lad named Pompeio, who shortly became his favorite lackey. This young man possessed a good figure, and had the appearance of being the descendant of some respectable family. His mind corresponded with his prepossessing appearance, and he conversed with an elegance which showed that he had been well brought up. He came every morning to bring me a billet from his master; and I most commonly amused myself in conversing with him. I did not at first perceive that he took pleasure in my conversation, though it was my business to have remarked it; for Master Pompeio, when talking to me, regarded me with an air so tender, that if I

6

were not on my guard against him it was no fault of his. At last, however, I opened my eyes and beheld my work."

Here I interrupted Francisca. " Just heaven, sister ! " exclaimed I, " what are you going to tell me ? Is it possible that this lackey had attracted your regard ? "—" I did indeed become distractedly enamoured of him," replied she. " However, suspend the reproaches which this avowal appears to give you the right of making. Attend me to the end.

"As soon as my feelings became known to myself, I was overwhelmed with confusion. I was ashamed of being vanquished by a servant, although I had heard that such things had sometimes happened to women of more dignified descent than my own. I called my pride to my aid, and, willing to stifle an unworthy love in its birth, would no more indulge in conversation with him. I coldly received from him the notes of which he was the bearer ; I spoke not a single word to him ; I denied myself even the pleasure of looking in his face.

" The poor boy was visibly mortified at this change, of which he did not penetrate the cause. He thought that I had read his temerity in his looks ; that I was incensed at it, and that it was in order to punish him I declined speaking to him. This caused him so much grief, that he excited my pity. I began to renew my conversations with him. I went further ; I engaged him to open to me the secrets of his heart, or at least I imagined it for him. ' Pompeio,' said I one day, ' do you love me ? ' This question, for which he was unprepared, quite disconcerted him. To give him time to recover himself, I continued : ' If you love me, you will repose in me a confidence which I promise you not to abuse. I suspect that you are nothing less than the character you represent : your manners betray you. Acknowledge it : you are some young man of family, who have a design in hand which cannot be accomplished without resorting to your present disguise.'

" Pompeio was so troubled at this, that he remained some moments unable to speak. ' Your embarrassment and your silence,' continued I, ' inform me that I have discovered you. Confide the whole to me, and I will keep the secret.'—' Madam,' replied Pompeio, after having a little recovered from his disorder, ' if you be absolutely determined that I should satisfy your curiosity, I will obey you ; but I warn you that I shall no sooner have done so than you will be displeased with me.'—

'Never mind,' replied I eagerly, 'speak: you do but render me more curious.'

" The Commander's lackey then, placing one knee upon the floor before me, like a theatrical hero before his princess, said, with the air of a declaimer : ' Well, madam ! well ! I am about to reveal myself, since such are your commands. I am not, it is true, a wretch reduced by fortune to a state of servitude ; I am a man of quality in disguise. I am called Don Pompeio de la Cueva. I had discovered that the Commander loved you, and not being able to imagine that he was loved by you in return, I resolved to endeavor to win your affections, rather encouraged by his age than by my vanity. I had the address to get received into his service, and by this stratagem have obtained admittance into your house.

" ' Yes, it is love, adorable Francisca,' pursued he, in a tone of voice full of sweetness ; ' it is love which has inspired me with this stratagem to make you acquainted with my flames. If you contemplate them without anger, nothing can be comparable to my happiness ; but if, too faithful to my rival, you will listen but to him, however great the ardor with which I burn for you, I will remove myself from Cordova forever.'

" If my heart had not been already prepossessed in favor of this young cavalier, I should have been on my guard against his discourse, and the air of persuasion with which it was accompanied ; I should have remembered that Don Gregorio de Clevillente had addressed me in exactly the same strain ; instead of which, enchanted with Don Pompeio de la Cueva, I doubted not for a moment his sincerity. I went still further, and added to the weakness of believing him, that of acknowledging that I was sensible to his love.

" The joy which he manifested on learning his victory was excessive, and mine was no less at seeing him so well pleased. It was thus I fulfilled the oath I had made the Commander, not to give him a rival. But how is it possible to keep oaths of this kind made to an old gentleman ? It is as much as we can do for the youngest and most accomplished gallants. I will say, however, in my defence, that I did not become faithless without remorse. I pitied him, and (what a jilt in my place would not have done) I resolved to leave him, making a scruple of conscience of receiving his presents and having a lover at the same time. As for my aunt, she was less scrupu-

lous; and, considering the custom of a Commander more profitable than that of a lackey, she advised me to give the preference to the former; or, at least, to retain them both, one for
the useful, and the other for the agreeable; a thing which
would not have been without example.   But I chose rather to
follow the counsels of love than hers, and to go off with Don
Pompeio, who pressed me to yield to his desire of carrying me
to Grenada, where he said a life full of pleasure awaited us.   I
therefore left my old adorer, as well as my false aunt, to whom
I abandoned all my effects to console her for our separation,
and keep her up until she could get another niece; and taking
nothing with me, as I may say, but my youth and charms, I
left Cordova one morning privately with my new lover, and we
both arrived the next day at Grenada.

CHAPTER V.

" It was not necessary to press Don Pompeio to espouse me.
He was so impatient for our marriage, that from the moment
we arrived at Grenada he occupied himself with nothing but
the measures requisite to facilitate it. In short, we were married ; and the morning after our nuptials, we had the following
pleasant conversation together.

"'My dear Francisca,' said he, embracing me tenderly,
'here we are, bound together in the soft bonds of Hymen.
Now is the time, my dear, that we ought to speak to each other
with sincerity : lovers only are allowed to behave with duplicity ; people who are married should speak the truth. I am
going to change my style, and shall now conceal nothing from
you. When I told you in Cordova that I was only acting the
part of a valet, and that love had inspired me with this stratagem to introduce myself to you, I told you the truth ; but when
I took the name of Don Pompeio de la Cueva, I will confess
that I imposed upon you, and that I only borrowed this fine
name to render my temerity the more excusable. However,'
added he, 'though not of noble birth, I do not derive my existence from among the dregs of the people. I am called Bartolo
de Mortero, and I owe my birth to a venerable apothecary in
the celebrated city of Saragossa. It is therefore, my princess,
but a slight fraud that I have practised upon you, and which
the daughter of a village judge ought to pardon.'

"'I pardon you willingly,' replied I ; 'accident does not
always couple people so well. But tell me whether you prac-
85

tise pharmacy.'—'I did dabble in it a little at first,' replied he;
'I made some decoctions, and that disgusted me with the business. I discovered that I was born for something more elevated. I became a prince: sometimes I am a Moorish hero,
and sometimes a Christian potentate. You are to understand
by this that I am an actor. I play principal parts: that is my
employment.'—'I am much in doubt,' replied I, ' whether the
revenues of your principalities be very considerable.'—'It is
true,' said he, 'they are a little slender, except now and then,
that our new pieces, whether bad or good, dazzle the eyes of
the public, and bring them in crowds for about a couple of
months, which good fortune, I admit, is but casual. As for
our princesses,' continued he, 'they are infinitely better off
than we. Whether the theatre be productive or no, they always
live in ease and abundance. One cannot, without witnessing
it, believe their happiness. They are adored by the nobility in
all the towns through which they pass. For instance, the
actresses of the company which is now in the capital of
Grenada, are all perfectly well established, from the most handsome to the ugliest among them. It seems as if the theatre
girls possessed a talisman to enchant men who are distinguished
by the highest birth or the greatest portion of wealth.'

" When my husband had thus vaunted to me the happiness of
the actresses of Grenada, he proposed to me to augment their
number. 'Attend to my advice, my fair Francisca,' said he;
'embrace the profession. Young and handsome as you are, you
will find in it nothing but what is agreeable.'—'You are laughing at me,' said I; 'one must have talent to go on the stage,
and I have none at all.'—'You have enough, and to spare,' replied he. 'I remember to have heard you sing some ballads
before the Commander. I was no less enchanted than he at
the softness and power of your voice. Not a syren of the Cana-
ries has a finer pipe than yourself.'

" ' Is it possible,' said I, laughing, ' that my singing has made
such an impression on you? What, then, would you say if you
were to see me dance? I am persuaded that you would feel
still more satisfied with my steps than with my voice.'—'Impossible,' exclaimed he, with surprise. 'Ah, my queen, pray
have the complaisance to execute a few steps before me. Let
me see in what way you will acquit yourself.' To satisfy him,
I danced a saraband, and he was actually enraptured at my exe-

cution. 'My dear,' cried he, in the excess of his rapture, 'what a treasure is it to me to have a wife who unites two talents, which may be called, nowadays, two mines of gold and precious stones! Let us hasten to put them to profit. To-morrow I will assemble the actors, and introduce you to their company as a person capable of enriching it.

" ' For my own part,' continued he, ' I have but to show myself to these gentlemen to be received among them. They have heard of the fame of Bartolo de Mortero, and will be delighted to have me. When I was passing through Cordova, where your beauty detained me, I had just come from Seville, where I had been shining three years; and I should still have shone there, had I not been obliged to disappear on a sudden, in consequence of some information I got of my creditors growing impatient.'

"In fine, my husband taught me to see so many advantages, so many pleasures in a theatrical life, he urged me so strongly to make a trial of it, that at last he succeeded in persuading me to it.

CHAPTER VI.

DONNA FRANCISCA JOINS THE COMPANY OF PLAYERS AT GRENADA
—HOW SHE WAS RECEIVED BY THE PUBLIC, AND OF THE GREAT
NUMBER OF NOBLEMEN WHO WERE CAPTIVATED BY HER TALENT
AND HER CHARMS—HER HUSBAND PROCURES HER THE COUNT
OF CANTILLANA FOR A LOVER—SHE RECEIVES HIM IN OBEDI-
ENCE TO HER HUSBAND.

" ALTHOUGH my husband had inspired me with some confidence, by the excessive praises which he had bestowed on me,
it was not without trembling that I presented myself the following day at the theatre, where all the company, curious to see
me, had not failed to assemble. The women, among whom
were some tolerably pretty, considered me with critical attention, finding in me more defects than I really had ; and to the
men I appeared more lovely than I really was.

" We passed a great many compliments on both sides, and
embraces were bestowed with as much prodigality as if we had
all been the best friends in the world. It was then debated
what employment I should undertake. ' 'Gentlemen,' said my
husband, ' my wife dances and sings to perfection. I believe
that with these two talents she will not be the most useless of
our party. As for declamation, that is what she has yet to
learn ; but, beside the talent I know her to possess for sustaining an amorous part, she will have Bartolo de Mortero for her
instructor, who promises you that in the course of six months
she shall become an excellent actress.'

" It was agreed on all hands, that if I were what Bartolo had
represented, I should be of great use to them, as they had a great
many very agreeable pieces, which they were unable to represent
for want of an actress who could sing and dance. I was then
requested to sing ; and when I had finished, they applauded
me, as if in emulation of each other.

"'That is nothing, gentlemen,' cried my husband, delighted at hearing my voice so highly praised; 'you are now going to see that my wife is as capable of charming the eyes as the ears.' In effect, as soon as I had danced, the whole company honored me with unanimous applause by clapping their hands; and many were the compliments paid to my execution. 'This,' said one, 'is what may be called dancing.'—'What nobleness! How natural! Ah, rogue!' said another in an undertone, tapping my husband on the shoulder: 'where hast thou been to angle for such a woman as this? What showers of pistoles are about to fall within thy grasp.' In a word, every one agreed that I was a great acquisition to the company, and I was received by unanimous consent, as was likewise Bartolo, who beyond contradiction was an excellent actor.

" Both of us now thought of nothing but preparing for our appearance on the stage; a business which happened to be rather embarrassing to us, as we were without equipment, without clothes, and without linen: we were even so badly off for money that we had scarcely enough to pay for the furnished room in which we lodged. We should, therefore, have had a considerable deal of difficulty in putting ourselves in a state to make our debut had I not retained Don Gregorio's diamond; but fortunately this was still in my possession. This, therefore, we sold, and were thus enabled to give money on account to the workmen, who immediately made us theatrical dresses of peculiar grandeur and richness.

" The day for our first appearance being arrived, the actors, who lose no occasion of augmenting their profits, availed themselves of this. They announced us to the public with high encomiums in a bill, which stated that two incomparable actors, lately arrived at Grenada, would that evening appear in the Phœnix of Germany, a revived piece written by Don Juan de Matos Fragoso. The public, who everywhere are fond of novelties, came in crowds to the house, and were highly pleased with my husband, who sustained the part of Ricardo. I appeared in the character of a musician in the first act, and my voice was no sooner heard than the whole house rang with the applause of the assembly. I was still better received in the third act, which I finished with a dance. What clapping of hands! What enthusiasm! I cannot describe to you to what a degree I pleased the spectators, who remained a full hour after the performance discussing my merits.   Some said that I sang better than I danced ; others placed my steps above my voice ; and what astonished them all was to see me unite two talents which are so seldom found together.   There were also some who were struck with my youth and person, and among these some who formed the design of cultivating an intimate acquaintance with me.

" At the second representation we gave of the same play there was again a very crowded audience ; and as I had now more confidence, I sang and danced better than before.   Nothing was spoken of in the town but the new actress.   Have you seen this prodigy ? was the question from one to another.   The noblemen of Grenada began to solicit my good graces by presents.   I was every morning receiving, while at my toilet, jewels or other rich gifts, which were sent to me without any intimation whence they came.   Sometimes it was a gold watch, sometimes a collar of pearls with earrings ; then again a piece of rich stuff, or perhaps a basket filled with gloves, laces, silk stockings, and ribbons.

" The gentlemen who showed me these little gallantries soon declared themselves ; and the question was now who should obtain the preference in my favor.   One would watch me in the entrances to say something flattering to me as I passed ; another wrote me billets-doux every day, and essayed to engage my heart in a commerce of love, foolishly imagining by that means to arrive at his ends ; another, taking a better course, sent an old actress, one of my friends, to invite me to supper, at which he did not fail to be present.   But none of these gallants obtained an equivalent for their expenses.   Besides that I grew more vain in proportion as I saw myself more applauded by the public, my husband, from whom I concealed nothing, continually exhorted me to listen to none but a nobleman, or at least some very rich man.

" It seemed as if he had a foresight of the good fortune which attended me.   About this time the Count de Cantillana came to Grenada.   As soon as he arrived, he was desirous of going to the theatre in consequence of the high character he had heard of the company.   I was in the piece that night.   I sang in it, but did not dance.   However, I needed no more than my voice to make a conquest of this nobleman : so Bartolo informed me two days after.   ' You have,' said he, ' placed in

your chains the Count de Cantillana. You cannot have a lover
of more utility to you; he joins to a fortune of ten thousand
crowns a year, a most noble manner of spending it. He is so
generous that he begins, I have been informed, with enriching
a mistress before he speaks to her. For the rest, he is a nobleman of about forty years of age at most, and very agreeable in
his person.'

" ' How do you know,' said I, ' that the Count de Cantillana
has fallen in love with me ? You think so, perhaps, because
you wish it.'—' No, no,' said he, ' I have it from his own mouth ;
and I can inform you that they are now furnishing, by his
orders, a handsome house which he has hired for you, about
two hundred yards from our hotel.' I only laughed at this piece
of intelligence, not imagining that he could have been serious
in relating it. However, he did not jest.

" ' I will tell you besides,' continued he ; ' we are to have a
cook, an under-cook, and a scullion, who will all be hired by
this nobleman ; and who, without our having to embarrass ourselves with cares of any kind, will defray our expenses, and keep
us a table of six covers. *Item.* He does not design to be tiresome to you : he will not place any old duenna to watch you
and observe your actions. He knows too well how to love, to
show a want of confidence, which cannot fail to be odious although a woman may not wish to be unfaithful ; he will depend
on your fidelity, and on his own attentions to you.

" ' *Item.* Besides the presents you will receive from him
every day, you will have a good carriage, the horses for which
will stand in the Count's stables, and in which you will go
superbly to the theatre, to the great uneasiness of heart of those
of your companions who are obliged to go there on foot or in a
hackney-coach.'

" ' To hear you talk,' said I, ' one would suppose that you
would not be displeased that I should have on my hands this
nobleman of whom you speak.'—' There would be reason for
thinking it,' replied he ; ' and in reality I would rather that you
should have a rich and noble lover like this, than see you foolishly engaged with an actor or an author. I repeat, I should
be delighted with it. If I thought otherwise I should be hissed
by all the husbands of our company.'

" I then assumed a serious tone, as if my virtue had become
fortified by my theatrical life, and reproached my husband for

wishing, himself, to engage me in a commerce of this kind. But he laughed at my scruples, and told me, by way of silencing them, that an actress who had but one lover at a time, was as well conducted as another woman who had none at all. 'On that footing, then,' said I, laughing, ' I choose for mine the Count de Cantillana, whom you so willingly propose to me, and ratify by my consent the treaty of alliance which you have made with him.'

" Although I did not appear to pronounce these words seriously, my husband did not fail to take them most literally. He assured the Count that I was in the disposition he desired; which so pleased that nobleman, that he sent me about ten thousand crowns' worth of jewellery ; at the same time requesting permission to come and see me in my furnished apartment, until I could go to reside in my new house. One morning while I was at my toilet he arrived, conducted by Bartolo, who, the better to enable us to converse with freedom, immediately withdrew, like a husband who understands good breeding.

" ' Madam,' said the Count de Cantillana, ' I shall make no excuse for coming thus indiscreetly to pay my homage to you at your toilet. I know very well that it would be choosing my time badly, with the greater part of your companions; but for you, lovely Francisca, there is no moment in which you are more redoubtable than the present.' After this compliment, so flattering in its nature, he launched out into other conversation, which was no less so. I found in him all the politeness of the Commander of Montereal, with something more; I mean a person so handsome that I should have given myself credit for obtaining the love of such a nobleman, even though he had not been master of all the riches which he really possessed.

" After a very long and tolerably lively conversation, he retired highly pleased, as far as I could judge, with his visit. I was presently confirmed in my opinion by Bartolo, who, having joined me as soon as he had gone out, assured me that he went away quite enchanted with my wit and behavior. ' He has just told me so,' said he, ' and I would wager that you, on your part, have no complaint to make of him.'—' I am very well satisfied with him,' replied I; ' he is one of those noblemen with whom a woman makes her fortune very agreeably.'—' It is true,' replied my husband, ' there are some of them so flat and disagreeable, that their mistresses may truly say they earn their money.'

CHAPTER VII.

OF THE FRESH PRESENTS WHICH THE COUNT DE CANTILLANA MADE
TO DONNA FRANCISCA—THE ATTENTIONS HE PAID HER—ONE
OF HER OTHER LOVERS SENDS HER AS A PRESENT A BOX OF
DIAMONDS OF GREAT VALUE—SHE REFUSES IT—HER FAVORED
LOVER, IN GRATITUDE FOR THIS REFUSAL, BESTOWS ON HER A
MAGNIFICENT COUNTRY SEAT—IN WHAT MANNER THIS SO TEN-
DER ENGAGEMENT WAS TERMINATED.

" WE removed into our new house as soon as it was in a state
to receive us. Had it been furnished for a princess, I do not
think that it could have been done more magnificently. Richness and good taste were visible in every part of it. There
were two separate apartments, one for my husband, and the
other for myself, the Count having so ordered it out of delicacy. Mine glittered with gold and silver, which shone in all
parts of it; and that of Bartolo, though more modest, would
have done honor to a knight of St. James.

" We visited every part of the house from top to bottom,
and it was not without pleasure that we found, in a kitchen
supplied with every necessary utensil, three persons employed
in preparing our supper ; that is to say, a cook, an under-cook,
and a scullion. I imagined, from the great number of dishes
which I saw preparing, that we should be a dozen persons at
table ; or, at least, I thought that the Count, who, in order to
install us in our new habitation, was to come and sup with us,
would bring some of his friends. Nevertheless he came alone,
and I had a second conversation with him, in which I confirmed his chains by exercising on him the charms of my voice ;
I mean by singing airs from some of the most tender of our
theatrical pieces, applying them to him, and looking at him
with so languishing an air as penetrated his very soul.

" If he were pleased at our private interview, he was not less

93

so during supper. I practised a thousand little tricks to raise his ardor, and succeeded so well that he sent me in, next day, plate to the value of a thousand pistoles. Three days after, I had brought me, by his order, two superb dresses for the stage. What do I say? it did not rest here; there was every day some new present.

"All these gifts, joined to the emoluments which my husband and I derived from the theatre, which, thanks to us, was now much frequented, made us so well in our circumstances, that we began to make a more brilliant figure. We took into our service two lackeys and a lady's maid; and I never went to the theatre but in a handsome carriage of which I was the mistress, and which, notwithstanding, I had not the trouble of keeping.

"As soon as this change was remarked, it roused the railleries of our company, and made many of them envious; but they soon left off talking, and became accustomed to it. For me, who saw in it nothing but what was quite agreeable, I imitated those of my companions who were in the same circumstances. Far from having any confusion on the subject, I braved the prattle and malignant looks of the public; and in truth, if there were anything ridiculous in our equipages, it was not on us that the ridicule should fall.

"I no longer saw, but at the theatre, the other actresses, with the exception of Manuela, who rolled about in a carriage on the same terms as myself. She had for a lover Don Garcia de Padul, a gentleman of Grenada, who enjoyed a very considerable fortune, which he spent nobly in her company. This girl sought my friendship, and obtained it, in return for her own. We became so much attached, that no sooner were we separated than we were all impatience to see each other again. I do not know whether we were not better pleased to be together than with our lovers. So very intimate a friendship between us became the means of Don Garcia and the Count getting acquainted; and when that took place, we formed all four a society, in which were seen predominating gaiety, pleasure, and good cheer. We supped every night at my house or at that of my friend. We respired nothing but joy, and we all lived so familiarly, that it would be hard to decide whether the noblemen had stooped to us, or we had raised ourselves to them.

" While we were leading a life so agreeable, I was making wretches elsewhere : I mean some young men who came every day to the theatre to see me, and who burned with a flame which they concealed, or which, if they gave any signs of it, procured them no return. Among these was one distinguished by his birth, and still more by his personal merit. This was Don Gutierrez de Albunuelas, eldest son of the Governor of Grenada, and the most handsome cavalier of his time. He had just returned from finishing his studies at Salamanca. He had no longer either tutor or governor, and was now beginning to feel the pleasure of being master of his own actions.

" This young nobleman never failed to be at any play in which I was to perform. He contented himself for a long time with ogling me and applauding me on the stage, whether from timidity, or that he despaired of supplanting so formidable a rival as the Count de Cantillana. He at last grew tired of keeping silence ; and not being able to make up his mind to speak to me, came to the resolution of making me a detail of his sufferings in a letter, which he had the address to get secretly conveyed to me, and to which, you may be well assured, I returned no answer. I even affected, in order to deprive him entirely of hope, to turn my eyes another way as often as by accident they encountered his own.

" All this rigor could not repel him, and imagining that presents would have a greater effect on me than either his love or his beauty, he sent me a jewel-box in which there were precious stones to the value of four thousand pistoles, that he had contrived to steal from his mother. I consulted Bartolo on the conduct which I ought to pursue in a conjuncture so delicate. 'You have only one way of acting,' replied he, after musing a few moments ; 'you must, without loss of time, send back these jewels to Don Gutierrez : we should both be inevitably ruined if we were so imprudent as to keep them. The Governor's lady (for I doubt not for a moment that it is from her he has stolen them) cannot be long ere she discover the theft. She will then seek for the perpetrator of it, and by diligent inquiries will discover him. The Governor will interest himself in the business ; he will be desirous of getting at the bottom of it, and that will incense him against you. I believe,' added he, 'I need say no more upon the subject. You know that actresses, however great may be their talents, venture a high stake when they make enemies of persons in power. After the treatment you received from the Corregidor of Seville, you ought to fear these gentlemen a little.'

" ' Your advice is too judicious for me to neglect,' replied I. ' I have represented to myself all the inconveniences which you have just laid before me, and I have no hesitation about return-ing the diamonds ; I am' even persuaded that that will have the happiest effect in the world on the mind of the Count de Can-tillana.'—' Never doubt it,' replied my spouse ; ' he will feel himself indebted to you for the sacrifice you will make of Gutierrez, and you will perhaps gain by it more than you will lose.' As I could not then, without danger, retain the jewels, I had them returned to the Governor's son, informing him politely that I sent them back to him, not finding myself capable of the gratitude with which his present should be repaid.

" We had not been in the wrong in thinking that the Count would be sensible to the sacrifice I had made him of so dan-gerous a rival. When he became acquainted with it, he was transported with joy. ' You prefer me,' said he, ' to the most amiable cavalier in Grenada. Ah ! charming Francisca, why can you not read the bottom of my heart at this moment ! you would find how deeply it is penetrated by this glorious prefer-ence.'—' Count,' replied I, regarding him tenderly, ' I do not pretend to make a merit of it with you : can a heart that is enamoured of you ever cease to be faithful ? No, Count,' I added, with a passionate air, ' be assured that neither Don Gutierrez, nor all the men in the world, can ever win me from you.'

" The Count, on hearing all this flattery, threw himself on his knees in transport, and broke out into an effusion of love and gratitude. After this he took another strain far more to my taste than the commonplace expressions of gallantry. ' To make you amends,' said he, ' for the jewels which you refused out of love for me, I make you a present of a castle which I have on the banks of the Guadalquivir, between Jaën and Ubeda. This castle is not very high rented, but it is a most agreeable residence.' I thanked my generous lover for this new present which he had made ne, and on the same day the deed of donation was made out and delivered over to me in due form.

" Nothing could equal the joy of Bartolo when I announced
to him the new acquisition which my charms had just made.
'I knew well,' cried he, 'that you would not give up Don
Gutierrez for nothing. What, the deuce! a castle! it must be
admitted that the Count has a noble way of doing things.' In
fact, my husband could not contain his joy; and yielding to his
impatience to see the estate which had cost so little, he hastened
thither and took possession of it. On his return, a few days
after, ' The Count,' said he, ' has made you a handsomer present than you are aware of. Learn what description of building
is this castle; it is a house which appears to have been built by
the fairies.' He than proceeded to give me so magnificent a
description that I could not help interrupting him five or six
times to reproach him for exaggerating its beauties. ' Quite
the contrary,' he always replied; ' instead of embellishing it by
my description, I rather weaken its advantages, since it is completely a *chef-d'œuvre* of art and nature. Besides that it has
wherewith to please the eye, it is farmed for three thousand
crowns to the richest peasant in the country: this is a certain
fact; I have seen the lease. Add to that, that you and I are
lord and lady of the village of Caralla, and that we may take
the wall of all the hidalgos in the parish; no trifling preroga-
tive. It is true that they will laugh a little at first at our expense on account of our profession, but we shall be quit for
that, and enjoy at a cheap rate our revenue and seigniorial
rights. Now let the affairs of the stage be at the disposal of
fortune: let our new pieces have what success God pleases; we
have an asylum inaccessible to famine.'

" It was thus my spouse felicitated himself at seeing us secure
of a retreat which is seldom the fruit of long and laborious
exertions among those of our profession. I was as well satisfied as he, and very soon the public began to feel the effects of
it. I began to put myself on a footing of not going so often
on the stage, and came insensibly to omit it altogether; and
this in pattern of some great actors, who, under pretence of
consulting their health, neglect their duty. It appeared to me
that a lady who possessed a manor of three thousand crowns a
year might give herself the same airs. Bartolo, after my example, would play but very seldom. This displeased the
rest, who leagued themselves against us; and discord spread
throughout the company.

7

"I am now arrived at the epoch of an event rather unfortunate for me. The Count de Cantillana received despatches
from the Court: the Duke of Lerma, with whom he was a
favorite, ordered him to repair immediately to Madrid, this
minister having cast his eyes upon him to replace a counsellor
of state who had just died. Although the Count was the more
pleased with this news, as his love was beginning to decline,
he failed not to represent to me that he was quite in despair,
and that he was almost inclined to refuse the place which was
offered to him; but, at the same time, he represented to me
that if he were to decline it, he should offend all his family, and
perhaps lose forever the friendship of the Duke of Lerma.
Lastly, by way of gilding the pill, he assured me that he should
always remember his dear Francisca. I affected to be the
dupe of these protestations; and as crocodile's tears cost
nothing to a good actress, I shed an abundance of them at our
last adieux.

CHAPTER VIII.

" THUS separated the Count and I.   Manuela, on her part, almost at the same time was abandoned by Don Garcia ; one nobleman not being more constant than the other.   Padul, under pretence of going to see a sick uncle at Badajos, removed himself from her and from Grenada.   Happily we were both of us well fledged, and of an age to console ourselves for the loss of our flighty lovers.

" Scarcely had they quitted us ere others presented themselves to fill their places; but, besides that we should have been embarrassed in making a choice, the divisions which reigned in our company augmented to such a degree, that we became disgusted with the theatrical life, and resolved to renounce it.   ' My dear Manuela,' said I one day, ' I am tired of exhibiting myself on the stage, and of diverting the public.   I will retire to my seat at Caralla, and act the lady of the parish. May I flatter myself that you love me sufficiently to accompany me ? '

" ' Such a doubt offends me,' replied Manuela : ' you know that nothing in the world is so dear to me as your friendship ; I should be unworthy of that if I could refuse to go and partake with you the comforts of your retreat.   Let us go, my dear Francisca, let us go ; I am ready for your sake to sacrifice all the gallants of Grenada.'   We both, therefore, left the company, as did also Bartolo, who, preferring the character of lord of the village to that of a theatre prince, willingly conducted us to Caralla, where we all three arrived quite happy in a good coach, purchased with our own money, or, if you will,

99

with that of the Count. A chaise in which were my servant and Manuela's followed us, with six valets who led so many mules loaded with our baggage. After which came our cook and Bartolo's lackey, both mounted on very good horses : all which composed a suit worthy the admiration of the peasants, and the envy of the hidalgos.

"I did not find the house inferior to the description which my husband gave of it. It appeared to me well built, well furnished, and kept in as good order as if the Count had made it his ordinary residence. I was in particular struck with the beauty of the gardens, and of the vast meadows which extended on the north to the very banks of the Guadalquivir. Nor did I consider with less satisfaction the wood on the southern side. Bartolo, seeing that I was charmed with this dwelling, said with an air of triumph : ' Well, my love, have I deceived you in the account I gave of your mansion ? Is there in Spain a place where one can breathe a purer air, or behold more smiling prospects ? '—' No, unquestionably,' replied my friend, still more delighted than myself with the beauties of my retreat ; ' it must be acknowledged that this is truly the present of a nobleman. We shall pass our days here very agreeably if the country gentlemen will be but a little sociable.'

" ' It is true, indeed,' replied Bartolo, ' that the hidalgos are a consequential set : when they have a common person over them, it can scarcely be expected that they will treat him with much respect or consideration. However, we every day see rich merchants, after becoming bankrupts, retire to estates which they purchase at their creditors' expense, and even tradespeople as well as ourselves ; but it being our business to be good actors, we shall be able to accommodate ourselves to their pride. That will not cost much ; and we may, by flattering them, enjoy ourselves at the expense of what is ridiculous in their behavior.'—' I have a better opinion than you of these gentlemen,' observed I in my turn ; ' I think that there are some among them of amiable character. However, be they what they may, we will oblige them by polite and engaging manners to render us our due.'

" It is certain that we were not prejudiced in favor of these nobles, of whom the greater part inhabited mere cottages. We had imagined that they were stupid and clownish ; and we were astonished, when they came to visit us, to find them so civilized as they appeared to be. Their wives, in particular, gave us to understand by their compliments that they did not want for wit ; and I remarked among them some whose behavior was very prepossessing. We gave them all so gracious a reception that they had reason to be very well satisfied with us ; and this they testified by protesting that they were delighted to have over them persons who treated the nobility with such becoming deference.

" We went to see them in their own houses ; and in the visits which we paid them, we made it our principal care neither to say nor do anything by which their vanity could be hurt. With this circumspection, which was absolutely necessary to live among them on good terms, we gained their friendship. After this there was nothing but feasting and amusement. There came four or five gentlemen, with their wives and sisters, to sup with us every evening; and we had after the repast a kind of ball, which sometimes lasted all night. I commonly passed the day at home, at play, or in conversation with the women, while my husband was hunting with the men in the neighborhood. Such were my amusements, and very soon it depended only on myself not to have others.

" Among our small nobles was one who was named Don Domingo Risador.* He perfectly justified his name by his character, being an unpolite opposer, an angry disputant, a wrangler, an arrant brute, and withal insupportably proud. No lady till then had been able to subdue him: so difficult a conquest was reserved for me. He was pleased with me, and avowed his passion with the confidence of a gallant who imagines that his love does honor to the object on whom he bestows it. However great was my aversion for this personage, I heard him with patience. I however assured him coolly, in clear and distinct terms, that I did not feel the least inclination to love him, and I begged that he would never again set foot in the house.

" You will think, perhaps, that, mortified with the ill success of his declaration, he retired full of fury, and converted his love to hatred. Not at all. He laughed in my face, telling me that he would persist in loving me whether I would or no. ' I am not,' continued he, ' so easy to be put off. I am acquainted

* This surname signifies a quarrelsome person.

with women, and do not take all their grimaces for proofs of virtue. Come, my princess,' continued he, 'change your tone if you please; make not so much ado about it; it becomes you less than another.'

"At this insolent language I could no longer suppress my rage, and in my first transports I treated Risador like a negro; but he slighted my invectives, and went out, replying only with laughter, which redoubled my fury. I actually cried with rage, and I had my eyes still bathed in tears when Manuela surprised me. 'What is the matter with you?' asked she, perceiving the state I was in. 'What cause of grief can you have in an abode where everybody is striving to make you happy?'

"I gave her an account of what had passed between Risador and myself; and when I had concluded, instead of participating in my resentment, she only began laughing. 'You are wrong,' said she, 'to distress yourself about the coarseness and ridicule of a clownish lover, which you ought rather to laugh at. The contempt with which you repay his passion revenges you sufficiently for his impertinence.'—'You are right,' replied I; 'in future, instead of taking it seriously, I design to divert myself with his extravagances.'

CHAPTER IX.

OF THE MISFORTUNE WHICH HAPPENED AT THE CASTLE OF CA-
RALLA, AND WHAT WAS ITS CONSEQUENCES—DONNA FRANCISCA
COMES TO THE RESOLUTION OF GOING TO MADRID WITH MANU-
ELA, HER THEATRICAL FRIEND—THEY PASS THEMSELVES FOR
WOMEN OF QUALITY.

" I WAS now determined to endure again the sight of Don
Domingo Risador, without at all changing my sentiments towards him ; but he refrained from coming to the house. His
pride at length revolting against my rigor, induced him, in
order to punish me, to form the design of no longer honoring
me with his visits.

" He did not, however, confine his vengeance to this ; he in-
sulted Bartolo, who, being more of a bully even than himself,
drew on him, and wounded him dangerously. However, Risador did not die, and this affair appeared to be passed over and
forgotten. But six months after, my husband being out hunting, and alone in a wood, was met by Don Domingo, who
treacherously fired at him with a carbine, and stretched him
dead on the ground. Although this assassination had been
committed without any witness, its cowardly perpetrator, persuaded that he should be suspected, and might be taken up,
took to flight to save himself from the rigor of the law.

" I mourned bitterly for Bartolo, and was the more afflicted
at his death as I could not have the satisfaction of avenging it.
I however consoled myself by the help of Manuela, who, ever
ready to offer her assistance, had the address to soften my
grief. But our pleasures were interrupted by this fatal accident, or rather we grew tired of living in solitude. " I do not
know,' said I one day to Manuela, ' whether you are in the
same disposition as myself ; I begin to be tired of the company
of country gentlemen and their wives. I am ignorant what can

produce this change in me; whether it be the effect of my natural inconstancy, or of my husband's death.'—'It is to your delicacy only that it is to be attributed,' replied Manuela. 'A girl accustomed, as you are, to the amorous discourses of noblemen, must very soon become disgusted with the conversation of such persons as we meet with here.

"'Do not imagine,' continued she, 'that I am better adapted than yourself for living in solitude. I will also tell you frankly, that I am growing tired of this place; I have not the same pleasure in it I had formerly. The different originals who come here, no longer interest me: the ridiculous may amuse at first; but it soon becomes disagreeable, and at length insupportable. If you will attend to me,' added she, 'we will pursue an idea which has come into my head, and which I have not yet communicated to you.'

"I asked her what was this idea. 'It is,' replied she, 'to abandon this dwelling for some years, and to go and establish ourselves in Madrid. We are rich enough to live there in a noble style; and we shall easily pass for women of quality, since we have all the manners of such. What do you think of this project? has it your approbation?'—'Doubtless,' replied I; 'I am infinitely flattered by it. How many agreeable images does it present to my mind! Let us hasten to execute it.' —'I am very glad,' replied Manuela, 'that you approve of this journey. I have a foreboding that it will not be unfortunate. Let us then prepare to set out. Leave the care of the house to your farmer, with directions always to forward you the rent to Madrid. I will join to that the spoils of Don Garcia, the better to support the figure which we propose to make in the capital.'

"We now employed ourselves in nothing but preparations for our departure, which were no sooner made than we commenced our journey, with our two waiting women, all four in a coach; and we were accompanied by two valets mounted on mules, and well armed. After a long and difficult journey, we arrived happily in this town, where we deemed it expedient to change our names. Manuela took that of Ismenia, and I, that of Basilisa; and representing ourselves as the widows of two gentlemen of Grenada, we hired this house, where we began receiving company. We have attracted many persons of respectability here by the dignity of our manners, and obtained their esteem by our prudent conduct.

" We see," continued she, " a number of noble cavaliers, and there is not one of them who does not hold us in esteem and consideration. You may judge of it by Don Manoel de Pedrilla, your friend. I am ignorant what he has said to you about us, but I know that he ought not to say anything bad. Although we allow him to come and visit us freely, we have no apprehension as to any report he can make of us. He has seen nothing which could give him an unfavorable opinion of us. If we do not follow the austere behavior of ladies who deny themselves the company of men, we have not for that the less virtue."

CHAPTER X.

OF THE CONVERSATION WHICH DONNA FRANCISCA HAD WITH DON CHERUBIN AFTER HAVING FINISHED THE RECITAL OF HER HISTORY—SHE PROPOSES THAT HE SHOULD COME AND LIVE WITH THEM—DON CHERUBIN CONSENTS.

DONNA FRANCISCA, my sister, here finished the recital of her adventures, and then said, with a smile : " Well, brother, what do you think of Bartolo's widow ? does she not appear to you a person of importance ? "—" Yes, truly," replied I ; " you have made your way in a very short space of time. I congratulate you on it, and thank Heaven that I have a sister in such good circumstances. But one thing occurs to me. We are subject in our family to sacrifice to love. I fear that among the cavaliers who visit you there may be some insinuating rogue through whose means you may lose your estate as easily as you gained it."— " Banish that fear," said Francisca ; " I am more capable of acquiring another than likely to give my own at the price it cost.

" But let us change the subject," continued she ; " since I have the pleasure of meeting my brother again, let us separate no more. I offer you a lodging in this house ; come and live in it with us. Ismenia will be no less pleased with it than myself. You will aid us with your good advice. Embarrassing circumstances may present themselves, in which your prudence will greatly assist us : you may save us from taking any false steps. Let us be under this obligation to you."

" The proposal, I confess, did not please me at first. I made a scruple of becoming the counsellor and guide of two beauties, whose prudence I was inclined to think very equivocal, notwithstanding all my sister could say. Nevertheless I could not excuse myself, and consented to it at the expense of whom it might concern ; reserving to myself, over and above, the right of separating myself from them if I should find any cause, however trifling, to grow tired of their company.

CHAPTER XI.

I WENT therefore to live with my sister and her companion,
who assigned me a small neat apartment in their house which
was unoccupied. I removed there the same evening, and took
with me Don Manoel de Pedrilla. "Come, my friend," said I;
"come and install me in my new abode, where I protest it will
be the greatest pleasure to employ myself in advancing your
suit to Ismenia."—"I refuse not your good offices," replied he;
"but I know not whether I shall benefit by them. Although
Ismenia appears to have some tender sentiments for me, she
will not put the seal to my happiness. I doubt whether your
friendship can do more than my love."

There came that evening to sup with the ladies two knights
of Santiago, who gave me a thousand embraces as soon as they
heard that I was the brother of Basilisa. "Permit me, sir,"
said one, "to embrace you for the sake of your charming sister."
—"He is your living image, madam," said the other, addressing
Bartolo's widow; "how rejoiced must you be at meeting each
other! I participate in your mutual satisfaction."

This discourse was but the commencement of an infinitude
of compliments which I had to undergo, and to which I answered in what is called the tone of good company, to show
these gentlemen that I was not to be put out of countenance on
such an occasion. They also appeared very well content with
the specimens of my wit which I displayed. They were still

more so by some happy sallies which escaped me during supper, and the merit of which they heightened by their praises.

These knights, one of whom was named Don Denis Langaruto, and the other Don Antonio Peleador, were very different in their characters and persons. Don Denis was a tall, skeleton-like figure, and Don Antonio a short fat man. The first, to show off as a man of learning, talked of nothing but the sciences; and the other, assuming the warrior, fatigued us with recitals of military affairs. As soon as one had discussed a passage in some author, the other, quickly taking up the conversation, gave us the relation of a battle. It appeared to be a contest which should tire us most. During this time Don Manoel and Ismenia were amusing themselves with an exchange of glances, which consoled them for the annoying conversation of the two guests, or rather which prevented them from hearing it. As to my sister and myself, we had so much politeness as not to lose a single word, and even to affect that we derived a great deal of pleasure from it.

In recompense, as soon as these gentlemen had withdrawn, I did not spare them at all. " If all the cavaliers who come to see you," said I, " be as unentertaining as those who have just left us, I do not think that in quitting your hidalgos of Caralla you have gained much by the change."—" It is true," replied Francisca, " that these are two suffocating mortals, but you will see others with whom you will be better pleased." I was, however, still less so with two secretaries from the office of the Duke de Lerma, who supped with us on the following evening.

These, being desirous of commanding as much respect as if they were secretaries of state, affected a most haughty gravity. When they were told that I was the brother of Basilisa, they did not launch out into panegyric, as the knights of Santiago had done; they contented themselves with honoring me by a simple inclination of the head, as dignified as if they had been members of the Council of Castile. Although they were enamoured of our ladies, they did not appear to be more animated towards them. Far from addressing them in a style of gallantry, they preserved a most dignified silence; or, if they broke it now and then, it was only by monosyllables.

I imagined that they would at least relax from their gravity when at table. I waited for that period to see them change their behavior, and give themselves up to pleasure, as grave personages generally do on such occasions. But neither my good humor nor the allurements of the ladies could make them lose their office sulkiness, nor draw from them a single smile.

As soon as they were gone, I again broke out in reproaches to my sister. " How," said I, " can you make such acquaintance ? you, who are yourself possessed of wit and taste ? These clerks were still more annoying than your two knights yesterday. Really, sister, since you are pleased to receive company at your house, it strikes me that you ought to make a better selection."—" Have patience," said my sister ; " you will meet here more than one cavalier, with whom you will not be sorry to form an acquaintance."

In fact, I did at last see several who might pass for the flower of gallantry, and whom I could not help looking on as so many brothers-in-law, though my sister protested every day that she gave none of them encouragement. There was one among them named Don Andre de Caravajal de Zamora, who united in his own person all the good qualities of which men the best born have in general only a part. As soon as this cavalier knew that Basilisa was my sister, he spared no pains to insinuate himself into my good graces. He had little difficulty in succeeding, being one of those agreeable men who easily prejudice persons in their favor. He was no sooner my friend than, wishing to be something more, he made me his confidant as follows : " Signior Don Cherubin," said he, " I love your sister. I am rich enough, and of a family sufficiently good, to induce me to hope that her wishes might correspond with my own ; but I perceive that she has an inclination for another gentleman, and I have every reason to fear the success of this rival."

I asked Don Andre who was the gallant of whom he appeared so much afraid. " You will never guess," replied he, " and when I shall have told you, you will find some difficulty in believing me ; for, in fine, it is not Don Felix de Mondejar, nor Don Vincente de Cifuentes ; it is Don Pedro Retortillo."— " Impossible ! " cried I, with astonishment. " Don Pedro, the ugliest of all of my sister's lovers, a capricious creature, a coxcomb ! No, I cannot believe that her taste is so depraved as to prefer such a man as he."—" You may say as you please of this cavalier," replied Caravajal, " but he is beloved by Basilisa : nothing is more certain. She looks on his imperfections with a woman's eye : to her he appears perfectly well made;

and it does not signify that his conversation is of the most absurd description ; she admires his wit."

I promised Don Andre to do my best to cross the love of Don Pedro ; and, not to be worse than my word, had a long conversation with Francisca the next day, the effect of which will be seen in the following chapter.

CHAPTER XII.

OF THE BAD SUCCESS WHICH DON CHERUBIN HAD IN HIS ATTEMPT
TO SERVE HIS FRIEND—HE LEAVES HIS SISTER'S HOUSE, AND
DOES NOT SEE HER AGAIN—DONNA FRANCISCA MARRIES DON
PEDRO—WHAT KIND OF MAN HE WAS.

"I DO not know, sister," said I, "whether you remember
that you begged me to aid you with my advice."—" Yes, doubtless, brother," replied she, "and I again beg you to do so."—
"Well, then," said I, "since it is what you wish, I am about
to take upon myself the office of counsellor. But first make
me a sincere confession. Do you love Don Pedro Retortillo?"

At this question Francisca became as red as fire, and was
quite embarrassed. "You blush," continued I, "and I need
no other reply to convince me of what I ought to think: your
embarrassment informs me but too well. It is then true that
you love Don Pedro! Oh, Heaven! Is it possible that you
have cast your eyes on him, who of all your lovers appears to
me most unworthy of possessing you!"

"Who," said she, "can have so well informed you of a love
which I had no idea of ever having manifested?"—"It is,"
replied I, "a rival of Don Pedro's, who has penetrated the
truth."—"And this so penetrating rival," replied my sister
hastily, "is, I suppose, Caravajal, for whom you have the goodness to interest yourself. Well, since he has discovered my
sentiments, I will not disavow them. Yes, I will not conceal
from you that Don Pedro has pleased me. I am sorry that you
do not esteem this gentleman; but know that I view him with
a favorable eye, and that I prefer him to Caravajal, as well as
to all the rest of his rivals."

"Oh! in that, sister," interrupted I, with some emotion, "I
can by no means agree with you in opinion. I can see nothing
in Don Pedro, pardon my frankness, but a tissue of bad qualities. He is clownish, consequential, full of caprices, and I believe withal of a jealous disposition."—"Let him be what you
please," interrupted Bartolo's widow in her turn, with a hasty

and mortified air, " whatever harm you may please to say of
him, he shall be my husband ; and it is the same thing as to
quarrel with me, to undertake to separate me from him."

My sister pronounced these words in a tone which imposed
silence on me. I no longer dared to combat her ridiculous
tenderness for Retortillo, nor speak in favor of Caravajal, who
was with all his merit obliged to give place to his unworthy
rival. I was the more mortified at this, as I every day found
my friendship for one and my aversion for the other growing
stronger. I detested the caprice of Francisca, and began to
fear that our union would be of no long duration.

In effect, after the conversation I had with my sister on this
subject, she changed her behavior to me. She abated greatly
in the attention and deference she had been accustomed to pay
me. She affected even to avoid my conversation, and when
she could not do so, she spoke to me with coolness. At last,
unable to pardon me for not having approved her design of
marrying a man who was detestable, she no longer viewed me
but as an inconvenient and perplexing censor, of whom it was
desirable to rid herself. As soon as I perceived this, I resolved
on my own course. I left the house, from which I had my
clothes conveyed to the hotel where I had formerly resided,
and rejoined my friend Don Manoel. After this, let them talk
of the force of blood : whatever friendship may exist between
brothers and sisters, it requires very little to break it.

After our separation I no longer saw Francisca, who did not
long delay uniting herself to Don Pedro in a marriage which
produced for her nothing but bitter fruits ; for, instead of meeting in her second husband with the commodious and complai-
sant humor of the first, she found that she had fallen into the
hands of the most jealous man in the world. From the morning after their nuptials, the appearance of the house was totally
changed ; no more admission for gallants; no more play ; no
more suppers. Don Pedro changed the servants, and placed
over his wife the most crabbed old duenna in all Spain. In a
word, he made a miserable wife out of the most happy of
widows. I heard shortly after that he had carried her into the
country with Ismenia ; so that Don Manoel was obliged to console himself as well as he could for the loss of his mistress, as
I for the loss of my sister.

END OF THE SECOND PART.

PART THE THIRD.

CHAPTER I.

DON MANOEL DE PEDRILLA BEING UNDER THE NECESSITY OF GOING
INTO THE COUNTRY, PREVAILS ON DON CHERUBIN TO ACCOM-
PANY HIM—OF THEIR ARRIVAL AT ALCARAZ.

As it is much easier to forget a sister than a mistress, in four
and twenty hours after I had separated from Francisca I thought
of her no more; instead of which, it took a full week to wear
out in Don Manoel's mind the recollection of his beloved Ismenia. By the time the ladies were forgotten, my friend received a letter from Alcaraz, in which he was informed that his
father Don Josef, having been taken suddenly ill of a malady,
from which there were no hopes of his recovery, wished him to
repair immediately to his presence, that he might die in his
arms. Don Manoel, sensibly afflicted at this news, immediately
prepared himself for obeying the orders of his parent; but
wishing at the same time to conciliate this duty with his friendship for me, solicited me so strongly to accompany him, that I
could not refuse to comply.

We set out from Madrid followed by a valet, all three
mounted on good mules, and took the road to Alcaraz, where
we arrived in less than six days. We found the good man Don
Josef just about to make his transit from this world to the other.
There were in his room two doctors, who, saluting Don Manoel
with an air of gaiety, informed him that his father ought, in the
course of nature, to have died three days before; but that,
thanks to the virtues of their medicines and the care they had
taken of him, his life had been preserved till his son's arrival.
" He desired," said one of them, " to have the satisfaction of

embracing you, and we have procured it for him." If these physicians had cured their patient they could not have manifested more satisfaction. However, the old man, who was drawing fast towards his end, had no sooner seen his dear son than he expired, and filled the house with mourning.

He left behind him an old sister, a young daughter, and Don Manoel. These three bitterly lamented his death, and had his funeral obsequies performed in a manner worthy of a gentleman who had been a general officer in the king's army in the preceding reign. When their grief had subsided, and Don Manoel had been put in possession of his father's property, he again appeared in the world, and did not deny himself the pleasures of society. He made it his chief care to introduce me to several of the most respectable persons in the town, as a gentleman of his acquaintance. This was the part I had to sustain, and I dare venture to say that I did not acquit myself badly. I was too well supplied with clothes and money not to make a good figure. I often gave entertainments to ladies, and, without vanity, drew no less of their attention than my friend.

One cannot long enjoy the company of fine women without paying the tribute which is due to them. Don Manoel soon became enamoured. Donna Clara de Palomar, a young beauty of Alcaraz, obtained the place in his heart which Ismenia had formerly occupied, and even lighted up a flame more ardent than which had been caused by her predecessor. As for me, I paid general court to all the ladies I met, without appearing to attach myself to any one in particular. My friend was much astonished at this. " Don Cherubin," said he, " is it possible that all the fair ones of Alcaraz should have exercised their attractions on you to no purpose? Does not some one among them revenge on you the mortifying indifference with which you treat the rest ? "

I laughed at these reproaches of Don Manoel's ; but, alas ! he would have been far from making them, had he known the real state of my mind. Very far from being insensible, I burned with the most ardent love for his sister, Donna Paula: I secretly adored her as one would adore a divinity. I feared to make known to her brother a passion so presumptuous : however great the friendship he manifested for me, I imagined that should I declare myself he would be offended at my rashness.

I therefore most carefully concealed my love. I even took the vigorous resolution of conquering it; nor did such a triumph appear to me impossible; for, notwithstanding my prepossession in her favor, I was sensible that Donna Paula was not a perfect beauty, and conceived that by separating myself from her I might be enabled to forget her. Having, therefore, come to the resolution of trying the effect of absence, conformably to the advice of Ovid, I told Pedrilla that I begged him to permit me to return to Madrid, but he most strongly opposed the idea of my leaving him.

" Are you," said he, " the friend who protested that he would pass his life in my company ? You tire, Don Cherubin," added he, " of this dwelling, or perhaps I have, without intending it, given you some cause to be displeased with me."—" No, my dear Don Manoel," replied I, " I have never been better pleased with you than I am at present."—" Why, then," resumed he, " do you wish to leave me ? " He then urged me so strongly to discover my secret, that I at last revealed it to him. " This then," added I, " is my reason for desiring to remove from Alcaraz, and you must approve of my resolution."

Don Manoel, after hearing me attentively, assumed an air of gloom and vexation. I thought that in spite of the friendship by which we were united, the pride of this gentleman had been roused at the temerity which had caused me to raise my thoughts so high, and, under the influence of this mistake, told him that he ought not to be offended at the avowal of a passion on the subject of which I had condemned myself to perpetual silence, and which he would still have been ignorant of had he not forced me to discover it. But in thinking thus of Don Manoel I did him injustice. " Don Cherubin," said he, " I am overwhelmed with despair at your not having sooner made me acquainted with your sentiments towards my sister; I promised her a week ago to Don Ambrosio de Lorca. How unfortunate that you were not beforehand with him. I would not have passed my word to this gentleman, though a match with him would perhaps be the most advantageous which my sister could possibly be offered."

I was overpowered by this news, and Don Manoel appeared to feel very sensibly the uneasiness it caused me. But suddenly brightening up, " My friend," continued he with an air of consolation, " the evil is not without remedy. I remember

that there is in my engagement with Lorca one circumstance
which may render it invalid: I only promised him my sister on
condition that she would subscribe without repugnance to the
treaty.   Regulate your conduct accordingly.   Pay your court
diligently to Donna Paula.   I will furnish you with frequent
opportunities of seeing and speaking to her in private.   Endeavor to obtain her affection, and if you succeed in that I
will take upon myself the rest of the business."   These words
recalled me in a manner to life.   I began to flatter myself that
I might after all become the husband of Donna Paula.   One
thing only alarmed me: I feared that this lady was prepossessed in favor of my rival, and it was upon that my fate depended.   Happily the very first conversation I had with her
dispelled my fear: I could even perceive that Don Ambrosio
was detested; a circumstance which my vanity induced me to
consider as a presage of love for myself.

CHAPTER II.

DON CHERUBIN OBTAINS THE AFFECTIONS OF DONNA PAULA—DON
AMBROSIO DE LORCA PRESSES DON MANOEL TO GIVE HER TO
HIM—HE CHALLENGES DON MANOEL AND DON CHERUBIN—
THEY ARE VICTORS.

In effect, I did not flatter myself with an unfounded hope.
By dint of acting, sometimes the languishing, sometimes the
passionate, sometimes the dying lover, I forced Donna Paula
to acknowledge that she was sensible to my tenderness. It is
true that her brother and her aunt contributed no little to render my attentions pleasing to her, by the praises they were
constantly bestowing on me; so that I had soon the satisfaction of finding myself in the happy situation of a favored lover,
who is on the point of being united to her he adores.

On the other hand, my rival, no less amorous than myself,
and relying upon the promise he had received from Pedrilla,
pressed him warmly to the performance of it. " Don Manoel,"
said he one day, " it appears as if you had lost the inclination
of becoming my brother-in-law. Speak candidly; can you
have changed your mind in defiance of the promise you have
given ? "—" No," replied Don Manoel, " but remember that
when I promised you my sister, I told you that I did not engage to marry her in opposition to her own inclination. You,
of course, understand me. I am sorry to inform you, but her
heart has escaped your endeavors to win it."

" Attempt not to put me off with this," interrupted Don
Ambrosio, reddening with shame and rage (for he was one of
the proudest and most self-important noblemen in Spain) ; " I
am not the person with whom it will pass : I am better informed than you think of what is going forward. I know it
all. You prefer to a man of my quality, the son of a petty

117

village judge; a mere commoner, to whom I will procure a
sound lashing, to punish his audacity and insolence."—"This
commoner you speak of," replied Pedrilla, "wears a sword,
and I must apprise you that his enemies are likewise mine."
—"In that case," replied Lorca, "be both of you to-morrow
morning at the entrance of the mountains of Bogarra, and there
you will find a man disposed to make you sensible that no one
may break his promise to him with impunity."

Having pronounced this with a menacing air, he retired full
of impatience for the morrow. My friend came to me with the
account of the conversation, and did not contribute very materi-
ally to my satisfaction by reminding me that we must prepare
ourselves for the combat. It was to no purpose that he showed,
himself, so much courage as even to laugh at this challenge;
to me it presented no image by any means so agreeable.
Nevertheless, although I felt my nature shudder, I failed not,
for the sake of my honor, to put on appearance of resolution.
I even affected an air of intrepidity, of which I am sure that
my friend was the dupe. But all this did not render me the
more valiant, and I should have had no objection to find our
party broken up.

I will confess more : to accommodate matters, I formed that
night a plan of pacification, by which I made a free surrender
of my mistress to my rival! I, indeed, afterwards rejected so
cowardly a thought : I represented to myself the contempt into
which I must sink should I display any want of firmness on
this occasion, and that with my good fortune, I should, at the
same time, lose the esteem of my friend and the love of my
mistress. These reflections warmed me by degrees, and so
inspired me with courage, that I became quite impatient to
engage.

I rose, fired with this excess of bravery, to fly to the place of
rendezvous with Don Manoel, who, although without the aid
of love to animate him, was exactly in the same mood as myself. We mounted our two best horses, and spurred towards
Bogarra. Don Ambrosio was already there with another cavalier. We joined each other, and, after salutations on both
sides, Lorca demanded of Don Manoel if he still persisted in
refusing him his sister, after having promised her to him.
"Yes," replied Pedrilla, "and your menaces have confirmed
me in my resolution instead of turning me from it."—"Then,"

said Don Ambrosio, "you and your friend Cherubin have only to dismount."

It was not necessary to repeat this intimation; we were instantly on foot. Our adversaries alighted likewise, and having fastened our horses to trees which grew by the roadside, each presented himself firmly against his opponent. Don Ambrosio attacked Don Manoel, and I had to contend with the other cavalier, who joined to the advantage of being a good fencer that of having to contend against a man who did not even know how to handle his sword. Nevertheless, I know not by what accident I contrived to wound this Hector so effectually, that I extended him at my feet. At the same moment that my antagonist fell, Don Manoel had the good fortune to despatch his own; so that we remained masters of the field of battle.

CHAPTER III.

THE first thing we judged it prudent to do after this melancholy event was to secure our safety.   Don Ambrosio was
related to the Governor of Alcaraz, and it was very natural to
conclude that this governor would set the holy brotherhood
after us as soon as he should obtain intelligence of the affair.
To this must be added that the cavalier who had the misfortune to feel my rapier, was of a family which possessed considerable interest.   On the other hand, into whatever part of
the world we might choose to retire, money would be a most
necessary article.   All this being well considered, we resolved
to regain Alcaraz before the death of Don Ambrosio could be
known, to supply ourselves with a good quantity of gold and
jewels, and then make the best of our way to Barcelona in
order to embark on board the first vessel which should sail for
Italy.

As soon as we had come to this determination we hastened
to return home, where, without loss of time, we loaded ourselves with as many pistoles and precious stones as we could
carry; we then bade adieu to Donna Paula and her aunt, after
arranging the means of holding a secret correspondence with
them by letter.   We set out for Barcelona followed by a single
valet; but not finding there any immediate opportunity of sailing for Italy, we were obliged, while waiting till it should present itself, to remain there for a few days.

It is impossible to conceive what I felt during this interval.
Without having been under the same circumstances, no one

could form an idea of the alarms and inquietude which troubled
my repose. Though I had killed my antagonist like a man of
honor, I was as much disturbed as if I had committed an
assassination. I expected every moment to see the archers
coming to seize me. Whenever any one looked in my face, I
took him for a spy employed to watch my motions. In fact, I
had a thousand terrifying thoughts by day, and a thousand
dismal dreams by night.

Besides the constant fears to which I was a prey, I could
not reflect without remorse on what I had done. I repented
having killed a cavalier instead of following the plan of pacification which I had contemplated on the evening before the
duel. My regret was the stronger because I began to fancy
that I was not so deeply in love with Donna Paula as formerly :
a change which must be attributed to the horrible situation I
was in; for love delights in holding undivided empire, and
cannot even endure the trouble and inquietude which he himself causes in the hearts of those who own his influence.

While Don Manoel and I were thus agitated with all the
terrors common to men whom justice is pursuing, Mileno, our
valet, augmented them one day by telling us that he had seen
alight at the door of an inn some persons of suspicious appearance, and that he thought he recognized among them an alguazil of Alcaraz. " But," added he, " I may be mistaken : in
order to ascertain the truth, I will go and slip quietly into the
inn and get an opportunity of observing them."

We allowed our servant, with whose address we were well
acquainted, to pursue his own plan ; and he, returning in about
a couple of hours, told us that the information he had given
was but too true. " An alguazil and a party of archers," continued he, " are after you. They are now coming to search,
one by one, every inn in the place ; and you need not doubt
that they will soon be here : you have no time to lose, if you
wish to escape. Hasten to demand an asylum in some monastery ; it is the only place in which you can now be in security."

We judged that Mileno was right, and immediately sought
refuge among the Barefooted Carmelites, the Superior of whom
received us with open arms when he understood that we were
two gentlemen whom an affair of honor had obliged to seek
concealment. It is true that, the better to engage his hospitality, we gave him to understand by our discourse that we were

in a state to make him remuneration. He was desirous, above
all things, to be made acquainted with the particulars of the
adventure which had placed us under the necessity of seeking
a retreat. We concealed nothing from him; and as soon as
he had heard our relation, " Your affair," said he, " may easily
be made up, for the gentlemen who have fallen beneath your
swords brought their misfortunes on their own heads. Think
no more of embarking for Italy; you need not go so far for
safety. Remain quietly here: you will be secure from the resentment of your enemies; and I hope, by the interest of my
friends, to be able to remove your embarrassment."

We thanked his reverence for his kindness in thus interesting himself in our affairs; and it was, in fact, a great piece of
good fortune in our way. This Superior directed the con-
sciences of some of the principal persons in the town, and
among others the Governor Don Gutierrez de Terrassa, by
whom he was highly respected. The name of Father Teodor
carried with it in Barcelona the idea of a good man, or rather
of a man of God. To this the Carmelite added a good understanding; but what was the most to be admired in him was,
that he possessed a fund of good humor, which he knew how
to reconcile with an austere and mortified life. He passed
three-fourths of the night in prayer and meditation; he employed the morning in listening to sinners who sought conver-
sion through the aid of his ministry; and after dinner, in his
hours of recreation, he indulged with his visitors in discourse,
in which he displayed all the wit and gaiety of a man of the
world. A monk of such a character is a rarity.

Father Teodor (such as I have just described him) ordered two
cells to be appointed for us, in which were two couches, each
composed of a straw bed and mattress of scanty materials, and
which, notwithstanding, hard as they were, might be accounted
soft in comparison with those of the monks. " Gentlemen,"
said this holy Superior, " you must not expect to find in this
asylum all the conveniences which you would meet with in the
world: besides that you will be but roughly lodged, you will
have to subsist on our slender pittance, which is adapted only
to satisfy the cravings of hunger, without much gratification of
the palate. But," added he, smiling, " I believe you will have
no objection to undergo this little mortification, in order to
appease that Heaven which you have irritated against you by

your duel." We readily submitted to this slight penance, and I can add that in a few days we accustomed ourselves to the hardness of our beds, and to the frugal portion of the monks, as well as if we had never slept softer, nor been better nourished.

CHAPTER IV.

WHAT WAS THE TERMINATION OF THE AFFAIR WHICH HAD PLACED
DON MANOEL AND DON CHERUBIN UNDER THE PROTECTION OF
FATHER TEODOR—OF THE SUDDEN RESOLUTION TAKEN BY THE
FORMER, AND IN WHAT MANNER IT WAS EXECUTED—HE IS
PRESENT AT AN EXHORTATION MADE BY ONE OF THE CARMEL-
ITES TO A DYING MAN—EDIFICATION WHICH DON CHERUBIN
DERIVED FROM THIS PIOUS DISCOURSE—HE DECLARES HIS RESO-
LUTION TO DON MANOEL, AND THEY SEPARATE.

OUR business was not neglected by the good Father Teodor.
In order to get it settled, he applied to his penitent the Governor of the principality of Barcelona, who, finding his reverence
greatly interested about it, spared no pains towards bringing it
to a favorable issue. He wrote in the strongest terms to the
relations of Don Ambrosio de Lorca, and among others to the
Governor of Alcaraz, who, by great good fortune for us, was
his intimate friend.

As Don Ambrosio had been the aggressor, his relations were
not so much incensed against us as they would probably have
been had he had more justice on his side. They easily sacri-
ficed their resentment at the intercession of Don Gutierrez and
of the family of Don Manoel. They ceased all further prose-
cution, and this business was entirely settled at the end of
about six months. The reader will doubtless imagine that
after this my friend and I returned gaily to Alcaraz to espouse
our mistresses, but this was not the case. I continued in Barcelona, where there occurred what I am about to relate.

While the necessary measures were proceeding for extricating
us from our difficulties, I had frequent conversations with
Father Teodor; and the more I saw of him, the more I was
pleased with him. There was in him an air of satisfaction
which I very much admired. This I often remarked to him,

and he has often told me that if I desired to have the same, I had only to pass my life in a monastery. " Take notice of our fraternity," said he, " and you will read in their countenances the tranquillity of their minds. You are," added he, " so much occupied in your own affairs, that you have not attended to this, though, believe me, it is a subject well worthy of observation."

I accordingly turned my attention that way, and was in reality edified by it. I was astonished to see men so content, who were condemned to a life so austere. I began to solicit their conversation from curiosity. I urged them to talk, in order that I might discover whether they really enjoyed an internal tranquillity, unalloyed by any secret care. I found their language in perfect unison with their countenances, and I had every reason to believe that they were as happy as they appeared to be. Hence arose the most agitating reflections. " What then ! " said I to myself; " there are mortals sufficiently detached from the wealth and pleasures of the world, really to prefer the solitude of a cloister ! How much is the happiness of such deserving of envy ! "

Among these venerable monks was one distinguished by a talent equally useful and uncommon. He appeared to have but one occupation, and that consisted in hearing the confessions of the sick, and exhorting them to repentance. He was constantly called on, at all hours of the day and night, to attend persons who were dying, and dispose them to make a Christian end. Having heard that he acquitted himself in a most extraordinary way in this melancholy employment, I had one night an inclination to accompany him. He had on this occasion to exhort to confession an old gentleman of Catalonia, who for forty years at least had been living among the banditti of the mountains of that province. Two ecclesiastics had already abandoned him, being unable to bear the offensive terms with which he overwhelmed them as soon as they appeared in his apartment.

This hardened sinner gave our old Carmelite, at first, a reception not a whit more gracious. " Retire, monk," cried he ; " the sight of thee offends me ; " and abused him in the most furious terms. The monk, instead of suffering himself to be repulsed, replied but with the utmost mildness, and seemed to have armed himself with indefatigable patience. The sick man was astonished. " For what are you come here, father ? " said he; "retire. So great a sinner as I should spare you the trouble of spending your breath in vain : I am too guilty to escape the wrath of Heaven."

Father Seraphin (this was the name of the monk) now extended his arms, and put up the following prayer, in a tone which affected every person present: " O Divine Saviour, Father of mercies ! thou seest one of thy creatures ready to sink into the abyss of despair. Be graciously pleased to render me instrumental in saving him from so dreadful a calamity. Cast upon him, I beseech thee, an eye of pity. Let thy mercy, O Lord ! preserve him from thy justice." The sick man was terrified at this apostrophe, and asked if it were allowed to entertain a hope of mercy, after having committed so many sins as he had been guilty of.

The Carmelite, zealous in the discharge of his duty, then approaching the gentleman, expatiated on the mercy of God in terms so consoling and so pathetic, that all who heard him melted into tears. To render his exhortation still more touching and efficacious, he himself accompanied it with tears, with which he bathed the cheeks of the sick man, as he every moment embraced him. There was balm in the very manner in which he spoke. The gentleman was moved, and when he had a little recovered himself, confessed his sins, and died, to all appearance perfectly converted.

I could not after this contemplate Father Seraphin but with admiration. I cultivated his friendship, which he was by no means inclined to deny to a man in whom he could perceive so great a disposition to become a devotee, as, in fact, I every day felt my inclination become stronger to retire from the world; and the conferences I had sometimes with this holy father, and at others with the Superior, insensibly inspired me with a wish to pass the rest of my life in a monastery. This wish was shortly converted into a resolution. I imparted my laudable determination to Father Teodor, who opposed it at first, not so much for the purpose of turning me from it, as to prove the firmness of my sentiments. "My dear son," said he, " when your affair shall be made up, you will think otherwise than at present."—" No, father," returned I, " no; I will die in this monastery, and beneath your habit."

Whilst this humor lasted, our business was settled. The Superior, after announcing this piece of news, asked me gaily,

"RETIRE, MONK," CRIED HE; "THE SIGHT OF THEE
OFFENDS ME."

" Well, my dear son, which now predominates in your mind—
the love of the world, or the love of solitude? Which now
do you prefer—poverty or plenty? It now rests with yourself
to return to Alcaraz, where the hand of a young and lovely person awaits you. Can you prefer to such a desirable lot, the
rough labors of penitence? Consult your feelings thoroughly
before you determine on a point of so much moment."

I replied that I had most thoroughly reflected on it, and that
I was determined to augment the number of his monks. I
added that I would, on assuming the habit, make over to him
all the property I possessed, of which I would make a present
to the convent. To this he made some objection at first, "for
fear," he said, "that he should be accused of having seduced
me." I combated his delicacy, which held out a long while
against my pious intentions; nevertheless, as his reverence
desired nothing but that the will of Heaven should in all things
be completed, he had the goodness to sacrifice his repugnance
to my entreaties.

I had not yet mentioned my design to Don Manoel, who
was very far from entertaining the slightest notion of it. He
saw very well that I had put on an outward appearance of
devotion; but he by no means supposed that it was such a
devotion as would lead me to adopt the habit of a monk.
Imagining that I was still constant to his sister, as he himself
continued to Donna Clara, he was not a little surprised when
I make known to him the change which had taken place in my
mind, and my determination to enter into the order of the Barefooted Carmelites.

" I had," said he, " calculated that you would return with me
to Alcaraz, that you would espouse my sister, that we should
form but one family, and that only death would separate us."—
" That," said I, " is the hope which I myself indulged when we
entered this convent. I formed to myself a delightful picture
of the life I should enjoy with you and Donna Paula; but
Heaven has otherwise ordained it. It has spoken to me in the
tone in which it addresses those hearts which it would wean
from the allurements of the age. I am no longer moved by the
idea of the softest pleasures Hymen can bestow; or rather I
make a sacrifice of them all. Happy if such a sacrifice can
expiate the irregularities of my former life!"

I redoubled Don Manoel's astonishment by this discourse.

" If it were permitted," said he, " to murmur against Heaven, I should reproach it for having deprived me of the dearest of my friends."—" Instead of complaining of Heaven," returned I, " dread that it should place among the number of your greatest sins, having neglected to profit like myself by the good example of the brotherhood of this monastery. However, my dear Don Manoel, it is not yet too late. Leave your property to your sister, and courageously renounce Donna Clara. Love is not an invincible passion, and the recollection of a mistress cannot here hold out long against the succors which the divine mercy will lend you to subdue it. Come, my friend," continued I, " make an effort to break the ties which bind you to the world. Remain in this convent, to partake in it with me the sweets of a tranquillity which only retirement can bestow. How happy should I be to see you taking such a resolution !"

" Hope it not," replied Don Manoel; " I admire, without being able to imitate you. We are not all born for the cloister. It is right, for the honor of Christianity, that there should be persons detached from the world and devoted to a life of austerity ; but we may, in all situations of life, work our salvation by fulfilling our duties with regularity and justice. Remain then," continued he, " in this holy solitude, since Heaven detains you here ; but for me it has other designs, and is pleased that I should return to Alcaraz, and preserve the faith I have sworn to Donna Clara."

This was the last conversation I had with my friend in Barcelona, and we finished it with mutual embraces. " Adieu, Don Cherubin," said he, with an air of tenderness. " May you ever persevere in the fervor which animates you now !" I sustained our separation with more firmness than he, and no sooner was he gone than I began to forget him; by which I was induced to believe that I was in a fit disposition to divest myself of all earthly affections, and that I might in time acquire that religious stoicism, which renders a monk insensible to the appeal either of blood or friendship.

CHAPTER V.

HOW, AFTER SIX MONTHS OF NOVITIATE, THE FERVOR OF DON
CHERUBIN BEGAN TO DECLINE—OF HIS QUITTING THE CON-
VENT, AND THE NEW COURSE HE ADOPTS—HE ACCIDENTALLY
MEETS WITH THE LICENTIATE CARAMBOLA—HIS CONVERSATION
WITH HIM—HE RESOLVES AGAIN TO UNDERTAKE THE BUSI-
NESS OF INSTRUCTION—WHAT PREVENTS HIM.

I WORE the habit of a novice for six months with pleasure,
acquitting myself with ardor of all my duties, and perfectly
assured that I should pass the rest of my life in the monastery.
Unfortunately for me, Father Teodor was called from Barcelona to Madrid, to fill the place of Superior in the principal
convent of the Barefooted Carmelites. To add to my mortifications, I lost about the same time the good Father Seraphin, who died of a pleurisy, which he had got by over-exert-
ing himself in exhorting to repentance a dying alguazil.

The loss of these good fathers most sensibly affected me.
Deprived of these two guides, who were safely conducting me
on the road to salvation, I was now given up to my own management. Nor was it long ere I again began to feel the tyranny
of those passions, from which I had fancied myself delivered:
so strong were their temptations to overpower my vocation, that
I could not long resist them. Nevertheless, before I yielded, I
exerted myself to the utmost to persevere in my godly course.
I sought for succor against my weakness, and fancying that
I should find it in the conversation of some novices, who appeared to me to have embraced the monastic life from feelings
of the utmost devotion, I one day said to one of them : " My
dear brother, how happy are you to have forgotten the world,
and to be able so courageously to pursue your pious career !
Alas ! why can I not resemble you ? "

" If," replied the novice, " you could see into my heart, you

would not find much cause to envy my situation. My family
have forced me to become a Carmelite, and I am obliged to
make a virtue of necessity: judge if I can be so content with
my situation as you were inclined to think." Another novice
told me, that having resolved to become a monk in consequence
of his grief for the loss of a lady whom he loved, he felt that
he was indeed consoled for his misfortune, but that there were
moments when he regretted not having sought some other
method of forgetting her. I believe, if I had examined all the
novices round I should have found them not much better satisfied with their condition.

Be this as it may, I became disgusted with a monastic life,
and resuming my secular habit, left the convent as I would
have left a prison, delighted to find myself at liberty, though
wholly unencumbered with money; for I had given all that
formerly belonged to me to these good monks, and getting it back
again was a thing not to be thought of. I could not determine
to return to Alcaraz, being ignorant with what eyes Donna Paula
would regard me. I rather chose to lose the pleasure of again
beholding her, than run the risk of being ill received; besides,
I was by no means too well assured that in the married Don
Manoel I should still find a friend.

I was deliberating, therefore, what course to pursue, when
the Licentiate Carambola, whom I never expected to have seen
again, all on a sudden presented himself to my eyes passing
along the street. We were both equally astonished at thus
meeting together in the capital of Catalonia. "You in Barcelona!" cried I, embracing him. "You too are here," replied
he; "what has brought that about?"—"A silly business,"
replied I, and at the same time acquainted him with my late
exploit. After hearing me to an end, he told me that I had
been in great haste to get rid of my money, and that I ought
by no means to have given it up, but on condition that it should
be returned to me if I should fail to finish my novitiate. "The
error is committed, my friend," replied I, "so let us say no
more about the matter. One thing I have to console me, which
is, that these good fathers, on bidding me adieu, assured me
that I should have a portion in their prayers for the benefactors
of the convent."

To induce the Licentiate to relate to me in his turn what had
happened to him since our separation, "Why," said I, "did you

leave Madrid, and the illegitimate slip confided to your care?
Did the Counsellor of the Indies, his reputed father, dismiss
you through caprice?"—"No," replied he, "it was I who
quitted him, and not without good reason. I will explain it to
you.

"'Signior Licentiate,' said he one day, 'I am in the habit of
having every night some one to read to me till I fall asleep, and
without this I cannot close my eyes. The person who does it
in general is taken ill: have you any objection to supply his
place until he shall have recovered?' I answered that I would
willingly do so, not knowing to what a deal of trouble I was
about to expose myself; and that very evening, as soon as he
was in bed, I seated myself by his bolster, having before me a
small table, on which were an old worm-eaten book, called by
way of distinction, 'his lordship's soporific,' with a slice of ham,
some bread, and a bottle of wine to refresh the reader.

"I took up the book, and had not read more than a dozen
pages ere my Counsellor showed signs of sleep. When I imagined him fast, I paused to take breath, or rather to refresh
myself with a glass; but he instantly awoke, and I was compelled to resume my reading. Astonishing prodigy! ten lines
of this admirable book were sufficient again to set him asleep;
on perceiving which, I seized the glass with one hand and the
bottle with the other, and swallowed one good draught of Lucena
wine. I would then have eaten a bit of ham, imagining that the
Judge would give me time to do so; but I was deceived: he
again awoke so quickly that I was unable to eat a morsel.

"Again I resumed my book, a third time I set my good man
asleep, and to render his slumber more profound, I did not
cease till I had read three mortal pages more. After having
administered so strong a dose of opium, I thought my Counsellor must now be secure for a time. No! no such thing; the
barbarian instantly awoke; and, observing that I had the glass
to my mouth, cried out gruffly: 'Hey! what the deuce, Signior
Licentiate, you do nothing but drink!'—'And you, Signior,'
replied I, 'do nothing but fall asleep and wake again. You
must, if you please, supply yourself to-morrow with another
reader: I would not employ my throat so disagreeably, though
you should double my salary.'—'It is, however,' replied he,
'what you must resolve to do, if you wish to continue the education of my son.' Seeing that he had thus brought it to a

point (you know the Biscayan vivacity), I replied haughtily, ' We will not contest the matter ; ' and on the morrow we separated.

" A few days after," continued the Licentiate, " one of my friends proposed to me to undertake the education of the son of a Catalonian gentleman.   I accepted the offer, and he introduced me to the father, who engaged me, and has brought me from Madrid to Barcelona, where I have now been six months."   I asked him if he were satisfied with his host. "Very much so," replied he; " the parents of my pupil are a good kind of people, and it appears probable that I shall remain with them a long while.   The child, who has but just entered into his eighth year, is idolized, and consequently spoiled by his parents.   Whatever mischief he does, they only laugh at it, and pass over everything.   I am forbidden not only to come to blows, but even to scold him for fear of injuring his health, instead, therefore, of correcting him when he merits it, I applaud everything he does.   In a word, I burn incense to the idol, and find my account in doing so : by that means I make myself beloved by my pupil as well as by his parents, who have an infinite deal of respect for me."

I congratulated Carambola on his happy situation ; after which, having reciprocally embraced, we separated with promises of seeing each other again.   Thus left once more to myself, I plunged again into reflection.   " What plan shall I adopt," thought I, " to extricate myself from the indigence into which I am sunk ?   If I had my Bachelor's habit, I would again essay the business of education.   But may I not in my present dress do pretty nearly the same thing ?   Why not ?   I have only to look out for some great house where they are in want of a governor to conduct some young man on his first entry into the world.   I am as fit to fill such an office as that of a tutor."

I resolved therefore upon this employment, which I was determined to exercise as soon as the opportunity should present itself.   Providence, however, which had other views for me, ordained it otherwise, and changed the appearance of my fortune all at once, by means of an event which I should never have expected, and which was preceded by a dream, too singular not to be related.

CHAPTER VI.

DON CHERUBIN'S DREAM, AND THE SUDDEN CHANGE WHICH TOOK
PLACE IN HIS FORTUNE—INCIVILITY OF THE MONKS—HE BE-
COMES A RICH HERITOR—HIS INCLINATION FOR NARCISSA.

I DREAMED that I was in the city of Mexico, in a superb
apartment, where I beheld my brother Don Cæsar in his dress-
ing-gown, sitting in an arm-chair, and dictating the articles of
his will to a notary who was writing. He had near him a
strong box, from which taking out several bags filled with gold
pieces, he showed them me, saying: "Here, my dear brother,
Don Cherubin, here are the fruits of my travels, and of the
measures which I have taken to enrich myself since I have
been in the Indies. I am now dying, and this wealth I be-
queath to thee; it is now thine own." He then gave me over
the doubloons, which I was so delighted to touch, that I awoke
with the pleasure, imagining I had my hands full of this
enchanting load.

This dream made so strong an impression on me, that I was
all in a tremor when I awoke. Instead of reflecting on it as a
chimera, I seriously contemplated it as a secret intimation,
given me by my good angel, of something favorable which was
to happen to me. "Such may be the case," thought I. "After
all the tales which I have heard on such subjects, I believe
that there may be dreams which convey some secret and mysterious meaning; and if that be the case, mine must certainly
be one. My brother, perhaps, is dead, and has left behind him
wealth which probably appertains to me." I was so strongly
impressed with this idea that, had I been well supplied with
money, I should, I believe, have travelled to New Spain in
search of my supposed inheritance. On the faith, however, of
my dream, I rose full of joy, and with a foresight of good
fortune, went out to walk about the town.

133

As I was crossing the market-place of our Lady del Mar, I saw at the door of the church of that name, a great number of persons who were attentively reading a placard which had just been stuck up. Feeling some little curiosity, I made my way through the crowd, and was not a little surprised at finding it couched in the following terms: " The public is apprised that an individual, named Don Cæsar de la Ronda, who lately arrived from the West Indies with money and merchandise at Seville, died there two days after his arrival. Those who may have any claim to his succession have only to repair to Seville with the proofs of their title, and his effects will be delivered to them, conformably to the inventory which has been taken by the order of our Lords the Judges of Commerce."

I read this bill no less than four times, not daring to trust the evidence of my eyes; nevertheless, being at length beyond doubt convinced of my good fortune, I went into the church to return thanks to God: nor did I forget Don Cæsar in my prayer. I lamented his death, but in such a way that it could not easily have been distinguished whether my tears were in-dicative of grief or joy. It would rest but with myself to do honor to my good nature, by saying that I was sensible only to my brother's death ; but, besides that there is a possibility of my sincerity being doubted, I am an enemy to falsehood, and I will candidly acknowledge that I mourned for Don Cæsar as a good younger brother generally does for an elder whose death has enriched him.

All my uneasiness now consisted in the want of money to enable me to go and take possession of what Heaven had so opportunely sent me. I had come out of the convent with empty pockets; and being without any resource, I found my-self, rich heritor as I was, cutting a very silly kind of figure. After reflecting a long while, however, there came into my head a plan by which I deemed myself secure of obtaining the means of travelling to Seville. The Carmelites, thought I, will willingly lend me fifty pistoles for this purpose. They are good and holy persons, who will desire nothing so much as to serve a man from whom they have received so considerable a gift.

Confident on this point, I addressed the Superior who had succeeded to Father Teodor, and making known to him my situation, begged him to let me have fifty pistoles, promising to repay him with interest as soon as I should have obtained possession of my brother's property. The good monk, after having heard me with attention, answered me coldly, that he could not do me this favor without having first held a chapter of the order ; and then put me off for a fortnight, that is to say, till the Greek calends. I could not have expected this refusal, after having made them a present of all I had when I was about to join their number ; but I now perceived that those who like very well to be obliged, have not always the same disposition to oblige others in return, and this was particularly the case with these good monks. Nothing, among them, can be done without holding a chapter, with a promise of which they lay asleep the greater part of those who have any favor to expect from them.

Very ill satisfied with monastic gratitude, I returned in a melancholy mood to the inn where I lodged. My host, whose name was Jeronimo Moreno, taking notice of my gloom, asked me the reason of it. Of this I made no mystery, and nothing more was necessary to set him railing at the monks, a thing that he was constantly in the habit of doing as often as he heard any of them mentioned, be they of whatever order they might. With the exception of this, he was a good kind of man enough, candid, obliging, and generous. "Signior Don Cherubin," said he, "console yourself for the ingratitude of these reverend fathers. You have no need of their purse to enable you to undertake your journey, since Jeronimo Moreno is not, thank God, too needy to lend money to an honest man. If you want but fifty pistoles to go to Seville, I have them here at your service. I am satisfied you are a young man of honor, and I would lend you all my property with no other security than your word."

I returned thanks to my host for his offer, and took him at his word. He told me out fifty pistoles, for which I delivered him an acknowledgment, and two days after embarked on board a Genoese vessel which was on the point of sailing for Seville. There were several passengers on board, and among others an old merchant of Tortosa, whom some commercial affairs had called to Andalusia. With this Catalonian I formed an acquaintance; and the similarity of our dispositions soon gave birth to a friendship which became so strong, that when we arrived at Seville he begged we might not separate, telling me that he knew an inn where we could be well lodged and meet

with pleasant company. I assented to his proposal, and we
went to lodge together at the sign of the Parrot in Lonxa
Street.

The master of this inn, his wife and his daughter, appeared
so rejoiced at seeing the merchant of Tortosa, that I was
induced to think they had been a long while acquainted.
" Here," said he, " is a cavalier whom I have brought you, and
whom I entreat you to regard as my second self."—" It is sufficient," replied the host very politely, " that the gentleman is of
the number of your friends, for him to merit the utmost attention it is in our power to afford him." The hostess, who might
be about forty years of age, and who by no means belied the
reputation which the women of Seville had acquired of being
flatterers and coquettes, could not refrain from adding to this
compliment of her husband's, " that a cavalier of my figure
must be satisfied that they could not fail to treat him with all
possible regard."

In the evening, when it was time to sup, the host, who was
called Master Gaspard, asked us if we wished to be served in
private. " No, no," replied the old Catalonian, " we will sup
with you and your amiable family; we are fond of company."
We therefore sat down to table with the host, the hostess, and
Narcissa their daughter, the latter of whom joined to a youthful
appearance, regular features, an air of gaiety, and eyes full of
a fire which fascinated the beholder. Mine were, of course,
frequently directed towards her during supper. For her own
part, she was by no means sparing of her glances, and she
favored me with some which failed not to afford me a subject
for reflection. I thought I perceived in them a desire to please
me which was not long without its due effect. I was troubled.
I felt agitated by some tender sensations; and my heart, which
my residence in the convent had only rendered more combus-
tible, was presently inflamed by the beautiful Narcissa.

The merchant of Tortosa, who perhaps perceived and wished
to serve my growing tenderness by making me pass for a man
of opulence, began speaking of the affair which had brought
me to Seville. He dazzled by this means the eyes of the
father and mother, and multiplied the favorable glances of
the young lady. Master Gaspard now offered me his services.
He proposed to take me on the following day to a lawyer of
his acquaintance, whose principal employment consisted in

securing justice to strangers who came to Seville on commercial pursuits. "This man," said he, "will instruct you what measures to take, to avoid being cheated out of your property by the officers whom you must employ to obtain it; or rather, he will, if you prefer it, take upon himself the whole trouble of the business, and you will be quit for a trifling remuneration; for he is a man of the most disinterested temper."

The old merchant persuaded me to accept this offer of the host's, which I did without the slightest hesitation; after which, it being bedtime, the Catalonian and I retired to the rooms which had been prepared for us, and which for the apartments of an inn were decent enough. I went to bed, where I employed my thoughts on the charms of Narcissa, in preference to the brilliant fortune which I was on the point of enjoying; but the image of Gaspard's daughter yielding in turn to the idea of riches, I fell asleep upon gold and silver.

CHAPTER VII.

On the following day my host, to convince me that he was a
man of his word, took me to the lawyer of whom he had spoken,
and introducing me to him, " Signior Don Mateo," said he,
" here is a gentleman who is lodged in my house. He is not
very well acquainted with business, and will stand in need of
your advice." The lawyer now gravely demanded what had
brought me to Seville, and I made him acquainted with the
circumstance. " In the first place," said he, " it is necessary
beyond all things to have a copy of the register of your baptism in proper form, with a certificate to prove that you are
really the brother of the said Don Cæsar de la Ronda, lately
deceased in Seville. Lose not a moment; set out immediately
for Salamanca to procure these documents. Bring them to me,
and rest assured that I will forthwith procure the property of
your brother to be delivered to you, in spite of all the chicanery
which can be practised to keep it from you."

My impatience to procure these papers, which were necessary
for extricating from the clutches of the Seville justices the
property to which I was entitled, did not allow me to delay a
single moment unnecessarily, and induced me to make such
good haste, that in the course of a fortnight I returned with
the register of my baptism, and with certificates both of the
Corregidor and of all the other magistrates in Salamanca ; so
that it was impossible to deny that I was my father's son,
and consequently the brother of Don Cæsar. As soon, therefore, as Don Mateo had read them, he cried out with rapture :
" Blessed be God ! these are, indeed, victorious documents. I

have further to inform you," added he, "that I have during your absence been with the Judges of Commerce, who told me that your brother had made a will the evening before his death, and left you his sole heir. You will, therefore, very shortly be in possession of your property, or I will never more interfere in any cause, however good I may have reason to consider it."

As this lawyer appeared to merit my confidence, I placed an implicit reliance upon him; and I had no reason to repent it, for in about three weeks he put me in the entire possession of Don Cæsar's effects, which consisted in bars of silver, Spanish pistoles, and various kinds of merchandise. To speak the truth, it was not without considerable discount that I was enabled to extract these riches from the hands in which they were deposited; and they were not delivered to me until after so many formalities, that it might truly have been said the officers of justice were my coheirs. Nevertheless, after all the moisture which these doves had drawn from my substance, my lawyer honestly renumerated an infinitude of duties paid, after all this reckoned, all deducted, I still found my inheritance amount to clear eighty thousand crowns.

What an inconceivable blessing! The first use I made of this good fortune was to give public marks of gratitude to my brother's memory. I ordered masses for his soul in every church in Seville; I paid the clergy, both regular and secular, to offer up their prayers in his behalf; and in fact made it plainly appear that Don Cæsar had not chosen an ungrateful brother for his heir. When I had discharged the duty I owed to his ashes, I turned my attention to my own affairs. I sold my merchandise, and deposited the money, by advice of the merchant of Tortosa, in the hands of Signior Abel Hazendado, who had the reputation of being the safest banker at that time in Seville.

While I was thus putting my affairs in order, Master Gaspard, at whose house I still lodged with the old Catalonian, treated me with the most unwearying complaisance, as did also his wife and his handsome daughter, from the latter of whom I was honored with a profusion of tender looks. In the meantime the merchant was incessantly expatiating to me on the merits of this girl. He was always praising her wit and amiable character, not forgetting her virtue. I saw very plainly the point to which he would bring me; he wished, as well as the host and hostess, to see me espouse this very amiable lady, to whom he was god-father, and perhaps something besides. I was well enough inclined to commit this folly; and I believe that I should have committed it, if I had not had the good fortune to be saved from it by a piece of intelligence which I received, and which will be read in the following chapter.

CHAPTER VIII.

DON CHERUBIN MEETS WITH MILENO—WHAT HE LEARNS FROM
HIM, AND THE NEWS WHICH PREVENTS HIM FROM ESPOUSING
THE DAUGHTER OF MASTER GASPARD, AND CAUSES HIM TO
LEAVE SEVILLE AS PRECIPITATELY AS IF HE HAD BEEN GUILTY OF
SOME CRIME.

IT is certain that I was enamoured of Narcissa, and, imagining that I alone was beloved by her, I was on the point of asking her from her father, when by accident I one day met with
Mileno, whom I supposed to have been still in the service of
Pedrilla. " Ah, my dear Mileno," cried I, " is it you? Is
Don Manoel in Seville? "—" I am no longer with him," replied he ; " we separated on account of a quarrel I had with his
cook, about a waiting maid of Donna Paula. The cook and I
were both very fond of this young person ; and, becoming
jealous of each other, we fought, and I having wounded my
man desperately, was obliged to fly. I came directly to Seville,
where I have the honor of serving a young canon, who con-
trives to reconcile with his breviary the pleasure of having a
mistress. He secretly visits, through the agency of an officious old woman and myself, the daughter of an innkeeper."

These last words made me shudder, and I tremblingly asked
Mileno if he knew the name of the innkeeper. " He is called,"
said he, " Master Gaspard, and his daughter's name is Narcissa.
You know them, I presume," added he, " since you change
countenance at hearing their names. You take some interest
in this lady? "—" More than you imagine, child," replied I.
" I am enamoured of this perfidious beauty ; you have done me
a good office by giving me the information I have just obtained
from you, and of which I shall not fail to profit."

" If I had known," returned he, " that you were about to

unite your fate with Narcissa's, I would have taken good care
to have said nothing of her weakness for the Licentiate Don
Blas Mugerillo, my master.   We ought to injure no one, and I
should be extremely sorry that any report of mine should prevent you from espousing a charming girl who has only a little
matter of gallantry to be laid to her charge."—" Signior Mileno,"
replied I, " cease, if you please, your ill-timed raillery, and continue your very honorable services to your very chaste master.
Give me some information about Don Manoel.   Has he become the husband of Donna Clara ? "—" No, indeed, has he
not," replied he.   " You do not know then that on his return
from Barcelona to Alcaraz he learned that this lady was in a
convent of the nuns of Niñaterra, and had taken the veil; so
that in all likelihood she is lost to him forever."—" And in
what situation," said I, " did you leave Donna Paula ? "—" In
that," said he, " of a girl who would have been very glad to
have borne with you the yoke of Hymen, and who, conceiving
herself under the necessity of relinquishing such an expectation, has taken an aversion to marriage, and will no longer hear
of it."

I would willingly have had a long conversation with Mileno,
but he was unable to remain with me, and quitted me suddenly,
saying : " Adieu, Signior Don Cherubin ; pardon me for not
stopping longer.   I am in haste.   My master has invited five
or six of his intimate friends to sup with him this evening, and
I am going to order a repast worthy of their sensuality."

When Mileno had left me I fell into a train of reflection.
Zooks ! thought I, there are some confoundedly deceitful faces
in the world.   Who would not, like myself, have supposed that
this Narcissa was prudent and virtuous ?   It must be admitted
that my brows have had a most fortunate escape.   Then turning my thoughts to Don Manoel, and pitying him for having
lost a mistress so estimable as Donna Clara, I participated in
his affliction.   " If I were at Alcaraz," said I, " at this time, I
should be a great consolation to him.   What prevents me from
going ?   My esteem for my friend, and my regard for my own
happiness, both urge me to it."   Unworthy as Narcissa has
proved herself of my tenderness, I still find her influence over
my heart, and to forget her I must again return to the company of Donna Paula.   The result of these reflections was
that I determined immediately to take the road to Alcaraz.   I

set out privately from Seville ; but when I was on the point of going away, conveyed a billet to the daughter of Master Gaspard, in which I informed her that being under the necessity of quitting her for some time, I had left to a young canon of the cathedral the care of consoling her during my absence.

CHAPTER IX.

DON CHERUBIN RETURNS TO ALCARAZ—IN WHAT STATE HE THERE
FOUND DON MANOEL DE PEDRILLA AND HIS SISTER DONNA
PAULA—OF THE RECEPTION WHICH THEY GAVE HIM—HIS LOVE
FOR DON MANOEL'S SISTER REVIVES.

AFTER having been ill fed, ill lodged, and otherwise tormented during six days, I arrived at Alcaraz. I alighted at the residence of Pedrilla, who imagined that he beheld a phantom when I appeared before him. " Is this an illusion ? " exclaimed he. "Is it really Don Cherubin de la Ronda whom I behold ? "—" Yes, my friend," replied I, " it is himself. I am he whom you left at Barcelona in a habit which my feeble virtue did not permit me to persevere in wearing." I then informed him how my fervor had relaxed so much, that I was unable to complete my novitiate. " And I suppose," said he, " the monks gave you back a part, at least, of the money you had made over to them when you assumed the frock."—" No, no," replied I, " there was no thought of any such generosity ; but I should not have complained of them, had they not refused to lend me fifty pistoles, which I solicited from them a few days after I left the convent." At these words, Don Manoel gave a shrug of the shoulders, which was as good as a volley of the most violent declamations against the monks. " You must," said he, " permit my friendship to reproach you for suffering me to remain in ignorance of your situation. Do you not know that among good Spaniards it is an offence to a friend not to have recourse to him when one has need either of his purse or of his sword?

" By way of reparation for your fault, you shall always remain with me and partake my fortune. All that I exact from your gratitude is, that you will be convinced your misfortunes can never lessen my friendship. I will go further ; I promised you my sister, and I now renew my promise. She still preserves the same sentiments for you which she indulged before

144

you went to Barcelona; for think not that by leaving her you have in any degree lost the place you possessed in her heart. She has wept your inconstancy, but without complaining of you."

I could not hear Pedrilla speak thus without being most sensibly affected, and pressing him closely in my arms, " Ah, my dear Don Manoel," said I, " what a happiness for me to have a friend like yourself, and how delighted am I to think that I may still aspire to the possession of Donna Paula! My joy is the greater since I am not in the state of indigence which you imagine. I have eighty thousand crowns to offer her with my hand."—" Is it possible," cried Don Manoel, " that fortune has showered on you such blessings in so short a time?"

I then gave my friend an account of all that happened to me since I left the convent; and so delighted was he with the intelligence that he immediately conducted me to Donna Paula, to whom he cried out in a transport of joy: " Great news! Here is Don Cherubin de la Ronda, who has returned as much as ever devoted to you."—" Yes, madam," said I, " love has again brought me to your feet. Heaven, satisfied with the efforts I made to detach myself from your charms, has sent back the lover of whom it was not willing to deprive you."— " I pardon you for those efforts," replied she; " my pride is not offended by them, and I have too much respect for the motives of your inconstancy to reproach you for it."

" How happy are you both," cried my friend. " The moment is approaching which is to carry your pleasure to the highest; but for me, miserable sport of love, I have lost forever the hope of possessing Donna Clara. I have just heard that she has professed, and that the cruel girl has left me to the task of forgetting her. Don Cherubin," continued he, " this was news you did not expect."—" Nay," replied I, " I already knew it. Mileno, whom I met in Seville, informed me of it. I deeply lament your griefs, but I hope that by sharing them with you I shall at least contribute to soften them."

These two tasks, therefore, now devolved upon me, to console the brother and to make love to the sister. I acquitted myself so well in both, that I diminished the chagrin of one, and augmented the love of the other. It is true, that if by my exertions the passion of Donna Paula was increased, she failed not on her part to excite most effectually my own, and soon restored it to its original warmth.

10

CHAPTER X.

WHILE waiting till I should become the happy husband of Donna Paula, I passed my time agreeably among the most brilliant youth of Alcaraz. One evening that I was on a visit at one of the principal houses of the town, we were joined by a tall, thin man, to whom the company appeared solicitous to show a particular portion of civility. On taking notice of this cavalier, I recognized him as Don Denis de Langaruto, the Knight of Santiago, whom I had met with at my sister's in Madrid. He also recollected me, and throwing himself on my neck, "Signior Don Cherubin," said he, "will permit me to embrace him. I am delighted at meeting with him again." Not to be behindhand with this gentleman in politeness, I manifested as much joy as himself; and God knows at the same time how little either of us was interested by the meeting.

We supped together at this house. As there were ten or a dozen at table, the conversation was not always general, each from time to time addressing himself in an undertone to the person who sat by him. Being placed near Don Denis, we consequently often discoursed together. "Signior Don Cherubin," said he, "I felt, I assure you, the greatest possible concern for the accident which happened to your sister's husband, Don Pedro Retortillo." I demanded, with an air of surprise, what was the accident he alluded to. "How then!" said he; "are you ignorant that Don Pedro, while engaged in hunting about three months ago, was thrown from his horse, and hurt so seriously that he did not survive his fall two hours?"—"I was, indeed," said I, "unacquainted with this;

146

and that ought not to surprise you, for I have quarrelled with my sister ever since her marriage with Don Pedro, and all intercourse between us is entirely broken off. But," continued I, " pray be so kind, Signior Don Denis, as to inform me whether what you have mentioned may be relied on as fact."— " You need entertain no doubt on the subject," replied he; "this accident happened to your brother-in-law near Cuença, in his Chateau de Villardesaz, where he went to reside with his wife a few days after their wedding."

I was so much affected by this news, that my mind was full of it all the rest of the evening. My sister, towards whom I imagined myself totally indifferent, presented herself to my thought in such a way as made me sensible that I was still interested in her welfare. The cause of our rupture subsisting no longer, nature easily resumed her rights. As soon as I saw Don Manoel, I told him of the fatal accident of which Don Denis had informed me. I then expressed some curiosity to know in what state were my sister's affairs at that time. " I am not less curious than you," replied my friend. " We will, if you think proper, repair to Villardesaz, to console this beautiful widow for the death of her husband; and we shall at the same time see Ismenia, who I suppose is still with her. But," added he, " I am of opinion that it will be better to postpone this journey till after your nuptials." To this delay I assented the more readily, as I was extremely anxious to become the brother-in-law of Don Manoel de Pedrilla.

The preparations for my marriage were therefore made with the utmost magnificence, and I espoused Donna Paula, who united her lot to mine with a satisfaction which rendered my happiness complete. There was nothing during a fortnight but concerts, balls, and entertainments. Had I been the Grand Seignior, I do not suppose that my wedding could have been celebrated by more feasts and rejoicings.

CHAPTER XI.

WITH WHAT GENTLEMAN DON CHERUBIN BECAME ACQUAINTED,
AND WHAT ENSUED—HE SETS OUT WITH DON MANOEL FOR
CLEVILLENTE'S COUNTRY SEAT—WHAT HE MET WITH THERE.

AMONG the young gentlemen who were at my nuptials, there
was one who particularly struck me by his noble and agreeable
air.   As soon as I saw him, I demanded of Don Manoel who
was that handsome cavalier.   " He is called," replied he, "Don
Gregorio de Clevillente."
At the name of Clevillente I changed countenance and became exceedingly agitated, entertaining no doubt that this
gentleman was the seducer of my sister Francisca.   Nevertheless, I concealed my emotion from the eyes of Pedrilla, who
thus continued: "He is returning from Calatrava, and is passing through Alcaraz, on his way to his country seat, which is
near Alicant.   I am extremely happy at having become acquainted with him; he appears to me an accomplished gentleman."
If Don Gregorio pleased Don Manoel, Don Manoel was on
his side no less agreeable to Don Gregorio, who stopped a
fortnight at Alcaraz, during which time there grew up between
these gentlemen so intimate a friendship, that I was at first a
little jealous of it.   But my jealousy could not hold out against
the advances which Clevillente made to obtain my friendship;
so that forgetting what might have opposed it, I honestly met
the sincere and affectionate sentiments which he manifested
towards myself.   This cavalier, the evening before his departure, after expressing his regret at leaving us, proposed to carry
us to his castle for a few days, and urged his request in a
manner so pressing, that we consented.   I set out, therefore, for
Clevillente's abode, not because it was possible to derive any
pleasure from the sight of a house which the brother of my

sister must necessarily view with pain, but drawn thither by a
secret inspiration of heaven, which chose by my ministry to
accomplish its designs.

The first object which struck my view in this house was a
boy about ten or twelve years of age, who came to throw himself into the arms of Don Gregorio, who having affectionately
caressed him, presented him to us, saying, " You see here the
fruit of my earliest love." We thought this boy extremely
pretty. Don Manoel and I embraced him, and congratulated
Don Gregorio on having so promising a son. Clevillente
appeared grateful for the compliments we paid him on this subject. " This child," said he, " is so much the more dear to me,
as he is the offspring of a mother whom I cannot console myself for having lost."

He accompanied these words with a sigh which I re-echoed,
in order to induce him to relate a story in which I had but too
much reason to fear that my sister was interested. " It is
melancholy, sir," said I, " to have a beloved object snatched
from one by death."—" The person whose loss I lament," said
he, " is not yet dead; so, at least, I imagine : but it is now ten
years since she disappeared from this house, and, notwithstanding all the measures I have taken to discover her, I know not
what has become of her."

" You give us," said Don Manoel, " a great idea of her
charms : they must be ravishing, since after ten years you still
take so much pleasure in thinking of her."—" She was not,"
replied he, " a finished beauty; however, so captivating was her
whole appearance, that it was impossible to see without loving
her. You shall judge for yourselves," added he, " if you will
follow me." At these words he led us into his closet; where,
amongst a great number of portraits, was that of my sister. I
knew it immediately, so great was the resemblance; all the
difference I found being that the copy had a striking appearance
of youth which the original began to want.

" There," said Clevillente, pointing with his finger to the portrait in question, " are the features of Francillo's mother ! " I
did not pretend to recollect Francisca in this portrait, nevertheless I was persuaded that Francillo was her child. " I cannot,"
said I to myself, " refrain from thinking so, though she made
no mention of him in the relation of her adventures. She must
have deemed it most proper to suppress this circumstance,

thinking that such suppression rendered her tale more innocent." Then changing my thought, " And yet, perhaps,"
added I, " This natural son may be by some other lady, whom
Clevillente had seduced like Francisca."

To gain from Don Gregorio's conversation some satisfaction
of my doubts, I said to him: " You must, indeed, have been
sensible to the loss of so moving a beauty: but how did you
lose her? Did she quit you through inconstancy, or did you
give her cause to complain of you? "—" Alas ! " replied he
mournfully, " I am the cause of our separation. It is my own
fault, and that is what renders me inconsolable. If Donna
Francisca had abandoned me out of levity, I should long ago
have forgotten her; instead of which, sensible of my ill conduct
to her, I cannot dismiss her from my memory. I confess,"
pursued he, " that I can impute her fault only to my own per-
juries. When I carried her off from the convent in which she
was a boarder, I promised, I swore that I would marry her;
and she yielded less to the violence of my love than to this oath.
Far, however, from keeping my word with her, I deceived, and
finally wearied out her patience. After a year's residence she
escaped from this castle, unrestrained by a new-born infant
whom she left, that the sight of him might incessantly reproach
me with my perfidy and treason.

" I had Francisca sought for in every direction as soon as I
knew of her flight, but the persons who were entrusted with
this charge acquitted themselves so ill that they obtained no
intelligence of her. Since that time I have never been at peace.
Francisca is ever in my mind, and her avenging image pursues
me night and day. I think I see her; I think I hear her,
deploring her credulity, burst out into bitter invectives against
me."—" Perhaps," said I to Clevillente, " you do not paint her
to yourself as she really is; perhaps, accusing herself only of
her misfortune, the recollection of her tenderness to you excites
her tears. Perhaps, in short, you still reign in her heart in
spite of your ingratitude."

" Ah ! if I believed it," exclaimed he, " and knew where she
was, I would go and lament at her feet the unworthy treatment
she has received from me. Yes, I would seek her out, though
she were at the end of the world."—" It would not be requisite,"
said I, " to go so far in search of her, if you were in reality disposed to expiate by marriage the mortal blow you have given

her honor, and the affront you have offered to her family."—
" What do I hear ? " cried Don Gregorio, astonished. " Is it
possible, Don Cherubin, that you are acquainted with the lady
whom this portrait represents ? "—"Doubt it not," replied I ;
" neither is she unknown to Don Manoel."

At these words Pedrilla considered the portrait with more
attention, and distinguishing the features of my sister, " What
is it I see ? " cried he with emotion : " I dare not disclose my
thoughts ; I would rather think that my eyes deceive me."—
" No, no," replied I, " their report is faithful ; Donna Francisca,
who is known to you under the name of Basilisa, is the original
of that picture. Clevillente seduced my sister ; she herself
avowed it to me. He carried her off from a convent in Carthagena where she was a boarder, and brought her to this
castle. It is a rape which honor would impel me to revenge ;
but since Donna Francisca is a widow, there is a milder way
by which the matter may be accommodated."

" After the sentiments which Don Gregorio has just manifested," said Don Manoel, " I am persuaded that his dearest
wish is to marry Donna Francisca."—" I have no other intention," cried Clevillente ; " and the remorse to which I have been
a prey during ten years ought to convince you of it. Let me
only know what part of Spain this lady inhabits, and thither I
fly instantly."—" I propose to conduct you there myself," said
I, " to be witness of the joy you will both experience at your
meeting. I believe that Don Manoel will not refuse to accompany us."—" No, doubtless," replied Pedrilla ; " I have my
reasons also for making this journey, independent of the complaisance which you have a right to expect from my friendship."

CHAPTER XII.

OF THE JOURNEY WHICH THE THREE CAVALIERS MADE TO THE
CASTLE OF VILLARDESAZ—THEY DISGUISE THEMSELVES AS
PILGRIMS TO GET INTO THE CASTLE—IN WHAT MANNER THEY
WERE RECEIVED—SINGULAR CONVERSATION WITH A DOMES-
TIC OF DONNA FRANCISCA'S—SURPRISE OF THE LATTER.

WE accordingly all three took the resolution of going to the
Castle of Villardesaz, where I conceived that my sister must
be. We made preparations for our departure, and, followed by
three valets, mounted like ourselves upon three mules, we took
the road for Cuença, where we arrived in less than six days.

When we had reached this town, we deemed it prudent to
stop there, and inform ourselves on those subjects which we
were desirous of knowing, that is to say, what was going on in
the Castle of Villardesaz, which is but three-quarters of a league
distant. We learned that Signior Don Pedro Retortillo had
really been killed by falling from his horse in a hunting party,
and that his widow, still afflicted with his loss, was leading a
melancholy life at the castle, with no other consolation than
the company of a lady, one of her friends. When Don Manoel
heard of this friend, he was filled with joy, entertaining no
doubt that it was Ismenia, whom he was no less delighted to
see again, than Don Gregorio to recover his lost Francisca.

As we were all three consulting about the manner in which
we should go and present ourselves to these two ladies, a wild
idea came into my head which my companions approved, and
which we resolved to pursue. We got made three pilgrims'
habits, in which, after having left our valets at Cuença, we went
about the commencement of the night towards the Castle of
Villardesaz. We knocked at the door, and told a servant who
came to open it, that three Aragonese pilgrims, who were going
to Santiago, in Gallicia, begged permission to pass the night in

152

the stables of the castle. The servant went in to announce us, and then came and told us a moment after, that his mistress consented to it ; and thereupon, having taken us into the castle, and conducted us into the middle of a large hall, where there was some fresh straw and a lamp fastened to the wall in a corner, " Friends," said he, " when pilgrims come this way, which often happens, it is in this hall we put them to sleep. You will not be badly off ; and as I believe you do not want appetite, I am going to bring you something to satisfy it. You will see that in this castle we do not perform things by halves."

Saying this he retired, leaving us the liberty which we wanted to yield to our desire of laughing at the hospitality which was shown us. It was, in effect, pleasant enough to see pilgrims like us treated in this way, and the idea amused us infinitely. We waited the return of the same servant ; and were not a little curious to know in what consisted the supper to which he had welcomed us, when a quarter of an hour after he returned into the hall with a large basket, in which were bread, cheese, and onions. He was followed by another servant, who brought a large cruise of La Mancha wine ; and approaching us gaily, " Here," said he, " are refreshments which I bring you to renew your strength ; line your stomachs well with them, for that is what supports the feet."

This lad appearing to us a sprightly fellow, who wished for nothing better than to talk, we all three put him questions by turns, to which he answered like a discreet and affectionate servant. We gave him an opportunity of relating to us the misfortune of Don Pedro ; which he did without omitting the most indifferent circumstance. " And your lady," said I, " was she much grieved at his death ? "—" She is still so," replied he : " I could never have thought that a woman would mourn for her husband so long."—" Don Pedro, your master," said Don Gregorio, " was, it seems, a very amiable cavalier ? "—" Not too much of that," replied the servant : " he was a mortal of a disposition bad enough, jealous, a grumbler, and full of fantasies. However, in spite of all that, he had an inexpressible something about him which rendered him agreeable to my lady."—" Is there no person who seeks to console this beautiful widow, eh ? " asked Don Manoel. " I beg your pardon," replied the servant : " besides that Signora Ismenia, her friend, incessantly combats her grief, there comes here almost every day a young gentleman of Cuença, who appears to me well calculated to assuage the tediousness of widowhood.

"This cavalier," continued he, "is called Don Simon de Romeral. I have no doubt that he is inclined to succeed Don Pedro, and the thing is not impossible. For some days past my lady has appeared to me less afflicted than common, whether because the conversation of Ismenia has taken an effect on her, or that of Don Simon began to be pleasing."

The report of this servant induced me to fear that we had come too late, and that Don Simon had already rendered himself master of Francisca's heart. "If that be the case," thought I to myself, "my sister will not owe me much goodwill for the care I am taking of her honor: she will not be pleased with the sight of an old lover, if she be actually prepossessed in favor of another." Don Gregorio made much the same reflection, and we began both of us to doubt whether our pilgrimage would prove successful.

By dint of questioning the servant, who was no fool, we rendered ourselves suspected by him. "Gentlemen," said he, shaking his head, "you appear to me to be very fine pilgrims. You are not *picaros*,* as are the greater part of those who wear the habit, but have all the air of persons of importance. You are disguised in this manner for the purpose of acting some play, and perhaps you have also chosen this castle for the scene of action. If you want," added he, "a fourth actor for your piece, I offer you my talents."

We took him at his word, and perceiving that he was a man who might be useful to us, we discovered ourselves to him; and, the better to engage him in our interest, gave him thirty pistoles. He saw by that that he had not judged wrong of us; and charmed by our behavior to him, "Gentlemen," said he, "dispose of your servant Clarin; you have but to command him. What is your design? What can I do for you?"—"We are acquainted," said I, "with the mistress of this castle and her friend: it is long since we have seen them, and we wish to appear before them thus disguised, to try if they will recognize us. Go," continued I, "go and tell Donna Francisca privately, that if she be desirous of hearing news of her brother Don Cherubin de la Ronda, a pilgrim is here who can satisfy her

* Rogues.

curiosity."—"If you exact nothing more of me than that," replied Clarin, "it is but a trifle: I shall soon have acquitted myself of that commission."

In effect, after having left us for a few minutes, he returned and said: "Come along with me; my mistress would speak with you." At the same time he conducted me to a very handsome apartment, where my sister was with Ismenia. They both immediately recollected me. "Brother," cried my sister, "what an agreeable surprise to me, to see you again. But why offer yourself to my view in this dress?"—"Sister," said I, "you will cease to be surprised that I appear before you in this form, when you know the cause of my pilgrimage. But allow me first to express the sorrow I feel for the death of Signior Don Pedro. As I know you are most sensible to the death of your husband, I come here to participate in your affliction."

The widow on this found her grief renewed, and her eyes were filled with tears. I thought she was going to break out in fresh lamentations, and awaited the coming broadside; but happily Ismenia turned aside the storm. "My darling," said she, "you have wept enough; it is time to console yourself: your brother comes here with the intention of contributing to enable you to do so."—"Oh yes," replied I, "such is my intention; and I dare venture to predict that the face of things will soon be changed in this castle: I am accompanied by two good pilgrims who are resolved to make joy succeed to sadness."—"And who are these pilgrims?" asked Donna Francisca: "I will not see, unless I know them."—"Allow me," said I, "not to name them, that I may leave you the pleasure of the surprise. Give orders that they may be brought here." Ismenia having then called Clarin, bade him go and fetch the other two pilgrims, who were not a little impatient to show themselves on the stage.

The moment they appeared, Ismenia knew Don Manoel; but my sister did not so readily recognize Don Gregorio, who no sooner saw her than he ran and threw himself at her feet. "Madam," said he, "permit a guilty creature, brought hither by remorse, to solicit pardon." Donna Francisca, less struck with these words than at the voice of Clevillente, recollected him, and immediately fainted. I had expected that the sight of Francillo's father would affect her; but I was not prepared to see it make so lively an impression on her.

Ismenia and I gave her prompt assistance; and when she recovered the use of her senses, she remained for some moments silent. Then addressing me, "Brother," said she, "you see the effect of your imprudence. Ought you not to have given me notice before you brought Don Gregorio into my presence? You are not unacquainted with the reasons I have for avoiding him."—"I was wrong, my sister," I replied; "I confess that I ought to have prepared you, by a private conversation, for again beholding a lover on whom you have a right to bestow the most severe reproaches, and who is, notwithstanding, not unworthy of pardon. He has seen his fault, and has for ten years deplored it. Permit him to explain to you what he has suffered. Deign to hear him: I answer for his sincerity."

"Yes, madam," cried Clevillente, "give me, I entreat you, a moment's audience; grant it to the prayers of my friend Don Cherubin. However prepossessed against me you may be, what I am about to say will disarm your resentment."—"Ah! what can you say in your justification?" said the widow of Don Pedro. "Would to God that you were not one of the most perfidious and ungrateful of men!"—"I acknowledge my perfidy," replied Don Gregorio; "but what have I not done to expiate it." He then entered upon a detail of his sufferings, which Ismenia and I allowed him to continue to her private ear, and which did not fail to produce its effect, that is, to soften Francisca; from which it is reasonable to conclude, that if the passions first felt be not all proof against the effects of time, they are at least badly extinguished fires, which may be easily rekindled.

While these two lovers were entertaining each other in a low tone of voice, I observed them, and it appeared to me that the anger of my sister declined. I believe that my nephew Francillo was not forgotten in their conversation, and that that did not impede their reconciliation. During this time Don Manoel and I informed Ismenia in what manner we had become acquainted with Don Gregorio, and all that had passed between us and that cavalier at the Castle of Clevillente.

"You delight me," said Ismenia, "in announcing to me the return of a perjured man, whom my friend could never entirely banish from her memory; but, by my faith, you could not have brought him here at a more critical moment: it was full time. A month later you would have found Francisca married. She began to entertain a liking for Don Simon de Romeral, and I was about to advise her to espouse him."—"Heaven be thanked," replied I, "we have then arrived fortunately indeed, provided my sister will not be inclined to prefer a new-comer to an ancient friend."—"Fie!" replied Ismenia, "do more justice to Donna Francisca. Even though her inclination should lead her towards Don Simon, she would without hesitation decide in favor of Clevillente: the suitor offered by love would yield to him presented by honor."

Notwithstanding all Ismenia could say to set my mind at rest on this subject, I did not cease fearing that my sister might be of a different opinion. My fear, however, was vain. Don Gregorio was a gallant of the first class; he possessed the happy talent of persuading ladies. Donna Francisca felt a renewal of all the tenderness which she formerly had for him; and on her part she was no less clever than this cavalier in the art of pleasing, she rendered him more amorous than ever he had been before. Nor did Don Manoel again find himself in Ismenia's company, without resuming the sentiments he entertained for her in Madrid; and this lady gave him sufficiently to understand by the obliging manner in which she received him, that his happiness depended only on himself, if he were disposed to have the pleasure of becoming her husband.

CHAPTER XIII.

THESE two pilgrims, who felt no weariness in the company
of their mistresses, were interrupted by the entrance of a servant, who came to apprise us that supper was ready. Hereupon
the widow of Don Pedro led us into a saloon, where there was
a table covered with all kinds of well-cooked viands. At the
sight of a repast at which reigned abundance and neatness, I
recollected the cheese and onions which Clarin had brought us in
the stable. "Brother-in-law," said I to Pedrilla, "here are
some eatables rather better than those which were offered us
awhile since. What do you think?"

This reflection excited a general burst of laughter, and put
us in the train for enjoying ourselves. "Gentlemen," said
Ismenia, "in your disguise we took you for three adventurers,
and we here regulate our hospitality by the mien of our guests;
but such pilgrims as you deserve that we should receive them
like honest folks; for which reason my friend and I are very
well disposed to afford you good treatment. I need not protest
it to you," added she, looking with a smile at my two companions; "you must already have perceived it." In short, our
pilgrimage afforded matter of amusement during supper, and
furnished us with a thousand pleasantries which entertained us
till midnight. Then a number of domestics, with lights, appeared to conduct us to the apartments which had been prepared for us; thus the three pilgrims, instead of retracing their

way to the stables, to sleep upon straw, went to rest, like
inquisitors, upon beds of down.

On the following morning, early, my sister sent to say that
she wished to have a private conversation with me.   I went accordingly to her apartment, where having made me seat myself
at the head of her bed : " Brother," said she, " I am satisfied
with Don Gregorio : he repents of having offended me.   For
these ten years past, he assures me that the stings of his conscience have pursued him like furies.   He sought me everywhere, to expiate his ill conduct by marriage.   He has found
me again ; he offers me his hand ; and, more taken with me
than ever, swears to me an eternal constancy.   He has rekindled in my heart all the fire to which he gave birth at Carthagena, and I accept his offer with transport."

I applauded this discourse of my sister's.

" You do well," said I : " Clevillente is the first who vanquished you, and the pledge of your love ought to make you
view him as a husband who rejoins you after a long separation."
Francisca blushed at these words, and said : " I believe, my
dear brother, that you will pardon me for having made a mystery of that pledge which you mention : when a fond girl relates her history, it ought not to be taken amiss that she sup-
presses some circumstance of it."—" Ay ! truly, my dear sister,"
replied I ; " I willingly pardon you ; but let me also be permitted to speak to you of Francillo.   There never was a more
lovely child.   When you shall have seen, you will pity him for
having been deprived of your caresses in his earliest infancy,
and you will acknowledge he well deserves that his father and
mother should recognize him as their legitimate heir."   In fact,
I pleaded so well the cause of my nephew, that Donna Francisca
was softened even to tears in reflecting on his lot.   " Francillo,"
said I, " is no longer to be pitied, since Heaven has brought his
parents together, and that marriage is about to unite them both :
they will fix his state, and by that means give a new member to
the nobility of Valencia."

After having talked a long while of Francillo, we spoke of
the death of my brother, Don Cæsar, and of the rich inheritance
which he had left me.   My sister (I owe her this justice), instead of evincing an avaricious regret at not having come in
for a part of it, was generous enough to congratulate me on it
with sincerity.   It is true that, being even yet better off than

myself in her circumstances, and on the point of marrying an opulent gentleman, she had a right to be content with her fortune. Our interview concluded with questions which she asked me about my marriage, and she had every reason to judge by my answers that I did not repent of the step I had taken.

After this conversation, I had another with Don Gregorio, who, finding his love every moment increasing, appeared all impatience to possess Francisca. While I was with this cavalier, Don Manoel arrived. "I have," said he, "just left Ismenia. I am enchanted with her, and dying with desire to join my fate to hers."—"Well, gentlemen," said I, "since you are so amorous, we must hasten your happiness. That is a care which I take upon myself. I am going to seek your ladies, and point out to them the impatience you feel to become united to them. I do not think they will have the cruelty to make you languish long." In effect, as soon as they perceived that their lovers submitted with so good a grace to the yoke of wedlock, they complied without hesitation with their wishes.

When I saw that the four parties interested were agreed, we held a council as to what was proper to be done, and it was resolved that this double wedding should be celebrated at the Castle of Clevillente, for more reasons than one. This being settled, we sent for our servants from Cuença, with our equipage, and prepared to set out; which we were soon ready to do. We quitted our pilgrim's disguise, to resume our cavalier's dress; and my sister, having left to her farmer the care of the Castle of Villardesaz, took with us and the whole of her domestics the road to Alicant, where we arrived at the end of eight days, not having chosen to use more despatch, lest we should fatigue our ladies. We did not stop in this town, and speedily gained the Castle of Clevillente, where the widow of Don Pedro, recalling the recollection of the griefs, or perhaps the pleasures, she had experienced, could not restrain her tears, which were redoubled at the sight of Francillo. But this amiable child himself dried up the tears he caused, and inspired his mother with so much tenderness for him, that he became her idol. Besides that she beheld in him her living image, he was her only child, she never having had one by either of her husbands.

Nothing was going forward in the castle but preparations for the nuptials of my two brothers. Whilst these were proceeding, I went to Alcaraz to fetch my wife, Donna Paula, without whom the feast would not have been complete. It was but a journey of six days, at the end of which the Castle of Clevillente beheld my return with my wife, whose happy arrival augmented the joy which reigned there. Ismenia and Donna Francisca caressed her in emulation of each other, and found in her a person disposed to live happily with her sisters-in-law.

Don Manoel and Don Gregorio exerted themselves so much to hasten the day which was to crown their happiness, that it shortly arrived. They received the nuptial benediction from the hand of the Bishop of Origuela, a relation of Clevillente; his excellency, who was a Dominican, having been kind enough to come to the castle for this purpose.

Such was the manner in which Ismenia and my sister were married. After having given themselves abundance of time, they married two gentlemen, who, through an excess of regard for them, raised them into ladies of importance. What an admirable thing is love! It draws the curtain over the past life of a coquette when it chooses to marry her to an honest man.

These two marriages were followed by rejoicings which lasted three weeks. After this, Don Manoel and I begged of Don Gregorio and his lady that they would permit us to retire to Alcaraz; but we had abundance of trouble to induce them to consent to it. My sister had so long lived in a close union with Ismenia, that she could not make up her mind to this separation. They, however, ceased to oppose our departure, on condition that in order to be together half the year, Don Manoel and I should go with our wives for three months to the Castle of Clevillente, and that Don Gregorio and my sister should come and pass three months of the winter at Alcaraz. They let us quit them at last, on the promise we made of faithfully observing this convention.

11

CHAPTER XIV.

AFTER having testified by mutual caresses how much we were
affected by our separation, Don Manoel and I set out with our
charming spouses, leaving Don Gregorio and my sister very
melancholy at our departure from the castle. As for us, the
possession of what we held dearest in the world consoled us,
and we derived infinite pleasure from our little journey.

As we were obliged to sleep on the road, we stopped at a
small town, where we had the diversion of a theatrical piece
played by a company of strollers; they had designated it Ines
de Castro. Relying on the reputation this piece had acquired
in Madrid, we procured our ladies the pleasure of seeing it;
but we were completely in despair when we saw appear in the
room of the inn in which this play was performed, a woman
in a state peculiarly unfavorable to elegance of shape, who
uttered a parcel of nonsense of which nothing was heard.
Then came an actor about sixty years of age: he represented
Don Pedro. In fact, this piece, which could be called neither
tragic nor comic, lasted but a quarter of an hour, to the great
satisfaction of the audience. They afterwards gave us an enter-
tainment, consisting of dancing, leaping, and tumbling; and to
close the spectacle, he who had played Don Pedro began fencing
with his right foot, standing on his head; and, as he acquitted
himself well, he was much applauded. But the most comic part
of the adventure was, that the Lady Ines, who while playing had
made a number of wry faces, presented an addition to the company before the audience had retired. The actors begged us

to excuse them for not giving us a Chinese ballet, which had
made great noise in Madrid, but which the unexpected incident
that had taken place prevented them from representing. We
had a great deal of amusement at supper in consequence of this
business. On the morrow we arrived safely at Alcaraz. Our
wives were in want of rest, and on our parts we wanted it also.

We enjoyed the most perfect felicity: though we had been
married three months, we loved our wives more than ever.
Too happy, had our felicity in my own case lasted for life.
But it was written in the table of destiny that there should happen to me misfortunes greater than those I had yet experienced.
The adventures of my sister occurred incessantly to my mind,
and I admired the providence which had never abandoned us.
" For a woman who has been so great a coquette to enjoy such
brilliant fortune," said I, " is indeed extraordinary. How many
persons who have more merit and more virtue than my sister,
do we see in ignominy and misery. What a world is this!
An immoral girl, an actress, become the wife of an honorable
gentleman! This is not often seen. The honor of my sister
is repaired by this; she is rich, and her husband not particularly so: thus one balances the other. May fortune allow us
long to enjoy her bounties! I will not again take it into my
head to put on the frock, and give my property to monks:
those with whom I had to do were too grateful for the wealth I
left among them against my will. (Perhaps I was wrong in
talking thus, for I might have derived my present fortune from
the efficacy of their prayers.) Don Manoel puts the finishing
stroke to my happiness by giving me the half of his castle; the
most distinguished persons in Alcaraz honor us with their
visits; and walking, hunting, fishing, playing, reading, are our
occupations and amusements."

Our pleasures were troubled by an accident which happened
to us. The castle one night took fire, and nearly the half of our
effects were consumed. Happily we had time to remove the
most valuable; and some repairs put things in their former
state. We should easily have consoled ourselves for this loss,
if we had not been robbed of money and of our wives' jewels,
which together amounted to a considerable sum. We did not
suspect any of our domestics, and yet it was notwithstanding
one of them, who was discovered by a shopkeeper to whom the
rogue had applied to sell a part of what he had taken. Don

Manoel would have delivered him over to the hands of justice ;
but out of consideration for me, he contented himself with dis-
missing him, ordering him, on pain of being prosecuted, to leave
the kingdom within two days.   We liberally recompensed our
honest dealer: he was of a kind not often met with.

Some days after, there offered himself to our service a youth,
whose physiognomy and figure spoke in his favor.   He came
to us with a recommendation from one of our friends.   We
hired him the same day.   His name was Alvares.   His mildness, his complaisance, his regularity in fulfilling his duties,
secured him our esteem.   He had that spirit of modesty and
humility which made him beloved by everybody; but notwithstanding the excellence of his disposition, he was frightfully
melancholy, and constantly sighing.   I conceived a great interest
for him.   This lad evinced an affection for me, and I returned
it : it was sufficient that he was unhappy, to render him dear
to me.

I esteemed Alvares so much, that I took it into my head
to dissipate his chagrin ; for his sombre, melancholy air
disturbed me.   I made him come one day into Don Manoel's
apartment, in order that he might discover to me the cause of
his grief.   I began by asking him if he were displeased with
us, and told him that we were well satisfied with him ; and that
the melancholy in which he was absorbed would sooner or later
bring him to the tomb.   Alvares heard me with a sigh, and said
nothing.   " You are in love," I continued, " and your affection
is not returned.   Confess it to me : if the person whom you
love be dependent on me, or reside in our neighborhood, do not
constrain yourself ; open your heart to me ; I am sufficiently
your friend to obtain you the object of your desires."—" I am
in love, it is true," replied Alvares, " but without any hope,
though I am loved by the most amiable creature that Heaven
could ever form."   These words surprised me from the mouth
of a valet.   " Your excessive kindnesses for me," continued
he, " are so reiterated, that I feel no difficulty in confiding in
you, and letting you know who I am."

Don Manoel, who heard us from his closet, and could not
restrain his curiosity, came out and joined us.   Alvares was
surprised to see him so near, and would have left us.   Don
Manoel stopped him, telling him that he had heard our conversation, and that the interest he felt in it had engaged him

to leave his closet for the purpose of hearing the rest ; and that he might look upon us in no other light than that of his friends. " Oh ! gentlemen," cried he, " how much am I confused by your kindness !

" My family is noble, but nobility is but a very trifling matter when it is not sustained by a good fortune. I had a mother who, by her coquetry and the great airs which she gave herself, ruined my father in a very short time. Happily I was the only fruit of their marriage. My father, who was called Don Alvar del Sol, died of grief by reason of this ; and my mother, unable to bear up against the distress which she had herself brought on, followed him shortly after."—" What ! " interrupted Don Manoel, " are you the son of Don Alvar del Sol ? Ah ! my dear Don Carlos, let me embrace you." Don Manoel threw himself upon his neck, and recalled to his recollection that they had studied together at Madrid. I was delighted within myself at this discovery, and begged Don Carlos to make known to us his misfortunes. My friend asked him news of Don Lopez, whose wealth was immense, and who had resided at Madrid. " Alas ! " replied Carlos, " he is the author of all my misfortunes, and by the means I will relate."

CHAPTER XV.

TRAGICAL HISTORY OF DON CARLOS AND DONNA SOPHIA.

" AFTER the death of my parents, Don Lopez de la Crusca, my maternal uncle, took charge of my infancy; and it was under his eyes that I performed my studies. In spite of his extreme avarice, he loved me, and had taken me home with him, where I lived happy, and without inquietude; but love came at last to trouble my repose. My uncle procured me all the pleasures which can gratify a young man who has just left college. We went frequently to the Prado together, and this promenade was our principal amusement. One day when we were there, my uncle, being tired of walking, sat down, and out of good breeding I sat down with him. There was opposite to us a bench, on which was seated the most lovely person one could behold. She cast a look at me now and then, and her looks were so many arrows darted at me by love. Her companion, however, whom I supposed her mother, arose, and she followed her. Seeing that they left the promenade by the side on which we lived, I feigned indisposition to induce my uncle to return home. He complied with my wish, and I had the happiness of following at a distance the person who of all the world had become dearest to me. What was my surprise at seeing them go into the house exactly opposite our own ! I asked my uncle if he knew the ladies who lived opposite; but he replied that, having never chosen to visit his neighbors, he did not desire to know them. I told him that there was, however, a treasure in that house, since it enclosed the most lovely person in the world. ' That may be,' said my uncle, ' and yet I take no interest in it.'—' If you be interested for me, my dear uncle,' replied I, ' you will introduce me at that house.'—' No, nephew,' replied he, ' I have taken care of you till this time, and I do not repent it, since you have always obeyed me. At-

tend to my advice. Do not go to that house: I have my
reasons.' He then retired, and left me alone.

"I was not unmindful of what my uncle had said; but love
obtained the victory, and on the following day I went to pay a
neighborly visit to the parents of the lady whom I had seen.
The reception which they gave me enchanted me. I perceived that the daughter at sight of me had blushed exceedingly; I believe, on my side, I was not too free from the same
weakness, being sensible of a flame which had been hitherto
unknown to me. The father and mother of Donna Sophia
(this was her name), knowing me to be the nephew of Don
Lopez de la Crusca, reproached me for not having been to visit
them before. I excused myself in the best way I could, and
told them that my uncle was so extraordinary a man that he
saw nobody; that, for my own part, I had done myself a great
deal of constraint in not having called on them before, and that
they might rely upon me for the future, since they permitted it.
Donna Sophia, while I was speaking, ceased not to gaze on me,
and I went out the most enamoured of men.

"I continued my visits during six entire months. No happiness could equal my own; I loved and was beloved. I
formed the design of asking Donna Sophia from her parents in
marriage. They granted me, without hesitation, their consent,
on condition that my uncle would subscribe to it; for without
that they retracted their word, since I had no expectation of
property but from him. I went to make known my happiness
to Donna Sophia; she blushed, and for the first time embraced
me. I read in her eyes that I did not displease her as a husband. Her father and mother came to interrupt us, and I returned to my uncle's. I there threw myself on my knees, and
confessed that in spite of his prohibition I had been to see
Donna Sophia, and was madly in love with her; and that her
parents had consented to give her to me in marriage, provided
he opposed no obstacle to my felicity. 'Nephew,' replied he,
'I oppose none. Espouse your mistress; I consent to it. I
know that for six months you have been regularly in the habit
of visiting her. I have never spoken of it; you this day avow
it to me; be happy; but never hope, while I live, for any part
of my property'—'Ah, uncle,' cried I, 'your consent suffices,
and I prefer Donna Sophia to all the wealth in the world.'
The next day I acquainted my mistress with my uncle's reply,

and she informed her parents, who immediately went to visit Don Lopez, that they might concert together the arrangements for our marriage. They left me with their daughter, and went to my uncle's, who on his part was much surprised at their visit. He let them talk as long as they pleased, and then replied, 'that he readily consented to the honor they designed me, but that I had nothing to expect from him during his life;' such were his intentions. It was in vain they represented to my uncle that I did not merit this injustice; this implacable old man would not swerve one jot from his opinion, and turned his back upon them. The parents of Donna Sophia were cruelly offended, and returning home, told me that my uncle would do nothing for me, that they begged me never more to set foot in the house, and ordered their daughter never to see me again.

"A criminal who hears his sentence read, was never more struck with terror nor more troubled than I at this dreadful news. I was taken so ill, that they were obliged to have me carried home; it was long ere I came to myself, and my uncle, whom I may justly call cruel, left me alone, and went to his country house. I inquired after Sophia, and was informed that her parents had sent her to Carthagena, to a convent of which an aunt of hers was abbess. As soon as I was in a state to go out, I directed my steps thither, but it was impossible for me to behold the object of my love. Despairing, without resource, without support, I would not set foot in my uncle's house, nor see him. I wandered during two years from town to town, where, not knowing what to do, I devoted myself to service, until such time as it shall please Heaven to release me from my misery. Death only can put an end to my misfortunes."

Our ladies came to interrupt us by bringing us news from Madrid, which were, that Don Lopez de la Crusca was dead, and that having left his property to Don Carlos de la Sol, it remained for him to make himself known. Don Carlos mourned his death, which certainly showed his good nature. Our wives, not being apprised of the change in Alvares, were surprised to see him weep, till we informed them who he was. They then congratulated him on his good fortune. Carlos a moment after cried out, "I can now be happy; my uncle is no more." He immediately wrote to the parents of Donna Sophia, informing them what had happened; and in the interval which must elapse before he could receive an answer, set out to secure his succession. After having thanked and embraced us, he went away, more amorous than ever. We caused him to be accompanied by one of our servants, at whose return we were informed of his fate. On asking for him, which was our first care, what was our astonishment at learning that he was no more! The servant informed us, "that while at his uncle's country house to take possession, he there received intelligence that the parents of Sophia agreed to his marrying her, and that he had only to repair to Madrid for the purpose, for that they had written to Carthagena to have her return from the convent. This news was so great to him, and the joy he felt so violent, that after a thousand demonstrations of it, and a thousand extravagances, he died in the arms of several friends to whom he had imparted his happiness.

"They sent me to Madrid," continued the servant, "to inform the parents of Sophia of what had taken place, and they wrote immediately to the abbess of the convent where she was, that Don Carlos had died of joy. They learned, in reply, that Sophia had received with great indifference the news that she was going to be married to Don Carlos, as she said she was fond of solitude. Nevertheless when, some days after, she heard that Don Carlos was dead, she fell down in a swoon and remained eight days without recollection. She had raised her eyes to Heaven, and they heard her pronounce these words: 'O Heaven! is it possible! He is no more!' The sighs which she uttered, and the tears which flowed from her in abundance, prevented her from saying more. In this state she continued, refusing every kind of nourishment, until her sufferings were terminated by death."

We were much afflicted at this news, and could not refuse our tears to the misfortunes of the unfortunate Don Carlos and Donna Sophia. They were dissipated by the visit of Don Gregorio, my brother-in-law, with my sister. They remained with us a month, and took a deal of interest in the tragical history of Don Carlos, of which we gave them a recital. We procured them all the pleasures we had formerly enjoyed. It was thus we preserved, by our reciprocal visits, the friendship which reigned between us.

END OF THE THIRD PART.

PART THE FOURTH.

CHAPTER I.

DON CHERUBIN DE LA RONDA, FIFTEEN MONTHS AFTER HIS MAR-
RIAGE, BECOMES THE MOST AMOROUS OF HUSBANDS—DON GA-
BRIEL CARRIES OFF HIS WIFE—HE PURSUES HER RAVISHER IN
VAIN—HE GIVES UP THE PURSUIT, AND RESOLVES TO GO TO
MEXICO.

IN this manner then did my two brothers-in-law and myself
live with our wives. Don Gregorio and Don Manoel gave me
every day new proofs of their esteem, as I, on my part, failed
not to treat them with the most respectful deference and attention. What is most worthy of notice is, that our ladies were
not less united than ourselves. They scarcely ever contradicted each other, and when such a thing did happen, it was
always without bitterness, and their disputes were always terminated by laughter.

To crown our happiness, we were soon made sensible that
Heaven had blessed our marriages. Ismenia in about ten
months was delivered of a boy, Donna Paula of a daughter,
and Donna Francisca, my sister, brought into the world two at
once, as if to make amends for her former sterility, or perhaps
to convince Clevillente that it was in his arms alone she could
be fruitful.

Our society, delighted with these fortunate accouchements,
celebrated them by feasts which formed occasions for rejoicing
to the whole village. In fact, we had now no wish ungratified.
In whatever spot we were, joy reigned incessantly among us;
and though our pleasures had in our own families an inexhaus-
tible source, we had notwithstanding a great number of friends
who came to augment them by partaking them with us. When

170

we were at Clevillente's house, the hidalgos of the environs afforded us good company there; and when we resided at Alcaraz, Don Manoel's house became the rendezvous of the gentry of the town, as well as of the illustrious strangers who came there.

We enjoyed a felicity the most perfect, and I in particular was satisfied with my lot: in Donna Paula's arms I found a source of the most pure and inexpressible pleasures, and though married, I loved her more than ever—too happy had the blessings I enjoyed been of longer duration. I thought I had arrived at the end of my misfortunes; but I had not yet undergone my destiny, which had evils in store for me greater than any which had yet befallen me.

Among a number of cavaliers who joined in our parties of pleasure, there was one who called himself Don Gabriel de Monchique. He stated himself to be from the kingdom of Algarves, and gave himself out as a relation of the Count of Villa Nova. In travelling through Spain out of curiosity, he had stopped at Alcaraz, and we had become acquainted with him. Besides having the equipage of a grandee, he was extremely ceremonious, and his manners were so noble, that he could not be suspected as a man of a common class; one would rather have taken him for a young prince who was travelling incognito through the Spanish monarchy, than for a private gentleman. I never saw a man who had a better air or more agreeable figure; nor was his mind inferior to the elegance of his person. My brothers-in-law and myself were charmed with him from the first moment, and spared no pains to acquire his friendship. We took pleasure in introducing him to our ladies, who, perhaps, secretly taxed us with imprudence, in bringing into their presence so dangerous an object. As for us husbands, instead of being alarmed for the consequences, we acted like true Frenchmen, by admitting him into our society at all risks.

He soon gave us to understand that we had let the wolf into the sheepfold, and unfortunately for me, my wife was the sheep he took a fancy to devour. I saw very plainly that she was not unpleasing to him; but this circumstance was very far from alarming me: I only laughed at it. I sometimes congratulated Donna Paula, in jest, on having made a conquest of such a handsome man, and she in the same style would reply that she was happy in being able to make me a sacrifice so flattering. Nay more! I made myself an amusement out of Monchique's love. Far from having any inquietude on the subject, I congratulated myself in secret on seeing so amiable a rival sigh in vain. In a word, I conceived the sister of Don Manoel too prudent to step aside from the path of duty; but I relied on her prudence too far. The gallant, who had formed the design of seducing her, succeeded but too well, through the agency of an old waiting woman, who had obtained a great ascendency over the mind of my wife, and whose fidelity she found the means of corrupting.

The most singular circumstance in this seduction was that it was managed so secretly that I had not the slightest suspicion of it. My wife was even already far off from Alcaraz when I was informed that she had disappeared with Antonia, her maid, as had also Don Manoel, and that in all probability this cavalier had carried them off.

I gave no credit whatever to the first report which was brought me on the subject, in which, to my apprehension, there was not the slightest probability. "No, no," cried I, "it is not possible that my wife, whose virtue has been unshaken to this moment, should begin by carrying matters to such an extremity as that; this would indeed be a most extraordinary *coup d'essai.* I should have been less surprised at this adventure, had the wife of one of my brothers-in-law been the heroine of it; for such a thing would suit them better than Donna Paula, whose conduct has been hitherto irreproachable. Notwithstanding, it is she who, in spite of the excellent education she has had, has just covered herself with infamy. How could this possibly have happened? Don Gabriel must have employed force to carry her off. But by what dexterity was he enabled to tear her from the bosom of her family and the arms of her husband? By what enchantment has he been able to effect this crime, without leaving a single trace of it behind? This event confounds me."

Clevillente and Pedrilla, not knowing what to think of this rape, were no less astonished at it than myself. We did not, however, content ourselves with thinking about the business, but all three made the most vigorous exertions to discover the route which the ravisher had taken with his prey. We made, both on the side of Murcia and of Valencia, the most diligent researches, all of which were ineffectual. We concluded that Monchique had gained the coast of Carthagena, and embarked there on board some vessel, prepared by his orders to transport him to Portugal with his Helen. I stopped at this conjecture, and, resolving to follow this new Paris, I prepared to go and seek him in the kingdom of the Algarves, where I flattered myself I should find him.

Don Manoel, not considering himself less interested in obtaining satisfaction for the proceeding of Don Gabriel, was absolutely determined on accompanying me, notwithstanding all I could say to turn him from his design, wishing nothing so much as to convince me that a brother such as himself was not less sensible than a husband of the affront done to his family. I had no small difficulty in persuading him to leave to myself the care of our common vengeance. He yielded, however, to my persevering requests, which were seconded by the tears of his wife. I therefore prepared myself to follow Monchique ; but before my departure I begged Don Manoel to charge himself with the care of having his niece, my daughter, educated, and of the administration of my rents. Then, having plentifully supplied myself with gold and jewels, as with a foresight that I was to be a long while absent from Alcaraz, I took leave of my brothers-in-law and their wives, whom I did not quit without exciting their tears, nor without shedding them abundantly myself. The ladies in particular were much moved when we bade farewell, whether because they were really afflicted at my departure, or because they were still good comedians.

I proceeded to the port of Vera, where I embarked with a lackey, on whose courage and fidelity I could rely, in a vessel freighted for Lagos, a town which forms the point of the kingdom of the Algarves, on the sea-coast. I was no sooner arrived there than I began to make inquiry for Don Gabriel Monchique, and, as they informed me that he was not known in Lagos, I went from town to town endeavoring to obtain an account of him. I passed through Tavira, Faro, Sagres ; in a word, all the kingdom of the Algarves, without deriving any other fruit from my researches than the mortification of having made them in vain. I was in despair at not meeting my enemy, and respired only vengeance.

" What rodomontade ! " will perhaps exclaim some of my readers, who remember the business of Don Antonio de Lorca, and the difficulty I had to bring myself to a resolution of engaging in a combat, two against two. It is, however, a certain fact that I would willingly have discovered Don Gabriel, to expose myself with him to the chance of having my throat cut. I must have become brave since that time, or else my injured honor inspired me with a spirit of vengeance which supplied the place of valor.

Be this as it may, Toston, my valet, who began to be tired of so many useless journeys, said to me one day: " Signior, we are both tiring ourselves to no purpose. Let us leave off running over Portugal after a man who may have directed his course to Flanders, or perhaps to Italy. Besides, do you know whether the lady who has been carried off deserves that you should expose your life for her? As to me, if you will permit me to speak my mind, I fear that she travels without regret with Don Gabriel, or rather with an adventurer, for I am much mistaken if this gallant be not a new Guzman de Alfarache, or something like him. If such were the case, would it not be much better to abandon a faithless wife to her evil destiny, than to entertain the desire of living with her again? "— " Assuredly," replied I. " Do not imagine that I think otherwise than yourself about the matter. If I knew that she had voluntarily left me, my contempt for her would prevent me from seeking her any longer. What do I say? Instead of continuing my search, I should look upon her as an infamous wretch, from whom I could not possibly place myself at too great a distance. But I cannot believe her so guilty."

" What prejudice! " resumed my confidant. " Is it possible that you cannot, with the good sense you possess, imagine the possibility of a hitherto virtuous wife ceasing to be so when vigorously assailed by the attentions of a handsome man? What a mistake! I judge less favorably than you of Donna Paula, and I have particular reason for doubting her virtue. I must make you acquainted with it. I one day saw Don Gabriel and old Antonia conversing in private, with an air of mystery. I am sure that you were interested in their discourse, or rather that they were concerting together the plan which they meditated, and in which my lady was, in fact, in concert with them."

This zealous servant told me so many other things, and returned so often to the charge, that he came at last to persuade me that I had been deceived by a hypocritical wife. I no longer doubted it ; and immediately passing from one extreme to the other, " Toston," cried I, " you have opened my eyes. Yes, I have been the dupe of pretended virtue : certain circumstances which you have related convince me of it but too well. O Heaven! how great has been my blindness! Donna Paula is a perfidious wretch, whom I will no longer remember but to detest."—" I am delighted," replied Toston, " to see you in this mind. Heaven be praised for it! Come, my dear master, let us no longer run after one who has deserved your hatred ; let us return to Alcaraz, where Don Manoel and Don Gregorio, your brothers-in-law, and, what is more, your friends, will assist you in banishing her from your memory."

" Ah! Toston," replied I, " what have you ventured to propose to me? You ought rather to counsel me to pass the Pillars of Hercules, and go into the wilds of Africa, to hide my disgrace and my name. I feel an invincible repugnance to beholding Alcaraz again, after the mortal blow which my honor has received there. I would rather keep from it for ever, or, at all events, for a few years."—" Well," said he, " since you make so much difficulty about returning to your friends, let us take another course. Let us sail to the West Indies. After all the wonders I have heard of Mexico, I should be very glad if you would go and see that charming country, which deserves the preference over all the climates in the world ; a country in which reigns, according to account, an eternal spring, where sick persons are scarcely ever seen, where the entrails of the earth are silver, and where, in a thousand places, the rivers run over golden sands. It is there, my dear master, it is there you ought to go."—" You have inspired me with a wish to do so, my child," replied I. " I am pleased with the idea ; let us set out for New Spain. The thing is decided, and I am determined to undertake the voyage. Perhaps it will enable me the more easily to forget the unworthy sister of Don Manoel."

I had no sooner taken this resolution, which was in effect better than that of persisting in my search after a woman who shunned me, than I proceeded to Cadiz, where I had not to wait a week for an opportunity of embarking for Mexico. I found a merchantman which was on the point of sailing for Vera Cruz, and hastened to avail myself of this convenience.

CHAPTER II.

IN order to spare my reader a tedious journal of my passage
to the Indies, I shall content myself with stating that after having experienced some perils at sea, I arrived happily at San
Juan de Ulhua, otherwise called Vera Cruz. As it is customary to travel on mules from this city to Mexico, I begged the
master of the inn to recommend me a muleteer. He sent for
one, and presenting him to me, "Signior Gentleman," said he,
"here is, without contradiction, the best muleteer in this
country. He will supply you with very good mules, and will
take particular care of your property. He is, besides, a witty
and good-humored lad, who will amuse you with his songs, and
the recital of a thousand little tales with which his memory is
stuffed. Is not this the fact, Master Tobias ? " continued he,
turning to the muleteer.

"Yes, Signior Gutierrez," replied the muleteer, " I have,
thanks be to God, so great a quantity of those goods in my
bag, that the gentleman will be in no want of them between
this and Mexico, although we have eighty good leagues to travel.
It is now about two months ago," added he, " since I took
thither a fat friar of the Order of Mercy, and on the road I
related to him such a number of stories, that I thought he
would have burst with laughter."

I judged by this answer that Master Tobias was a babbler,
and I was not sorry for it. " He may," thought I, " sometimes
fatigue my ears with his songs and tales ; but in recompense,
he will sometimes divert me. I am even of opinion that he

will inform me on some matters which I am desirous of knowing. As for Toston, his joy was so much the greater, as he hoped that a man of his character might draw me out of the melancholy into which at times I fell in spite of myself, the image of Donna Paula in the power of Monchique incessantly arising in my mind.

On the morrow, as soon as it was day, Master Tobias, agreeably to our engagement, entered the courtyard of the inn with four good mules, of which there was one for me, one for himself, the third for my servant, and the last was destined to carry my trunk and a portmanteau, which contained all my effects. We set out on our journey, and were scarcely half a league on the road, ere Master Tobias gave employment to a strong voice which might have done honor to a chanter of the cathedral. He thundered forth a number of couplets composed in the time of Carlos V. upon the conquest of Mexico. I was too fond of my country's glory not to hear with pleasure the exploits of the valiant Cortez and his companions; but, besides that I had a thousand times heard the incredible recital of that conquest, the verses which Master Tobias was singing did not render it very agreeable to the ear; the poetry not being quite adequate to the dignity of the subject.

After having borne about twenty couplets of the same air, I interrupted the singer, who tired me, though, in fact, his verses were ridiculous enough to have amused me. For my sins it came into my head to say, " You sing marvellously well, Master Tobias; but enough of it for the present, my friend. Signior Gutierrez, my host, told me, as you know, that you have an infinitude of diverting histories : will you relate one ? "—" Most willingly," replied he, " and rather ten than one, to convince you that Gutierrez has told you the truth. I will even," continued he, with a malicious smile, " since he has made me welcome with the histories I am acquainted with, begin with his own, which will perhaps appear to you pleasant enough." He then made me his recital nearly in the following words :—

" The Signior Gutierrez, a native of Zamora, having made a journey to Portugal, married there the daughter of a citizen of Santarem, both young and pretty. About a month after his marriage, he embarked with her at Lisbon for Vera Cruz, with a design of settling there. Hoping to make a fortune in this town, he hired a house, the same which he now occupies, and

12

turned innkeeper. He soon perceived that he had done a very good thing in coming to Vera Cruz, for his house was always filled with guests drawn thither by the gentility of his wife. Nothing was spoken of in the town but the beautiful Portuguese (so she was called), and it might be said that she made as many conquests as there went young men to her house. Gutierrez, naturally jealous, could not without terror behold this concourse of gallants; and to withdraw his wife from the eyes of men, he shut her up in a room, where he had her food carried to her by an old black slave who possessed his confidence. You may easily imagine that a husband who treated his wife in this way, without having any reason to complain, and purely out of jealousy, could not fail to render himself odious to all who knew of his tyranny, that is to say, the whole town, for there was nobody ignorant of it. Every person, taking an interest in the fate of the beautiful Portuguese, put up prayers to Heaven that she might speedily be released from her tyrant; and this was speedily accomplished. The black, who alone was permitted to enter the apartment of this lady, hearing her every day groaning and lamenting, was touched with her distress; so that one fine night he released her from slavery, and disappeared with her from Vera Cruz, neither of them having been since seen or heard of."

The muleteer here stopped, to give way to his laughter at the expense of Gutierrez. As I was rather serious, Tobias thought that this story was not to my taste; and to put me into a gayer humor, he related a number of others, which, in his own opinion at least, were so extremely diverting, that I thought he would have burst with laughter, like the fat friar of the Order of Mercy whom he had conducted before us: as for me, I had little inclination to bear him company in his merriment, the story of a seduced wife having put me in a frame of mind little calculated for the enjoyment of buffoonery. Toston being well aware why I did not laugh, and remarking that I even wished Tobias and his tales at the devil, said to him, in order to change the discourse: "What you have been saying is extremely pleasant; but have you any objection that we should talk a little about Mexico? You, who are so well acquainted with that great town, must be able to inform us of some interesting particulars. What do you conceive is the most worthy of attention there?"—"Five things," replied Tobias; "the

women, the dresses, the horses, the streets, and the carriages of
the nobility, which surpass in magnificence and beauty those of
any other court in Europe, without exception. It is true that
to ornament them, they spare neither gold nor silver. They
even employ for that purpose precious stones, with the finest
silks of China. The horses have bridles enriched with fine
pearls: their bits are of silver; and one would suppose from
their proud movement, that they are sensible of their advantage
of being the most perfect animals of their species.

"Let us now come to the streets," continued he; "they are
of an uncommon width; a thing extremely necessary in a town
where fifteen thousand carriages are in motion every day. But
one must, at the same time, admire the good order of them, for
there is not a town in the world where they are kept cleaner;
and indeed it would be pity that it should be otherwise, on account of the shops, which present an air of opulence nowhere
else to be seen. Those, among others, in the Goldsmith's
Street, are filled with immense wealth, and most extraordinary
workmanship."

"I am most curious about the women, Master Tobias," interrupted Toston. "Your impatience is just," replied the
muleteer. "What I have to tell you about the women certainly
merits attention. The Spanish ladies of Mexico are generally
beautiful, and their beauty is considerably heightened by their
dress. They have such a prodigious quantity of jewels, that
they appear more brilliant than the stars. What luxury! what
magnificence! One ought to go and see them towards the
close of the day in the Alameda, which is the promenade for
the gentry and principal citizens. It is there you may judge of
the excessive expense they bestow on dress. But it is in vain
that they are naturally lovely, and richly attired; the most they
can do is to share the notice of the men with the Indian girls
of their suite, whom they have walking by the sides of their
carriages: these blacks are so pretty and delicate, that they are
often preferred to their mistresses."

"Fie! Master Tobias," cried my valet, distorting his features, "no joking. Can those tawny skins be looked upon with
any pleasure?"—"With any pleasure?" repeated the muleteer;
"ah! you talk like a man just come from Spain, and who has
never been in the habit of seeing brunettes! Go, go; when
you shall have considered them well, you will not think them so

disgusting. The gentlemen," added he, "and the officers of Chancery render them more justice. The Viceroy himself makes them extremely welcome; and his Excellency has so much pleasure in their conversation, that the wags say black has become his favorite color."

I could not help laughing at these words of Master Tobias; and, in order to engage him to tell me all he knew of the Count de Gelves, who was at that time Viceroy of New Spain, I asked him several questions about that grandee, to which he replied in a manner which made me sensible that the virtues and vices of men in power do not escape the notice of the public. "The Count de Gelves," said the muleteer, "is rather too fond of money, and of those black girls I was talking about. Though he has a hundred thousand ducats a year out of the king's treasury, and gets a million at least by the presents he receives from the country, and the commerce he carries on with the Philippine Islands, all this cannot satisfy his appetite for wealth. With the exception of this, he is a perfection of a Viceroy. He knows better than any of his predecessors how to make the laws and the king's authority respected; and he is so strict that he is called for distinction 'the Butcher of the Brigands.'

"In truth he well deserves this name," continued Tobias, "for the pains he has taken, and which he still takes every day, to clear the public roads of robbers; for, since he has been Viceroy, he has caused more murderers and malefactors to be executed than have been punished since the territories of the Great Montezuma changed their master. But we must conceal nothing. If the Government of Mexico do so much honor to the Count de Gelves, I believe, between ourselves, that he is a little indebted to Signior Don Juan de Salzedo, his principal secretary, who is a man of merit, and in whom he very justly confides for the management of some of the most laborious duties of the viceroyalty."

I interrupted Tobias, to ask him if Don Juan de Salzedo, of whom he spoke, had not been employed in the office of the Duke de Uzeda. "Yes, truly," replied he, "and he would be so still if the Duke de Uzeda had not been in exile since the death of our good King Philip III.; but immediately after the disgrace of that minister, Don Juan left the Court, to join at Mexico the Duke de Gelves, who was one of his old friends, and to whom he is rather a colleague than a secretary."

I was delighted to find by this news that I should in Mexico be in a land of acquaintance ; for Don Juan de Salzedo was that same secretary who had made choice of me to be the bearer of important despatches to Naples for the Duke de Ossuna, and who had the habit of quoting on all occasions passages from Latin authors. I told the muleteer that I knew Don Juan de Salzedo well, and that I could even boast of having been once among his friends. " Ah, Signior Gentleman !" exclaimed Toby, with great vivacity, " how happy are you in having a friend of so much importance. I know not what brings you to Mexico ; but with whatever view you may have come here, be assured of success, since you are acquainted with a man who disposes of all the employments which the Viceroy can bestow, and who, as one may say, is the mainspring of government."

When the muleteer Tobias had said thus much of the Count de Gelves and his secretary, he returned once more to the delights of Mexico. "When," said he, " you shall have seen this town and its environs, you will admit that if there be a country on earth which may be compared to a terrestrial Paradise, it is that. Andalusia and Lombardy, so praised by travellers, do not come near it." And on this Master Tobias gave us a description interesting enough, but so long that it was not concluded when we arrived at Xalapa, the first small town on our road, and in which there is an inn commonly well stocked with provisions.

CHAPTER III.

OF THE MEETING WHICH DON CHERUBIN HAD WITH A FRIAR OF
THE ORDER OF SAINT FRANCIS, ON ENTERING THE TOWN OF
XALAPA—CONSEQUENCE OF THIS MEETING—HE SUPS WITH
THE SUPERIOR OF THE MONASTERY—DESCRIPTION OF THE
MONKS WHOM HE MEETS WITH THERE—AFTER SUPPER HE
PLAYS, WINS, AND RETIRES AT MIDNIGHT FROM THE
MONASTERY.

As we alighted at the door of this inn, there .passed by us a
friar of the order of Saint Francis, whom my servant and myself viewed with as much attention as we thought he merited.
He was mounted on a good horse, and accompanied by two
Moorish slaves who walked at his stirrups. He wore a robe of
brown wool turned up and attached to his girdle by a silken
cord, exhibiting drawers of fine holland embroidered at the top,
silk stockings, and shoes of Spanish leather with red heels.
He had above his frock a hat of Canadian beaver, of which
the lining was of flesh-colored satin. So much grandeur in a
mendicant friar appeared to me a little out of order ; but having
learned that in this country it was customary to see such things,
I prepared myself for witnessing others of a surprising nature.

I was told that this Cordelier was the Superior of the convent at Xalapa, who probably was going to pay some visit at
the extremity of the town. I saluted him with a respectful air,
and he returned my salute with a great deal of civility. I had
no sooner lost sight than I thought no more of him ; and was
far from entertaining an idea that we should sup together that
evening, when, about three hours after, there came into the inn
a little friar who inquired for the muleteer Tobias. They spoke
together a moment in private ; after which coming to me,
" Signior," said the muleteer, introducing me to the friar, " here
is a little brother who comes to acquit himself of a commission

182

with which his Superior has charged him."—"Yes, Signior Cavalier," said the friar, "our most holy father Guardian entreats you will do him the honor to come and sup with his reverence." I answered the little brother politely, "that the proposition was too agreeable for me not to accept it with pleasure, and that he might assure his most reverend Superior that I would directly prepare myself for visiting his monastery," as in effect I did, leaving the muleteer and Toston at the inn.

I met at the gate of the convent the father Guardian, who was waiting to conduct me himself to his apartment. "Signior Cavalier," said he, saluting me with a dignified air, "pardon the liberty which one of your countrymen has taken in inviting you to supper; but it is my custom so to act with all the Spanish cavaliers who pass this way on the road to Mexico. It affords me an extreme pleasure to receive them, and to hear from them news of my country, for I am a native of Billao, the capital of Biscay, of which my accent will easily inform you. I am descended from the ancient Counts of Durango, who so signalized themselves in the wars of Fernando against the Moors, and in those of Carlos V. in the low countries."

I judged by this opening that the monk, in spite of the vows he had made, still preserved the Biscayan character. Accordingly, in order to flatter his vanity, I told him "that by his noble and majestic air, I was, from the first sight, inclined to believe that he must be a man of quality; that that struck the view at once; and finally, that I found myself highly honored by the invitation he had sent me."

Upon this the monk, who appeared to be a man of about forty and some odd years, introduced me into a large hall decorated with portraits which represented different saints of his order. From thence, having made me traverse a vast court filled with palms and orange-trees, he led me into a wing of the building separated from the rest, where he himself resided. To show me all the parts of his dwelling, he made me pass through several rooms hung with cotton tapestry, and full with cupboards furnished with vases of porcelain. This good father then opened a closet where he slept upon a simple woolen mantle, spread out upon a mat. "How then, my reverend father," cried I, "is it on that your reverence sleeps? I imagined you would have had a softer bed."—"You are very good," replied he with a smile. "Do you not find me much to be pitied?

Know that I enjoy upon that pallet, a slumber more profound than that of the inquisitors who sleep on down: admire the effect of habit. I have only," continued he, "my library to show you." At the same time he ushered me into a room quite unfurnished, and in which I perceived about twenty old worm-eaten books on the floor, thrown one upon another, ill bound, covered with dust and cobwebs, and on which there were a guitar, some pieces of music, and a great number of boxes of conserves. At this sight, which appeared to me to have in it something ridiculous, I had no small difficulty in keeping my countenance. I, however, suppressed my inclination to laugh; and I did well, for the reverend father was most perfectly satisfied of the importance of what he was displaying.

When it was time to sit down to table, we went into a saloon in which were three young monks who were to sup with us, and whom he introduced to me, with an eulogium on each of them. One, as he told me, had a fine voice, the other made good verses, and the third played on all manner of musical instruments. These were his courtiers, and his ordinary table companions when he received strangers. These young friars (what I should be wrong to forget) were dressed in the style of their Superior: they displayed under their large sleeves, doublets of white satin, and the wrists of their fine holland shirts were ornamented with lace. What is the most remarkable is, that after the fashion of their Guardian, they all laid claim to distinguished birth, whether they were really entitled to do so, or, being unknown to each other, all thought they might with impunity admit themselves into the order of nobility. To finish the description, they were intelligent men, and their manners rather military than monastic.

I was astonished at the number of dishes with which we were served; there were enough to satisfy a general chapter. All kinds of solid meat, of wild fowl and game, composed the first course; and the second did not less surprise me by the variety of fruits and confections, both dried and liquid, with which the table was covered. I remember among other things that, finding some conserves of an excellent flavor, I said to the Guardian, "These are admirable conserves. How fortunate are you, father, in having such clever confectioners in your convent!"—"These conserves," replied he, "were not made

in the house : they are the work of some good nuns, whose convent is in our neighborhood, and who give themselves the
trouble of making them for us."

During supper all these friars ceased not asking me questions
about the Court of Spain. One demanded, of what character
was the king, another, if the new minister, the Count Duke of
Olivarez, worthily replaced the Dukes of Lerma and Uzeda ;
and the Guardian in particular, assuming the man of importance, informed himself successively of all the grandees, with
whom he claimed relationship. He boasted of being cousin to
the Duke of Ossuna, nephew of the Dukes of Frias and Albu-
querque, allied to the Marquesses of Peguafiel and Avila Fuente.
In short, he summed up his genealogy, in which he modestly
included all the great names in the Spanish monarchy.

After the repast, some of the party proposed to play at
Primero, and this proposal was generally agreed to. Cards
were brought ; and the first who took them up to deal acquitted
himself with a good grace, and in a manner which showed that
he was well accustomed to handling them. Here then we were,
fairly engaged at play. Fortune at first seemed inclined to
favor no one in particular. Sometimes she flattered my companions ; but at last declared herself against two of the friars,
who, losing their coolness with their money, apostrophized this
divinity in a manner not the most guarded for persons of a
religious character, and rather adapted for a tennis-court than
a monastery.

The building occupied by the Reverend Father Guardian re-
echoed with their exclamations, when I heard it strike midnight.
Then addressing myself to the Superior, I begged him to permit me to retire, representing to him that I had a great journey
to perform, and that I must be on the road again before the
dawn of Aurora. He was polite enough not to endeavor to detain me longer. I took leave of his noble reverence, after having thanked him for his gracious reception, and returned to my
inn, to the great regret of the two friars, who would willingly
have kept me all night, in the hope of regaining some of the
pistoles which I had managed to carry off in spite of their
ingenuity.

CHAPTER IV.

OF DON CHERUBIN'S ARRIVAL AT MEXICO, AND IN WHAT PLACE HE
WENT TO LODGE—HE IS CHARMED WITH HIS HOST'S WIFE, NOT-
WITHSTANDING HER BLACKNESS.

As soon as I returned to my inn I went to bed to get some
repose; but scarcely had sleep taken possession of my senses,
ere the hoarse voice of Master Tobias awaked me. I instantly
rose; and as I finished dressing myself, my chocolate was
brought me; after which I mounted my mule, and proceeded
on my journey.

The muleteer, an enemy to silence, soon put an end to it.
He sang that day ballads made on the wars of Grenada. He
then related to us some little tales, the same perhaps which had
made the fat friar of the Order of Mercy laugh so much; but
they had not quite so good an effect upon us. On the contrary,
they annoyed us so much that we thought the road longer than
it really was. I shall, therefore, spare the reader the trouble of
perusing them, as well as those which he forced upon us on the
following days. Let us hasten to get to Mexico.

On entering this celebrated town, I asked Tobias to what
point he intended conducting us. "The quarter of the nobility," replied he; "to an inn where gentlemen who come from
Spain generally put up, kept by a Spaniard, native of Carmona
near Seville, and who is called Master Jerom Juan Morales.
Finding himself without property in his own country, he left it
to come to Mexico, where he keeps an inn with a young Indian
girl whom he has married, and who brings showers of gold into
his house."—"Beware the Moor," cried Toston, beginning to
laugh. "Oh! there is no Moor to fear," replied the muleteer;
"Morales, far from resembling your host at Vera Cruz, is by no
means jealous, though he has one of the most enticing of
Indians for his wife. You will acknowledge when you see her,

that there are tawny faces which may be looked on without horror."

"On this footing," said I to the muleteer, "his tavern ought not to be ill attended."—"Nor is it so," replied Tobias. "There are a number of honest folks who go there every day, less to drink than to see the hostess. She receives them with so affable an air that they are enchanted, and the conversations that she has with them, seldom fail to be followed by presents; a thing which is particularly agreeable to Morales, who is delighted at possessing a pretty woman, and seeing people caress her."

This discourse struck me, and made me wish myself at the inn, that I might have the evidence of my own eyes, not being able to conceive that an Indian woman was capable of fascinating Europeans. Master Tobias, seconding the impatience I evinced for arriving at the house of Morales, redoubled our pace. He took us into Eagle Street, in which reside none but gentlemen and the officers of the Chancery. We alighted at the door of a house which had for a sign a serpent, with these words: *Al Basilico, buena cama.** "Zooks!" said I to myself, "this sign appears to me droll enough; it seems as if it had been put up to apprise strangers that there is danger in going to lodge at this inn." But I thought the danger too agreeable to be intimidated at it: notwithstanding all Tobias had said, instead of fearing the Basilisk, I exposed myself without hesitation to her looks.

I sustained them at first with impunity: nay, more! her tawny skin displeased me. Nevertheless I soon became accustomed to it. What do I say? She insensibly fascinated my eyes by her dignified and thoroughly graceful manners; so that after a quarter of an hour's conversation, I found that hearts are not less in danger with such Indians, than with the most formidable beauties of Madrid. She resembled a little la Gitanilla, of whom I spoke in the first volume of these memoirs; I say a little, for the Indian was still more piquant.

It is true that when I saw her she was dressed out in a fashion which added considerably to her charms. She had a petticoat of Chinese linen thickly covered with silver, with a flame-colored ribbon, the ends of which, ornamented with gold

---

* To the Basilisk, good lodging.

fringe, came down very low both behind and before. She had above this a jacket of the same stuff with large sleeves, embroidered with red silk intermixed with silver, and fastened with gold cords. To this was added a girdle of blue silk enriched with jewels, a collar and bracelets of pearls, with earrings of fine brilliants.

It is certain that it was difficult to see her thus without emotion, or rather without being enamoured of her. I thought I should have suffered myself to be caught. At least, for the first day I was entirely taken up with her charms, which persisted throughout the night in presenting, themselves to my mind, but my reason, more obstinate than her image, prevented me from yielding to my tender emotions. " Well, friend," said I to Toston the next day, "what do you think of our hostess? Has she a little reconciled you to the Indians? "—" Perfectly," replied he; "Tobias was right in saying that I should change my mind. Last night I fatigued the muscles of my eyes by stretching them in contemplating the wife of Morales. What a sprightly girl! I could not be satisfied with looking at her, and she has, it may be said, changed my taste from white to black."

CHAPTER V.

I FELT so great a desire to see the town, and, in particular,
the palace of the Viceroy, that to have this satisfaction I went
out in the morning with my valet. Morales would absolutely
accompany me, to answer, as he said, the questions I might be
disposed to ask out of curiosity; and I did not refuse to be conducted by so good a guide. He made me cross the market,
the most considerable place in Mexico : one side of this is built
in arcades, beneath which are seen shops filled with all kinds of
merchandise.

As I was looking about on all sides, I perceived a large
house, and asked to whom it belonged. "It is the palace of
the Viceroy," replied my host; "you see it such as Cortez
caused to be built on the ruins of Montezuma's."—"Is it
possible," cried I, with astonishment, "that this should be the
palace, the magnificence of which I have heard so frequently
extolled? There are houses full as good in all the principal
towns in Spain. I expected to have seen a more sumptuous
building."—"You are mistaken," replied Morales; "it is not
this palace of which travellers give so splendid a description,
but that which was reduced to ashes; it is affirmed that it might
pass for the eighth wonder of the world."

"What exaggeration!" again exclaimed I. "I have no objection to believe that the walls were, as these gentlemen say,
composed of masonry intermixed with jasper, and of a certain
other black stone, mottled with red streaks as brilliant as
rubies. I also believe that the roof might be inlaid with cedar

189

and cypress ; but I cannot put faith in the extraordinary things which they relate of Montezuma, apparently to amuse their readers. They say, for instance, that there were in his Seraglio more than two thousand women, of whom there were always two hundred pregnant at the same time."—" Mercy upon us ! " cried Toston, bursting with laughter ; " he had then more than King Solomon."—" There is nothing in that which ought to astonish you," said Morales, " since Montezuma might have three thousand of them, having the privilege of carrying off the daughters of the principal Indians as often as he pleased."

Thus conversing, we approached the palace. There were at the gate some soldiers, who suffered every one to pass freely. We entered a spacious square court, to cross over to a large staircase which led to the Viceroy's apartments. We followed several cavaliers, who came to that nobleman's levee. We crossed with them three or four richly furnished apartments, and arrived at last at that in which the Count was being dressed by his *valets-de-chambre.* We all three placed ourselves in a corner, from which we could see with ease everything which was going forward.

I set myself at first to consider the principal person. He appeared to me about fifty years of age, and possessed the Spanish gravity in a remarkable degree. He had lank hair, black and very thick eyebrows, and a terrible and ferocious air. Nevertheless, I remarked one thing singular enough. While he conversed with some of the gentlemen who came to pay their court to him, he smiled occasionally ; and as often as that occurred, he became all at once so different from himself that he appeared as if he had two faces. In short, while he was serious he inspired fear, and when he smiled he appeared perfectly agreeable.

The conversation which he was holding with these gentlemen was interrupted by the arrival of his secretary, in whom I recognized my old friend Don Juan de Salzedo. He held in his hand a large bundle of papers ; an old piece of policy in the ministers of Spain, who, in order to appear overloaded with business, always showed themselves standing on end with waste-paper. The Viceroy had no sooner seen, than he came up to him. They both retired to the window, and conversed together nearly a quarter of an hour in private. During this time, I made an observation which agreed very well with what Master

Tobias had told me, and which marked very plainly the ascendency that Salzedo had over the mind of the Count: I know not what was the subject of conversation between them, but it appeared to me that his Excellency listened to his secretary with great complaisance, and approved of all he said.

I was determined not to leave the palace without saluting Don Juan. With this design I placed myself in waiting for him in an antechamber, very curious to see what reception he would give me. I doubted his behaving very kindly to a man who would not at Madrid profit by his kindness: nay, I even doubted that he would deign to recognize me. Nevertheless, he had no sooner fixed his eyes on me, than making his way through the crowd, he approached, and addressing me with a smiling air, "I believe," said he, "I do not deceive myself; you are Don Cherubin de la Ronda." I answered that I was delighted to find he still recollected me. "I have not banished you from my memory," replied he, "*tantum abest!* On your part you ought not to forget that I esteemed you in Spain. I remember that time with pleasure, and I feel at the sight of you all my former friendship revive."

Touched, penetrated with the friendship which he evinced for me, I would have broken out in grateful acknowledgments; but he cut me short, and drawing me aside, "Don Cherubin," continued he with a low voice, "let us have no compliments; you know well that I am a man of sincerity, though I have been all my life at court. Speak to me with confidence. What brings you to Mexico? I think I can guess: *auri sacra fames*, is it not? Avow it boldly. I am in a state to aid you." I again opened my mouth to thank the Secretary for his generosity, and he a second time closed it by saying: "I cannot stop with you any longer. I have some pressing affairs which will detain me the rest of the morning. Come and see me by and by, we will then converse at leisure. *Vale.*"

Pronouncing this word of Latin, which he accompanied with a close embrace, he quitted me to resume his labors, leaving me transported with joy at the reception he had just given me. All who had been witnesses of it, looking upon Salzedo as a second Viceroy, envied my happiness, and judged that I must be a Spaniard of distinction, since Signior Don Juan had done me the honor to embrace me. My host complimented me on the subject, and conceived a very high respect for me.

As to Toston, he was in inexpressible rapture. " Sir," said he, as we returned to the inn, " are you not now pleased with having come to the Indies? What may you not expect from the friendship of Don Juan? You may flatter yourself by his credit——"--" Hey! what hopes," interrupted I, " my friend, would you have me conceive? You know that I am rich enough to be contented with what I have."—" No, no," replied he, " abundance does no harm. Besides, consider that you have a daughter; you cannot amass too much wealth, if it be but for the sake of leaving her a rich heiress."

CHAPTER VI.

OF THE VISIT WHICH DON CHERUBIN MADE IN THE AFTERNOON
TO DON JUAN DE SALZEDO, AND OF THE SECOND CONVERSA-
TION HE HAD WITH HIM—THE RESULT OF IT—DON CHERU-
BIN DE LA RONDA IS RECEIVED AS GOVERNOR OF DON
ALEXIS, SON OF THE VICEROY—TOSTON'S JOY AT LEARNING THIS
AGREEABLE NEWS.

I DID not fail to return to the palace of the Viceroy in the
afternoon. I was shown the part in which Don Juan de Salzedo
was lodged, and went to present myself at the door. I there
found a *valet-de-chambre*, to whom I had no sooner told my
name, than he said to me, with a respectful air, " Signior, my
master is waiting for you in his closet, whither I will conduct
you." At the same time, he made me cross five or six rooms
at least, each one more sumptuous than another ; for the Secretary's lodging was as richly furnished as the Viceroy's, and
perhaps even more so. There were an infinite number of paintings by the best masters in Italy, with some of the finest works
of Mechoacan feathers and of rabbits' skins.

At last my guide opened the door of a closet, in which was
Don Juan, alone, and sitting on a sofa of Chinese silk. As
soon as he saw me he rose to embrace me, saying : " My dear
Don Cherubin, I was waiting for you with impatience, to
know what had been the means of bringing you into this country,
and to assure you again that if you be badly off in your affairs,
you shall not be so long. In a word, I take upon myself to
make your lot happy in Mexico."—" I am," I replied, " as sensible as I ought to be of your kindness ; but it would be only
abusing it if I were to tell you that the desire of enriching myself had brought me to Mexico. No, sir ! though I have but a
moderate fortune, I am satisfied with it ; and the desire of
seeing New Spain has alone induced me to undertake this
journey."

13   193

" Your sentiments are rather too philosophical," replied Don Juan. "To have but that which is precisely necessary to enable us to live, is not to be exactly at one's ease, and being confined to a certain expenditure is sad for a man of the world, however little he may be inclined to generosity. Attend to my advice; preserve what you have, and do not refuse the new favors which fortune is preparing to shower upon you through my ministry. An idea has come into my head," added he, "which may be useful to you. I will place you——"—"Do not propose to me," interrupted I, abruptly enough, "a place in any of your offices." My vivacity made Salzedo laugh. "No, no," replied he, "I know that you do not like a secretary's post. I design you another, which will suit you better; that of governor to the young Don Alexis, the only son of the Viceroy. Leave me to manage it for you. I will this day speak to his Excellency, and I dare answer for the success of my application."

As I had accustomed myself to a life of independence, and saw myself about to pass from that into the miserable occupation of a child's governor, I was not dazzled with Salzedo's project. I was even going to tell him candidly my sentiments on the subject; but what he added kept me silent, and appeared deserving of attention. "Do not imagine," said he, "that I have made you a bad offer. I know as well as yourself that at Madrid, and in the other towns of Spain, the office of governor is no very pleasing one, and that those gentlemen who fill it get barely enough to support themselves, particularly when they have the folly to dress themselves splendidly. God forbid that I should be tempted to procure you a similar establishment here! That would be rendering you no great service. But deign to hear me out. I design, in placing you over the conduct of Don Alexis, to establish you on another footing at the Viceroy's. I will have them look upon you as a Mentor, and treat you with distinction. In a word, you will there be considered, beloved, respected; and you will have a considerable salary, without counting the profits which you will obtain every year through my means."

The Secretary Salzedo said so much to me about it, that he prevailed on me. "I can no longer," said I, "hold out against such flattering promises; and what I am pleased with beyond all the rest is to see you take so great an interest in my fortune.

The only question is now whether I shall have the good luck to please his Excellency."—"That is a point on which I am under no apprehension," interrupted Don Juan. "The description that I shall give him of you will not fail to prepossess him in your favor, and your appearance will spoil nothing. Return," added he, "return hither to-morrow, and I will present you to his Excellency after his dinner."

Such was the second conversation I had with my friend Salzedo, who said to me the following day as soon as I approached him: "Your business is done; you are governor of Don Alexis. The Count de Gelves assigns you apartments in the palace, with twelve hundred pistoles a year for your salary. Besides this, when you desire to go out to pay a visit, or for exercise, there will be always two lackeys and a carriage at your disposal."

"Truly, Signior Don Juan," cried I, "I am confounded by the marks of friendship which you are giving me."—"Oh! that is not all," replied he; "I should not be satisfied with myself if I confined my desire of obliging you to that. I calculate on adding every year to your salary two thousand crowns at least, which will result from the commerce carried on by his Excellency and myself, both with Spain and the Philippine Islands, and in which I will give you a share."—"Ah! this is too much," said I. "What have I done to merit so many favors, and how can I repay them?"—"By esteeming me as much as I esteem you," replied he; "that is all I exact from your gratitude. But," added he, changing the discourse, "let us go and see my lord. He is in his closet, where he must by this time have finished his siesta. Let us seize the opportunity."

He conducted me directly as far as the door, and desired me to wait there a moment. He then went alone into the closet, where he remained nearly a quarter of an hour; then returning to me, he took me by the hand, and introduced me. The Viceroy ran me over with his eye from head to foot, and the *coup d'œil* was favorable. "I think," said his Excellency, with an air of condescension, "that Salzedo has not gone beyond the truth with me: you have a countenance which confirms the eulogism he has passed upon you. I confide Don Alexis to your care, confident that he cannot be in better hands. In regard to your interests, Don Juan has of course made known to you my intentions, and on what footing I design you to be in my establishment." I replied, "that I would make it my whole study to render myself worthy of the employment with which he was disposed to honor me."

I retired upon this with my Mecænas, who carried me to Don Alexis, whom we found in his apartment composing a theme under the eyes of his tutor, an old Gallician priest, who had, as they say, burned the broom. "My young lord," said Salzedo to Don Alexis, "here is the governor whom his Excellency has chosen to introduce you into the world, and form your mind to virtue. I can assure you that you will be satisfied with him, and I hope he will likewise be so with you." Don Alexis only replied by staring at me with open eyes. I addressed him in order to induce him to speak, and to enable me to judge of his mind, which appeared absorbed in the matter in which he was engaged. While I conversed with him, his preceptor, who was a man bristling with Latin, quoted passages from Virgil and Horace; and Don Juan, who desired nothing better than to do the same thing, overwhelmed us in his turn with Latin sentences. After they had thus amused themselves to their heart's content, Salzedo said: "Signior Don Cherubin, return to your inn, and prepare yourself for coming hither to-morrow to take possession of your new post. You will find here a lodging befitting the place which you are to hold."

I immediately made my bow to the company, and returned to the Basilisk, where I found my valet waiting with the utmost impatience to learn the success of my visit. "Toston," said I, "we must go and reside at the Viceroy's palace. I am governor to Don Alexis." I had no sooner pronounced these words, than, abandoning himself to an immoderate joy, he began to jump about like a madman. When he had tired himself, he stopped to take breath. "Here we are then," said he, "thank God, in train, you of enlarging your fortune, and I of commencing mine; for I calculate that one will not go without the other."—"You are right, friend," replied I; "if I acquire riches in this country, I assure you that I will give you a share of them." This promise revived in Toston the humor of jumping.

While he was cutting fresh capers, Morales, who came in, demanded why he was so exceedingly rejoiced. I told him the cause, and gave him a circumstantial detail of the advantages

THE BACHELOR OF SALAMANCA.

attached to my employment. My host was dazzled by this; and, already looking on me as a great and powerful lord, begged me to grant him my protection. The most amusing part of the business was, that I accorded it to him with a serious air, making him sincere protestations of serving him whenever I should find the opportunity. On the following day, after having charged Toston with the care of having my effects conveyed to my new dwelling, I bid adieu to my beautiful hostess, who appeared to me rather mortified at our separation, though she had no great reason to be so, as she only lost in me a man who refused to sacrifice to her charms.

CHAPTER VII.

I RETURNED to the palace, where I went in the first place to
see Salzedo, who, to install me in my new post, took me himself to my lodging, which consisted of three small rooms on the
same floor, well furnished, with a wardrobe where there was a
bed for my valet. " You will not be badly lodged, as you perceive," said Don Juan; " and you can dine in private with
Doctor Gaspard de Aldagna, preceptor of Don Alexis, if that
be more agreeable to you than to be served alone in your apartment. This doctor is a very honest ecclesiastic, of a very good
disposition, who does not want for wit, and who talks Latin
admirably." I replied, " that I should be happy to dine and
sup with such a colleague," and the arrangement was made
accordingly.

The first step which I considered I ought to take in the discharge of my duty, was that of paying my respects to the Vice-
Queen. Salzedo conducted me to her. I expected a reception full of haughtiness, imagining that the Countess was a
proud woman, and intoxicated with her grandeur. Not at all:
the good lady, on the contrary, received me graciously, and the
more particularly so as Don Juan had previously made her a
magnificent eulogium on my merit. She asked me several
questions, in order to judge by my replies if my understanding
had not been too highly represented to her; but happily for
me, she was so well satisfied with our conversation, that she
said to Salzedo in my presence: " I owe you thanks, Don Juan,
for having made such a choice. This gentleman appears to
me qualified for bringing up a young nobleman. Such is the

person required for forming the manners of my son, who, I confess, has but little disposition for becoming a perfect cavalier."—" That will come in time, madam," said Don Juan; " Don Alexis has a slow genius, which will develop itself by degrees with the aid of a good governor."

After having had this conversation with the Vice-Queen, I went to see my pupil, with whom I had one which afflicted me. I found I had to do with a scholar who was preparing me abundance of employment, with a most heavy subject, with an automaton. I expressed my chagrin on this subject to Doctor Gaspard, who, I thought, ought not to have had less than myself; however, he appeared to have made up his mind upon it. " I agree with you," replied he, " that it is disagreeable both for you and for me to have an imbecile scholar; for Don Alexis is in reality such. He is already in his fifteenth year, and he is not capable of making the most simple version, though for eighteen months that I have been his master, I have toiled myself to death to teach him the Latin language. Sometimes, tired of sowing upon sand, I have lost patience, and begged my dismissal from the Count; but he would never grant it to me. ' Signior Doctor,' he always said, ' pray do not abandon my son. I know very well it is not your fault, if hitherto he has not profited by your lessons. No matter! continue. By hearing the same things often repeated, he may retain some, and that will be enough for him, for I do not pretend to make him a man of learning.' To obey his Excellency, therefore," pursued the doctor, " I remain, and still go on in my old way. I give my little lord exercises and versions, which he gets through as it pleases God.

" In the meantime I live well in the palace. My salary, which is tolerably good, is regularly paid, and I shall perhaps in the end get hold of some good benefice; for when in the service of the great, one is not always ill recompensed. Imitate me, therefore, Don Cherubin. Hey! Why take things so much to heart? Conduct young Alexis into the world; reprove him when he is guilty of any reprehensible action, or says any foolish thing, and laugh at the rest. If our pupil be naturally a stupid animal, we cannot help it. Look at his other masters; are they more forward than ourselves? No, truly. One cannot teach him music, nor the other the principles of dancing, though they have been fifteen months instructing him. Do you think that grieves them? Not at all. They give the fool their lessons at all hazards, and make a milch-cow of him."

It was thus that the Gallician exhorted me to console myself for the stupidity of Don Alexis, and I conceived that he was in the right. I began, therefore, to discharge my duty as best I could. I set myself before all things to gain the friendship of my little man by mild and insinuating behavior, and in a few days succeeded in my endeavor. It is true that I only conversed with him in a manner more calculated to divert than instruct him, for fear of disgusting him by dogmatizing.

CHAPTER VIII.

HE GOES OUT WITH HIS PUPIL TO THE FIELD CALLED THE ALA-
MEDA, WHICH IS THE PRINCIPAL PROMENADE AT MEXICO—OF
THE OBSERVATIONS HE MADE THERE, AND THE EXTREME AS-
TONISHMENT THEY CAUSED HIM—TRAGICAL EVENT OF WHICH
HE IS WITNESS.

I PASSED three days in getting myself properly settled, with-
out going out of the palace; but on the fourth, towards five
o'clock in the evening, I got into a magnificent carriage with
Don Alexis, and we drove towards the field of the Alameda, as
I felt a great pleasure in seeing it, after the description that
Master Tobias, the muleteer, had given me of it.

This field is of vast extent. It contains a great number of
alleys bordered with trees, where one may walk without being
incommoded by the heat of the sun. The Zocodover of Toledo,
and even the Prado of Madrid, do not come near this promenade, which presents an enchanting spectacle to the eye. One
may see there as many as two thousand carriages, filled with
gentlemen, citizens and people of all conditions. The gentry,
those principally who are said to be descendants of the captains
of Cortez, have for the most part superb equipages, and are
followed by Moorish slaves in rich liveries, with silk stockings,
and wearing roses of precious stones on their shoes. Besides
this, these slaves are all armed; so that their proud masters
may boast of having guards like kings.

The ladies do not ride with less pomp than the gentlemen.
By the sides of their carriages they arrange their suites, which
are composed of those genteel black girls whom I formerly
mentioned, and who are so adorned that they frequently rob
their mistresses of the glances of the men. These, notwithstanding, omit nothing to render themselves charming. All
that can be done by art is exerted in their dress, and precious

stones are employed in it in the most coquettish taste of America.

On whatever side I turned my eyes, I saw nothing but gold and diamonds; which produced an effect so advantageous for the women, that they all appeared to me, one more handsome than another. "Where am I then?" said I to myself. "At seeing so many ravishing objects, little is wanting to believe one's self in Mahomet's paradise."

I was, in fact, dazzled by the brilliant beauty which offered itself to my view on all sides; but no one of these ladies made more impression on me than another: for the moment that I remarked one who struck me, there passed another who attracted my attention to herself; so that I beheld with impunity a number of faces, which I should have found very formidable had I seen them singly.

The pleasure which I felt in looking to the right and left was disturbed by an event which is but too common in this promenade, where jealous lovers, who cannot endure that their rivals should speak to their mistresses, nor even approach them too closely, often dart upon them sword or poniard in hand. I saw at two or three hundred yards from me, at the side of a carriage, two cavaliers who were fighting with so much fury that one of them speedily fell to the ground. In a moment twenty swords were drawn, some to avenge the vanquished, and others to defend the victor. The friends of the latter were the strongest; they delivered him from the hands of his enemies, and carried him to the nearest church, where he remained in safety, the immunity of churches being inviolable in this country. Whatever crime a man may have committed, if he be fortunate enough to save himself in one of these sacred asylums, he escapes the rigor of the laws, without even the Viceroy himself having the power to force him from it, to deliver him up to justice.

After having been witness of this melancholy adventure, I continued to ride about and view the ladies, until the night concealed them from my view. I then returned with my pupil to the palace, my mind much occupied with what I had seen, and unable sufficiently to admire the magnificence of the inhabitants of Mexico. When I drew a parallel between them and those of Madrid, the latter did not gain by the comparison.

CHAPTER IX.

HOW THE GENIUS OF DON ALEXIS WAS BRIGHTENED—THE CON-
VERSATION WHICH DON CHERUBIN HAD WITH HIS VALET
—WHAT HE LEARNS FROM HIS VALET ASTONISHES HIM—PRU-
DENT ADVICE WHICH HE GIVES TO TOSTON—THE LATTER IS
INCLINED TO PROFIT BY IT.

IF I had a scholar who was stupid, in recompense he was
gentle and obedient. If he did not well that which I wished
him, he at least tried to do it : his goodwill supplied by degrees
the talents of which he was deficient. At the end of nine or
ten months (what perfectly astonished myself) he appeared
quite another thing in the eyes of the Count his father, who
complimented me upon his improvement, as did also the Countess. *Macte animo,*" said my friend the Secretary to me one
morning; " they are well satisfied with you. *Perge,* and be
not in pain for the rest : that is my business."

Flattered with so fortunate a commencement, I attended
more closely than I had hitherto done to my pupil ; and each
of his other masters seconding my endeavors, we made of him,
in less than two years, a cavalier as good as most others. He
knew how to present himself with a good grace, and to sustain
a conversation in the style of the best company at Mexico. It
was an absolute metamorphosis, and did me peculiar honor, as
also Doctor Gaspard, who by dint of repeating the same things
over and over to Don Alexis, had at last succeeded in putting
a little Latin into his head.

We were all proud of the happy result of our labors. Nevertheless, whatever cause we might have to applaud ourselves
for having polished our scholar, I know not whether Toston
had not a greater share in the work than we. He at least contributed to it as much : a fact which he revealed to me one day,
when I was boasting in his presence of having made my pupil

a smart youth. " Sir," said he, with an arch smile, "you undoubtedly deserve praise, and I should be very much in the wrong were I to refuse it to you; but permit me, if you please, to say that you and Doctor Gaspard ought not to take all the merit to yourselves since I have labored at the same work; or rather, know that it is I who have brightened this young lord: or indeed, if you will, it is a miracle of love."

" Speak to me," said I, " more clearly ; explain the whole."— " That," said he, " is what I am about to do in a few words. There is, among the attendants of the Vice-Queen, a Creole of about seventeen, who is possessed of wit and beauty. This little person is the author of the change of which you attribute to yourselves the glory."

" What sayest thou, Toston ? " cried I ; " thou announcest to me a piece of information which astonishes me exceedingly. How did Don Alexis become enamoured of this Creole ? Has he made known to her his sentiments ? How, in short, does he stand with her ? "—" At the tail of the ballad," replied my valet. " I cannot get over my surprise," replied I hastily ; " recount to me, I pray thee, the means by which this intrigue has been carried on."—" I will faithfully detail it," replied he ; " do me the honor to attend.

" You know that I pay assiduous court to Don Alexis, and that we live together very familiarly. I am not less his *valet-de-chambre* than yours, and possess his confidence. Blandina, the most lovely of the attendants of the Vice-Queen, had charmed him. He made me the confidant of his love, and prayed me to exert myself to procure him private interviews with this nymph ; which I effect at night so happily, that no one has the least suspicion of it. This is what I had to inform you. Judge now whether these nocturnal interviews, or your lessons, have brightened up the wits of our young lord."

Thus spoke the officious and secret agent of Don Alexis ; after which I said, shaking my head : " Master Toston, if thou thinkest to have my applause for having thus contributed to the change in my pupil, thou art in error. God forbid that I should approve the culpable method thou hast used to rid him of his imbecility ! Better he had still continued in it. Besides, art thou well assured that thou will not repent of having been so obliging ? Thou knowest the severity of the Viceroy. He will not perhaps feel much indebted to thee for such services rendered to his son, if, unfortunately for thee, they should come to his knowledge; nor may the Countess think it altogether right that thou shouldest corrupt her maids. In short, my friend, thou art playing a game which may get thyself shut up in a dungeon; and me turned out of doors, to teach me to choose valets of a less vicious character. See to what thou exposest us both.

Toston allowed me to talk as long as I liked without interrupting me; but instead of being moved at what I said to him, he turned a deaf ear to my discourse; and when I had concluded, answered me, smiling, in the following terms: "Nothing is more reasonable than what you have been representing to me. You are a wise and prudent man. But you know not all. The Countess is not ignorant of what is going forward. I will tell you,—it is by her orders that I conduct this intrigue."

"What do I hear?" cried I. "Dost thou not deceive me? May I place faith in thy report?"—"Doubt it not, sir," said he; "it is a certain fact. If a lie sometimes escape me, at least it is not with you. The Vice-Queen," he continued, "having one day sent for me, said to me in private: 'My friend, I would employ thy ministry; but be discreet. Don Alexis has no longer the air of stupidity which he formerly had. His mind is brightening every day. There wants nothing to finish him but a little female conversation. An idea has come into my head. Do thou enable him to make a secret acquaintance with Blandina, who is the prettiest and most lively of my attendants. She will not fail to inspire him with love, and that love will produce good effects: it will perfect the cavalier, and prevent him from attaching himself, like his father, to the blacks; a detestable taste, from which I would preserve my son, and for which I cannot pardon Spaniards. For the rest,' added the Countess, assuming an air of reserve, 'if I charge thee with this commission, which perhaps appears a little delicate, it is because I am persuaded that Blandina runs no risk: she has prudence, and my son is too timid to alarm her virtue.'

"I would not tell the Countess," continued Toston, "that I had been beforehand with her, and that the parties already, through my interference, lived in the softest union. To give her the honor of it, I promised to execute her project, as if it had not been already done. This is what you were ignorant of," continued he: " now you need no longer tremble either for yourself or me."—" That does not set me at ease," said I; " if the Viceroy come to know that thou contrivest *tête-à-têtes* between his son and Blandina, a melancholy salary may probably be the reward of thy services; and the Vice-Queen, although thy accomplice, will leave thee in the net instead of drawing thee out of it. Make thou thy own reflections on the matter."

The advice appeared of importance to my gentleman intriguer, who, in order to profit by it, resolved to take his measures so well, that he might continue with impunity to serve the passion of Don Alexis; which, in effect, he did with so much good fortune and address, that during two entire years no person in the palace had any knowledge of it.

CHAPTER X.

DON CHERUBIN DE LA RONDA ROLLS IN GOLD AND SILVER—HE
EXPENDS A GREAT PORTION IN PARTIES OF PLEASURE WITH
LADIES OF HIS ACQUAINTANCE—HE GOES TO SEE A PLAY—
WHAT KIND OF PIECE THIS WAS, AND THE IMPRESSION IT
MADE UPON HIM.

ON the other hand, the Count de Gelves, delighted with the
polished exterior of his son, and imagining that it was my
work, did not know how to repay me. He did not content
himself, avaricious as he was, with having my salary exactly
paid, but loaded me with presents. Add to this, that Salzedo
was very punctual in keeping the promises he had made to me ;
so that I began to roll in gold. Had I had ever so little disposition to avarice, I should unquestionably have become a
miser in so lucrative a post : but this was not my vice ; and far
from hoarding up, I spent my money as I gained it.

I often made parties of pleasure, and gave entertainments to
ladies with whom I was acquainted. I used to go to their
houses to pass the afternoon in play ; which is carried on so
freely in Mexico, that it is the principal occupation of the
women. I sometimes took them to the theatre, the actors of
which were supported by the Viceroy, or, more properly speaking, by the public; for his Excellency allowed them such a
trifling pension that they could not subsist on it. Their company, which was composed of Mexicans, was tolerably good.
There were among them five or six excellent actors, a sufficient
eulogium of a comic troop, which commonly has not three who
deserve to be applauded.

One day, when these actors represented for the third time a
new play which had been very well received, I went to see it
with Don Juan and two ladies of his acquaintance. It was the
production of a celebrated author. It was much praised about

town, and was entitled La Nobia Sonsacada.* I suffered myself to be carried thither out of complaisance, or rather in spite
of myself, not feeling much curiosity to see a piece which
promised me more pain than pleasure. The connection which
the title had with my own adventure frightened me, and I
doubted not that there was something in the comedy of a nature
to cause a laugh at my expense.

Nevertheless, though struck with so reasonable a fear, I
mixed among the spectators, resolved, since my story was not
known, to put the best face on the matter, and even applaud
the first strokes of raillery which I should hear uttered against
unlucky husbands; but I was not under the necessity of going
so far as that, since, though it was a comedy, there was not a
single word throughout calculated to excite laughter. The
author was not one of those who take Plautus and Terence for
their models ; but, on the contrary, sworn enemy to mirth and
pleasantry, he admitted only sighs and tears in his pieces, which
he farcified with sentences and tirades of morality in rhyme, to
the infinite amusement of the gentleman Americans.

But if my ears were not struck with any raillery which I could
apply to myself, I was not therefore let off at a cheaper rate.
As the business of this piece consisted in carrying off a wife,
the rape of Donna Paula, which I was beginning to forget, came
in full force to my recollection, and caused me inconceivable
pain.   In vain I constrained myself, and exerted every effort
to overcome the secret emotions which agitated me; it was impossible to conceal them from Salzedo, who, remarking the
alteration of my countenance, said to me, with a smile: "Oh,
oh! it seems to me that this piece interests you."—"It is impossible to do so more," replied I, reddening. "The author
possesses perfectly the art of touching the passions. But it
must be admitted that these are admirable actors. I am principally pleased with him who plays the husband. He represents
so naturally a tender spouse from whom a wife has been carried
off, that I find his grief communicate to myself. I put myself
in his place. I imagine that I have lost a beloved wife. I
feel as much as he."

My answer excited the laughter of the Secretary and the two
ladies who were with us. They rallied me on the excess of my

* The seduced bride.

sensibility. I suffered them to make themselves merry at my expense; choosing much rather to sustain their pleasantries, than to make them acquainted with what I was extremely happy they should remain in ignorance of. Having recovered from the disorder into which my spirits had been thrown, I said to Salzedo when the play was ended: " The husband, instead of abandoning himself to despair, as I at first thought he was inclined to do, acts wisely in resolving to console himself "— " True, he does well," replied Don Juan, " since the wife appears to have acted in concert with her ravisher. If I had the misfortune to find myself in similar circumstances, I would not, I assure you, be fool enough to let myself die of grief for having lost a woman who had betrayed me."

As, upon this subject, I had no other opinion than Salzedo's, the impression which " La Nobia Sonsacada," made on my mind was speedily effaced; or rather I profited by this piece, in espousing the sentiments of the husband, and by renewing my resolution of forgetting Donna Paula.

14

CHAPTER XI.

OF THE GREATEST EMBARRASSMENT IN WHICH DON CHERUBIN
EVER FOUND HIMSELF—IN WHAT MANNER HE GOT OUT OF
IT—SALZEDO PROPOSES TO HIM HIS DAUGHTER IN MARRIAGE
—HE REFUSES HER—SURPRISE OF HIS FRIEND.

ABOUT this time, Salzedo, who had been a widower some years, took home his daughter Blanca from the convent in which he had placed her on his arrival at Mexico. She possessed a small lively person, very pretty, and a mind in which was discernible sufficient sense to afford the promise of her having a great deal at a future day.

To contribute on my part towards forming her, or rather to pay my court to her father, who begged me to see and talk to her as often as possible, I scarcely let a day pass without having some conversation with her, in which I gave her moral lessons, enlivened by discourse as sprightly as was necessary not to make them tiresome.

All this went on the best in the world; but there happened an accident which spoiled all: the preceptor could not help falling in love with his pupil. No sooner was I sensible of my sentiments, than I reproached myself with them. " What do you propose to do ? " said I to myself. " To show your gratitude for Don Juan's bounties, would you seduce his daughter ? " I was not satisfied with reproaching myself for this passion, I resolved to combat it ; which, however, I did at first without effect, for, continuing still to see Blanca, the sight of her always overpowered my reflections ; so that I was under the necessity of applying to the efficacious remedy recommended by Ovid upon such occasions, that is to say, absence.

I ceased therefore to pay such frequent visits to the young lady, and when I did go to see her, had not more than a moment's conference with her. Piqued at the change which she perceived in my behavior, she said to me one day : " You grow tired of me, I see very plainly ; you look upon me as a child who is not capable of amusing you." I knew not what answer to make, not having resolution to tell her the reason for which I shunned her, for fear of becoming more culpable in endeavoring to justify myself.

At last Blanca, perceiving that I every day took more and more pains to avoid her, complained of it to her father, who did not fail to reproach me for it. " How is this ? " said he ; " Blanca complains of her master. You grow tired, she says, of instructing her. Is it possible that, in proportion as she grows up, you find her company less agreeable ? This sur-prises me." I replied in the same tone, " That would indeed be a surprising consequence ; but may I not, on the other hand, discontinue my lessons because her company is beginning to grow too dangerous ? "—" Would to Heaven," replied Don Juan, " that it were for that reason you abandoned your scholar ! "—" And what other reason," returned I, " could make me abandon the charms of Donna Blanca ? Yes, Signior, if I fly her, it is because I find it impossible to view her with im-punity. After the avowal which I have just made you, I be-lieve you will applaud the care which I take to combat the birth of an affection which might, by augmenting, cause me to lose your friendship."

Salzedo smiled at these words, which were, in my opinion, calculated to make him assume a more serious air. " Don Cherubin," said he, " you show too much diffidence of your own virtue ; repose more confidence in it. Continue your lessons ; see my daughter every day : I believe you incapable of abusing the liberty I give you of conversing with her ; I have no un-easiness on the subject. I shall say no more about it."

This reticence plunged me in a profound reverie. " What could have been the thoughts of Don Juan ? " said I, " when he had quitted me. Would he be inclined to have me marry Blanca ? Such, it appears to me, must be the meaning of the last words he uttered. Could his friendship for me be carried so far as to afford me such a testimony ? But what folly in me to think of such a thing ! This Secretary is too rich not to have views more elevated by far ; and his only daughter is not made for a man like me. But whatever may be his intention in requiring me to revisit Blanca, he must be satisfied."

I determined then to obey him, fully resolving to keep myself on my guard against the charms of his daughter; a thing
more easy to say than to perform, for every day she became
more formidable. As she knew how very highly I was esteemed
by her father, she received me in a manner so familiar and
obliging, that I had to fear no less the marks of friendship she
bestowed upon me, than the power of her eyes. I was in a
situation quite embarrassing.

To add to my trouble, Don Juan said to me one day: " It is
now time to communicate to you a design I have conceived.
Learn the extent of my regard for you. My daughter is now
matura viro, and it is you whom I have chosen for my son-in-
law."

I could not hear this without being disconcerted. Salzedo
put a wrong interpretation on the embarrassment I evinced.
He thought it was caused by joy; and in this error continued:
" Yes, my dear Don Cherubin, I feel an extreme pleasure in
allying your lot with that of my daughter, to bind you more
firmly to myself." He even accompanied these words with an
embrace which pierced my heart. In the chagrin I felt at this
moment in not being at liberty to become his son-in-law, I
uttered a melancholy sigh, which he interpreted no better than
he had my agitation : he imagined that Blanca was not to my
mind, and that I felt a repugnance to espouse her. He was
highly piqued at this; and casting upon me a look in which
anger was depicted, said to me, in a tone of irony: " Signior
Bachelor, I am extremely sorry that my daughter has not found
the way to your heart: you love only beauties old enough to be
grandmothers; you should have to please you a Donna Luisa
de Padilla."

At this piece of raillery I looked in Don Juan's face with
such a mortified air, that he, judging something extraordinary
was passing in my mind, began to consider me with the most
serious attention.   " Ah, Signior," said I, " do you imagine
that I know not the value of the honor you would confer on
me ? Do me more justice. The possession of Donna Blanca
would have a thousand charms for me ; but, alas ! that is forbidden to me: I am married."—" You ! " cried Salzedo with
surprise, " you married ! Why did you not tell me so ? "—" If
I made a mystery of my marriage with you," I replied, " it was
because in speaking of it I should have been obliged to inform

you of the misfortune which followed close upon it, and which
I would have buried in eternal silence."—" Conceal not this
misfortune from me," returned he; " perhaps I may assist you
in repairing it."—"I must then reveal the secret," replied I;
" pardon me for not having done it before." I then confided
to him the whole story, and remarked as I related it, that he
participated in my affliction.

" Don Cherubin," said he, when I had finished my recital,
" I am sensibly affected with what you have told me. I am
no longer surprised at your appearing troubled at the representation of ' La Nobia Sonsacada.' This piece no doubt revived the recollection of your misfortune; but let reason
banish forever from your mind these gloomy images. With
regard to my daughter, we will say no more about her; ceasing
to see her, you will shortly cease to love her. I would
gladly have been your father-in-law; and I should doubtless
have been so, had not fortune thrown this insuperable obstacle
in the way. Let us then content ourselves with being united in
bonds of the most tender friendship."

CHAPTER XII.

THE easier to forget Salzedo's daughter, I began to pay court more strongly than ever to the most lovely of the Mexican ladies. I also saw a number of young gentlemen with whom I every day engaged in parties of pleasure. Among others, I formed a close intimacy with Don Andre de Alvarade, great-grandson to the famous Alvarade, of whom such honorable mention is made in the history of the conquest of Mexico.

Having one day gone to visit him, I found him in his room extended on a sofa of Chinese silk, and plunged in a reverie so profound, that I entered without his perceiving me. I remained some minutes before him, while he was so occupied with his thoughts that he was insensible of my presence; and imagining himself alone, pronounced aloud, " Yes, I believe that this creature will drive me mad." He then started from his reverie, and, seeing me, burst out laughing. " Ah ! my dear friend," cried he, " are you there ? You found me absorbed in my reflection ; and, since you have heard me, I will no longer make a mystery with you of the state in which I find myself. I love, or rather I adore, a lady who is driving me to despair."

" Hey ! " cried I, " who is this cruel, this ungrateful creature, of whom you complain ? "—" It is," replied he, " Donna Cynthia de la Carrera, daughter of Don Joaquin de la Carrera, Councillor of the Chancery. You have never seen her, and she is a new acquaintance, whom I have made to my misfortune. She is a lady of ravishing beauty ; but the hope of pleasing her is denied me. She is courted by Don Bernardo de Orosco and Don Julian de Martara, who are two young noblemen of great merit."

" I understand you," replied I ; " these concurrences give you pain ; you are alarmed at their courtship."—" Very little," replied he : " formidable as they are, I fear them less than the strange character of Cynthia : she is so proud and so disdain-ful, that she does not imagine there is on earth a man worthy of her attention. She becomes like a fury when any one speaks to her of love. Don Joaquin, her father, who is de-sirous enough of marrying her, but who will not constrain her inclination, finds her so opposed to his intention, that he dares no longer press her to take a husband. Would you believe it ? in the apartment of this cruel creature everything announces that she is an enemy to love. Nothing is to be seen there but the portraits of women, over whom this god could never triumph. On one side, you see Daphne flying from the em-braces of Apollo ; on the other, Arethusa, who chooses rather to be changed into a fountain than yield to the love of Alpheus. In a word, all the paintings which there meet the eye evince that she despises men."

" You are giving me the description of a most extraordinary lady," said I, considerably surprised to find that there was any such in Mexico, where the women are naturally less cruel than in any part of the world. " She has then, it seems, received very ill the declaration of your passion ? "—" I have not yet declared it to her," replied he ; " and, between ourselves, I know not what to do about it. If I break silence, she will close my mouth with some haughty answer, and if I hold my tongue, my fate will still remain uncertain.

" You see my embarrassment," pursued Don Andre ; " if you were in my place, what course would you pursue ? "—" An extreme," replied I. " Instead of burning incense to the idol, and nourishing her pride by flattery and attentions, I would op-pose it by a feigned indifference ; I would employ disdain for disdain ; I would go beyond her in the aversion she manifests for all tender engagements. It is thus I would act with a per-son of such a singular character. What say you to my way of thinking ? You perhaps consider it extravagant."—" Not at all," replied Don Andre ; " I approve of it highly ; and, to convince you of it, I am determined to act this part with Cynthia. I think I shall not acquit myself ill, though I burn with the greatest ardor towards her. We shall see what this artifice will produce. I will go and see her to-day, and will give you an account to-morrow of what shall pass between us."

We here separated, and early the following day Alvarade called upon me. I was no less impatient to hear the progress he had made than he to recount it to me. " Don Cherubin," said he gayly, " I shall be very much deceived if our stratagem do not succeed. Yesterday, when I went to Cynthia's, as I was going into the house I met her servant Laura, whom I have already engaged in my interest. I made her the confidante of our project, telling her the plan I intended to pursue with her mistress ; and nothing it appeared to her could have been more ingeniously conceived. Laura," continued he, " was not content with only applauding my design, but promised to second it ; and I rely a great deal upon this promise, for she is a girl of talent, and capable of serving me."—" But," said I, " did you not see Cynthia ? Did you not speak to her ? "—" Pardon me," said he, " I went to her apartment, where I found her with some ladies of her acquaintance, and Don Bernardo de Orosco. We began talking of marriage. Don Bernardo extolled the advantages of it, and made the happiness of life consist in the union of two persons bound by mutual affection. Don Joaquin's daughter, on the contrary, maintained that there was no condition more wretched than that of two persons bound together by the yoke of Hymen. ' I am of the lady's opinion,' cried I, ' on that subject. I think that no state can be more deplorable than that of married people ; and have therefore, ever since I attained the age of reason, looked with horror upon wedlock, as also upon love ; for it is this dangerous passion which commonly conducts to marriage.'

" All the company burst out laughing at hearing me speak thus. ' You are then,' said one lady, ' an enemy to our sex, Don Andre ? '—' No, madam,' replied I, ' do not make me more culpable than I am. God forbid that I should be a woman-hater ! I respect and honor them infinitely ; but that is all they are to expect from me. I will neither love them, nor be loved by them.'—' How, then ! ' said Don Joaquin's daughter, ' if any beautiful lady should cast her eyes on you, she might run the risk of being repaid with ingratitude.'—' Yes, madam,' replied I, ' doubtless ; she would have the mortification of loving by herself, were she as amiable as you.' The ladies redoubled their laughter at these words, which I pronounced with a very serious air, and with which Cynthia appeared to me to be a little moved. 'Ladies,' returned she, addressing her friends, 'you see that Don Alvarade will not deceive you, since he declares his sentiments so plainly.'—'But, Don Andre,' cried a lady, 'be consistent with yourself: you have been seen to give entertainments to ladies, which seems to imply that you are not so insensible as you would have us believe to their attractions.' —'That does not,' replied I, 'prove that I love them; it only shows that I am gallant, as every gentleman ought to be. I do not deny myself their company; but I view the ladies without suffering my affections to be engaged to them, and without feeling any desire to please them.'

"This is what passed yesterday with Don Joaquin's daughter," continued Don Andre Alvarade; "and to tell you my opinion of it, I thought I remarked in Cynthia's eyes a secret anger at meeting a man who seemed to bid defiance to her empire. I do not know, after all, whether I may not deceive myself in thinking so. I would not swear it; and the indifference which I affect out of pride, will perhaps answer no other purpose than that of making her despise me the more."—"No, my friend," said I; "I rather conclude, that to avenge her wounded vanity, she will be the more desirous of fixing you in her chains."

CHAPTER XIII.

CONTINUATION OF THE STORY OF DON ANDRE ALVARADE AND
DONNA CYNTHIA DE LA CARRERA—FINAL SUCCESS OF DON
CHERUBIN'S ADVICE—HE IS THANKED FOR IT BY DON ANDRE.

IN effect, on the very same day, Don Andre having met
Laura at a house appointed, he learned that her mistress had
fallen into the snare. " Yes, Signior Don Andre," said the
waiting-maid, " you have raised against you the pride of the
haughty Cynthia. She says she cannot pardon your insensi-
bility ; and I warn you that she is resolved to spare no pains to
triumph over it. She has not slept all night ; and has done
nothing but groan and sigh with rage, at your having braved
the power of her eyes."—" But, madam," said I, " what cause
have you to complain of Don Andre ? he is not more blamable
in being insensible to the charms of ladies, than you in despis-
ing the most accomplished cavaliers."—" Do not take his part,
Laura," replied she. " Seek not to excuse him. I detest him ;
and I shall never feel satisfied till I see this savage dying at
my feet. I would, if I possessed it, give all the wealth in the
world to have that pleasure."

" You of course judge by what I have told you," said the
maid, " that Don Joaquin's daughter is preparing to set every
engine at work to inflame you. Take your measures accordingly, and be persuaded that you have everything to hope for
in continuing the deception you have began. Adieu, Signior
Don Andre," continued she, " I am going back to my mistress.
Return here at six o'clock, and it is probable I may have some
information for you." Don Andre, having returned at the
appointed time, accordingly met the maid. " Keep yourself on
your guard," said she ; " my mistress designs to attack you
with her strongest weapons : as it is now Carnival time, she

designs to give a *Sarao* * to-morrow evening, in which it will be so contrived, that you will both wear sashes of the same color. She makes tolerably sure of enchanting you, with the flattering glances which she will abundantly bestow upon you. Distrust this syren, who has no other view in charming you, than that of overwhelming you with contempt. I fear that, transported with joy, and too full of your love, you will betray yourself."— " No, no, my dear Laura," replied Don Andre, " lay aside that fear: enough that I am apprised of the peril to enable me to shun it. Let me alone in the business; the haughty Cynthia will most probably be caught herself."

Alvarade, after having had this fresh conversation with Laura, came with an account of it to me; and we both congratulated ourselves upon it. Don Joaquin's daughter, on her part, meditating the conquest of a man who was already but too much taken with her beauty, employed herself in making preparations for her *Sarao* on the following evening. She sent tickets to the ladies whom she wished to be present; and as Don Bernardo and Don Julian were of the number of the cavaliers who were likewise invited, Don Joaquin was extremely pleased, flattering himself with the hope that one or other of these gallants might render himself agreeable to his daughter. Don Andre, as it may be well supposed, was not forgotten. He also received his ticket, and the next day when the hour for the *Sarao* had arrived, went there gaily dressed, and disposed to acquit himself well of his part.

As soon as he entered the saloon, the woman who held the sashes designed for the gentlemen, presented him with a green one. He immediately put it on, and looking out for the lady who should have one of the same color, he found her in the daughter of Don Joaquin. He advanced towards her, and accosting her politely, " Madam," said he, " I look upon this

* This is an assembly which takes place in the Carnival time. It is composed of young people of both sexes, who are in disguise, but without masks. A woman who has in her hand a basket of silk sashes of different colors, presents one to each lady as she enters the *Sarao* saloon. Another woman, supplied with sashes of the same kind, distributes them to the gentlemen. After this, each of the gentlemen seeking the lady who wears the color which marks her as his partner for the evening, accosts her, and remains at her feet all the time the *Sarao* lasts. He is allowed to address her in the most tender language without her being at liberty to take offence: such is the rule, which of course often occasions intrigues. The *Sarao* concludes with dancing.

day as the happiest of my life, since it falls to my lot to become
the partner of the charming Cynthia."—" Do not congratulate
yourself too much on your good fortune," replied she; "the
danger you are in ought rather to make you tremble. You
ought to complain of your chance; which would have been
more favorable had it assigned you another lady. You might
have been able to please her, instead of which you will derive
no advantage from the conversation we shall have together. I
will even apprise you out of charity, that if you have the misfortune to become enamoured of me, I shall treat you with the
utmost rigor. This is what you may make up your mind to."

" You think to frighten me," replied my friend, " but fear
yourself that your pride may be forced to stoop to mine; for,
in short," continued he, assuming a tone of tenderness, is it
possible that you will not be touched by my pains, when, profiting by the liberty which the *Sarao* affords me to speak to you
of love, I shall make known the deplorable state to which I am
reduced? Yes, lovely Cynthia, my heart is a prey to a thousand flames." So saying, he kissed her hand in transport.
" Alvarade," replied the lady, repulsing him gently, " you contradict yourself: you express yourself in such a manner, and in
such terms, as make me imagine that you really love me, though
you think you do not. You do not remember that I told you
I should repay your sighs with contempt and rigor."—" It is
you, madam," replied Don Andre, " it is you that forget we
are in a *Sarao*. All that I said was only affected."—" What ! "
cried the lady, " do you not feel what you have just been saying ? "—" Heaven preserve me from it ! " returned the cavalier,
changing his tone. " Who ! I augment the number of your
slaves? No, madam, though I were even capable of loving
you, shame would oblige me to conceal it."

" You can, then, counterfeit extremely well," said Cynthia.
" To perfection ! " replied Alvarade; " I borrow when I please
the eyes and language of the most tender love; for example, if
I wished to make you a declaration of love, I would say : Adorable Cynthia, it is not through gallantry, or to fulfil the duties
of the *Sarao*, that I tell you my heart was surrendered to your
earliest glances; it is to discover to you my secret sentiments,
since I can this day make you acquainted with them without
raising your anger at my presumption."—" And that was only
pretended ? " interrupted the lady hastily. " Say no more,

Alvarade: I see through your finesse; you pretend to be insensible to female beauty, flattering yourself that by that means you will render me more tractable. Have I not penetrated your design? Acknowledge it with a good grace, and you shall not repent it: rely on the promise which I make you."

Don Andre hesitated some moments before he answered; but determined at last to satisfy her at the expense of whom it might concern, he confessed the whole: after which he said: "Madam, I now await my doom; deign to pronounce it, decide my fate."—"I might," replied Cynthia, "be offended at your duplicity, and to punish you for it, treat you like my other lovers; but I pardon you for the sake of the invention, and give you the preference over all your rivals."

I leave it to the reader to conceive the rapture which these last words caused my friend, who as long as the *Sarao* lasted, which was till the following morning, ceased not to manifest his gratitude to Don Joaquin's daughter. No sooner had he quitted this lady, than he ran to me to communicate to me his joy. He returned me a million of thanks for having advised to assume the part which he had acted so successfully, telling me that I was the author of his felicity. In short, a fortnight after he married his mistress, in prejudice of his two rivals, who at bottom were preferable to him.

CHAPTER XIV.

A SHORT time after this marriage, it happened that a friar of
the Order of Saint Dominic came from Guatemala to reside at
Mexico. He preached at first in the cathedral, and made so
much noise from the time of his first sermon, that he became
the general subject of conversation in the town. Whatever
house I entered, I heard nothing there but the praises of
Father Cyril: the women in particular extolled him, and set
him above the most famous preachers of the Order of Mercy,
of Saint Francis, and even of the Jesuits, although among
these latter were some of great celebrity. When he preached
in a religious house, all the nobility flocked thither in crowds;
and the price of seats was enhanced. The congregation burst
out in exclamations of applause. They even clapped their
hands, and went out of the church praising the eloquence of
the preacher to the skies.

I could not hold out against the reputation of Father Cyril,
and was desirous of judging of his talents from my own observation. Having learned that he was to preach on the Day of
the Assumption at his convent, I went thither, and found a
numerous and brilliant congregation, though this monastery is
a league from the town. I took my seat for my money among
the rest of the auditors, and, while waiting for the sermon, conversed with a cavalier who was sitting near me. I asked him
if he had ever heard Father Cyril. " Twice," replied he; " and
I protest to you, that no preacher ever pleased me so much
as he.

" You will be astonished," continued he, " with his dazzling

222

style, and the beauty of his portraits. He has a choice of terms and an eloquence which set off everything; happy metaphors, judicious and charming allegories, beauties of detail, terms which are peculiar to himself, and, above all, the most nicely conceived transitions. I warn you only, that it is necessary to listen to him with all the attention you are capable of; for he has a volubility of tongue which it is difficult to follow. I was at his last sermon at the Convent of Mercy: I had the misfortune to sneeze, and my sneezing caused me to lose a period." I replied, "that there were some preachers who spoke so quick, that one must not even turn one's eyes from them for a moment, if one would not lose the thread of their discourse.

This conversation, however, redoubled the impatience I felt to see this celebrated personage. I saw him ascend the pulpit, and the church immediately echoed with a general acclamation; which gave me to understand to what a point the public were prejudiced in his favor. Father Cyril appeared to me not bigger than a dwarf; and was really so small, that we could but just see his head. I was struck with his features; and scarcely had he pronounced his text, ere I completely recognized him by the sound of his voice. "It is he," said I to myself. "Yes, faith, it is the Licentiate Carambola. What a pleasant adventure! It seems that we follow each other. We bade adieu in Toledo, and met again in Madrid; there we separated, and found each other at Barcelona. One would say that fortune takes pleasure in bringing us together." Then, doubting the report of my eyes and ears, "May I not deceive myself?" I reflected. "This is, indeed, his voice and figure, but do we not every day see men who exactly resemble each other? Besides, can it be possible that Carambola has assumed the frock and (what is beyond my comprehension) become a great preacher? This is what I cannot understand." Nevertheless, the more I heard and contemplated Father Cyril, the more was I convinced that he was my Biscayan licentiate.

Whilst waiting until I should be able to convert my doubt into certainty, I listened attentively to the friar, to ascertain if the public were right in admiring his eloquence; but he delivered himself so rapidly that, without sneezing, I lost more than half of what he said. I heard, however, enough to console me for this loss; I even made a remark which did not redound to the glory of the preacher; I observed that the auditors were only taken with his style, and that the orator spoke less to the heart than to the head.

When the sermon was concluded, I got myself conducted to the apartment of Father Cyril, who beheld me again with a surprise equal to that which I had felt on seeing him in the pulpit. We both embraced affectionately. " Signior Licentiate," said I, " thank Heaven that we once more meet; but acknowledge that this last rencounter is more astonishing than the rest. I should never have expected to find you in the habit of a Jacobin."—" My astonishment," replied he, " is equal to yours, and you may easily imagine that I am not a little curious to know what you are doing in Mexico. I suppose you are not less so to know how I became a friar, and what is more, a preacher of the first flight. We must satisfy each other. But let us put it off, if you please, till to-morrow, for two reasons: besides that I am fatigued, I have a long recital to make."—" And on my side," returned I, " I have also an infinitude of things to recount to you. Adieu, Father Cyril; repose yourself. We shall see each other again to-morrow."

Hereupon I left my preacher; and, having rejoined him on the following day in the afternoon, we shut ourselves up in his apartment, where we prepared ourselves for mutually recounting what had happened since our last separation. I spoke first; and persuaded that I need have no reserve with my friend Carambola, I told him everything. When I had concluded, he recounted to me his own adventures with equal sincerity.

END OF THE FOURTH PART.

PART THE FIFTH.

CHAPTER I.

THE LICENTIATE CARAMBOLA BEGINS THE HISTORY OF HIS VOY-
AGE TO THE WEST INDIES—HE MEETS WITH ONE OF HIS COL-
LEGE COMPANIONS—WHO HE WAS—HE RESOLVES TO FOLLOW
HIM, AND BECOMES A FRIAR.

"You know well," said he, "that you left me at Barcelona,
tutor to a spoiled child; I told you, if you remember, that I
was very well satisfied with my post, that I possessed in it
all the advantages which a pedagogue could anywhere have,
and that in all likelihood I should occupy it a long while.
Nevertheless, I was obliged to leave it. They gave me
my thanks; what do I say? They dismissed me unfairly
enough. This was the reason: one day being a little out of
humor with my young gentleman, into whose head I could not
drive the first principles of the Latin language, it happened
that I forgot I was forbidden to chastise him, for fear of griev-
ing and making him ill; and I pulled his ears rather roughly,
I must acknowledge. He screamed as loud as if I had been
burning him alive. His mother, who was within hearing, ran
to him, and, finding her son in tears, accused me of brutality.
The father, who was not master in his own house, was desirous
of interceding in my favor, but he was silenced as if he had
been a child, and I was turned out of doors without further
process.

"Some days after having been thus dismissed, as I was
walking alone on the wharf, musing on the unpromising state
of my affairs, I met two reverend fathers of Saint Dominic, of

whom I recognized one as having been my fellow-student at the university of Alcala. We accosted each other, and, after having cordially embraced, began to amuse ourselves with conversing on the little tricks we had played our professors at college. He then informed me that he had come from Salzona with his companion, in order to embark on the following day on board a vessel which was to sail for Cadiz, where they were both expected in their convent, one to be professor of philosophy, and the other of theology. 'I envy your happiness, fathers,' said I, sighing, 'and repent of not having embraced your life, instead of having made myself a galley-slave, for such I call a poor devil of a tutor.'

" My schoolfellow began laughing at hearing me talk thus. 'I did not know,' said he, 'that the condition of a tutor was that of a galley-slave.'—'I can inform you then that it is so,' replied I, 'and you may take my word for it. I acknowledge that there are no rules without exceptions, and that there are houses where the slavery of pedagogues is mild, or at least supportable. At the house of an old prudish devotee, for instance, a hypocritical preceptor is not badly off : he possesses the confidence of his patroness, who sees but with his eyes, and who, as the price of his interested complaisance towards her, sometimes makes generous mention of him in her will. But such places are rare, and as for me, I have hitherto met with none but wretched ones.'

" ' I am sorry,' replied the monk, 'that you are not content with your lot. I wish you were as much so as I am with mine. If everybody knew how happy we Jacobins are, our cloister would not contain the great number who would eagerly press forward to inhabit it.'—'Ah ! father,' cried I, 'you augment my regret for not having assumed the fortunate habit of Saint Dominic.'—' If you speak seriously,' said he, ' I will enable you to put it on when you please. It is not yet too late. Profit by the opportunity. Come with us to Cadiz : I will present you to the Reverend Father Isidore, prior of our house, and I am sure that he will receive you willingly among us, when he shall learn that you have made a noise among the schools of Alcala, where I have witnessed your brilliant studies. I still remember that they used to call you by way of excellence, *aquila theologiæ*.

" ' Yes, Signior Licentiate,' continued he, ' Father Isidore will look upon you as an excellent acquisition to our order, and will owe me much goodwill for having procured it such an one. Determine ; see what you will do ! '—' I will take you at your word,' replied I, ' and would set out with you for Cadiz, if I were sufficiently well off for cash to defray the expenses of my journey and my reception ; but I will candidly acknowledge to you, that all my property consists of a single doubloon, of which I owe three-fourths at the inn where I have been living since I was out of place.'

" 'You have no need of money with us,' said the other friar ; ' we are able to defray all the expenses on the journey : and as for your reception, be assured that it will be given gratuitously on consideration of your merit. Well ! are there now any more difficulties to get over ? '—' No,' replied I, 'there are none. Indeed, fathers, you inspire me ; I am ready to follow you.'

" My future companions appeared charmed to see me disposed to go along with them. 'We say not adieu, brother,' said my schoolfellow ; 'we shall have plenty of time for conversation. We leave you,' added he, pointing with his finger to a vessel which was lying in the port, ' to deposit on board that ship all the provisions necessary for our voyage ; for we are not folks to embark without biscuit. Come and join us then this evening : we shall sail to-morrow before day.' "

CHAPTER II.

" Not choosing to leave Barcelona like a swindler, I returned
to my inn, where I paid my host; then resuming my road to
the port in order to attend my appointment, I arrived there
with a small portmanteau, which I carried under my arm, and
in which were my clothes. The monks were already on board,
and waited for me with impatience. These good fathers, by
way of precaution, had provided themselves with an abundance
of viands, and a copious number of bottles of the best wines of
La Mancha, as if they had been going to the end of the world.
We weighed anchor the next day before the dawn of Aurora,
and our vessel soon left the port of Barcelona far behind. During the voyage, which, thank Heaven, was very fortunate, our
monks showed themselves so good-humored, that, far from re-
penting of having enrolled myself in their company, I incessantly congratulated myself upon it, persuading myself that no
mortals were happier. I will assure you that I am this day in
the same opinion.

" Arrived at Cadiz, we repaired to the monastery of the order
of Saint Dominic. The prior Isidore received my two companions with distinction, as persons of whom his house was in
need. He also gave me a favorable reception, as soon as he
heard that I was a learned licentiate who desired the habit of a
novice. He granted it to me without difficulty on their assurance that I was born to reside among them, as in fact I had
sufficiently let them see on board ship, where I accommodated
myself wonderfully well to their mode of living.

" I entered then upon my novitiate, and, thanks be to God, was not disgusted with the monastic life. After having professed, I was called Father Cyril. I attached myself to the study of theology. I then took holy orders ; and finding, in my own opinion, that I possessed talents for the pulpit, I composed a sermon, which I had the boldness to attempt delivering in the cathedral of Cadiz, before the Bishop and the Governor. But do you know how I acquitted myself? You shall learn ; for my sincerity ought to correspond with your own, and we ought on both sides to recount our disagreeable adventures with the same candor as the others. The assembly was numerous, and filled with monks of all orders. A congregation so enlightened, but at the same time so critical and jealous, agitated me to such a degree that I stopped short in the middle of my exordium. In vain I fatigued my memory to be able to continue ; the rebel obstinately refused me his aid, and I was obliged to vanish. But before I disappeared I said to my auditors, 'Gentlemen, I am sorry for you ; you lose a good sermon.'

" You may easily judge that these words, pronounced by a Biscayan," continued Father Cyril, " did not fail to produce laughter. The Bishop and the Governor lost their gravity. All the monks, if you except those of our order, left the church stifling their laughter, and better satisfied than if I had preached to perfection.

" So unfortunate a *coup d'essai* did not discourage me. On the contrary, to retrieve my honor, I armed myself with audacity, and three months after remounted the same pulpit from which I had so disagreeably descended. Those of my auditors who had been witnesses of the trick which my memory had played me the first time, expected perhaps again to see me stop short, and to laugh anew at my expense ; but they were deceived in their expectations ; my memory was faithful, and I was generally applauded. What do I say? they found me an orator complete, and from that day forward I was placed on a parallel with the most famous preachers of Spain ; a thing which proves that one may acquire a reputation at very little cost. This made me redouble my efforts to merit the praises which were bestowed on me, and which, in spite of my self-love, I was perfectly aware I did not merit. I composed other sermons, with which my auditors were so well satisfied, that my name became every day more famous.

"I was enjoying at Cadiz the general esteem of its inhabitants, when Father Isidore received a letter from America. The prior of Saint James of Guatemala begged him to send over two skilful preachers to support the reputation of our order in that country. I was desirous of being one of these holy laborers: less in truth from apostolic zeal, than from my desire to see those fine countries which had been subdued by the Spanish arms. I can affirm that it was not without repugnance Father Isidore permitted me to go to the Indies, not having at that time in his community a member of equal value. Nevertheless he had the goodness to yield to my request, on condition that after some years I should return to Spain.

"I set out then from Cadiz with Father Bonifacio de Tabara, who was appointed to accompany me. The wind continued favorable until we reached the Havannah; thence we proceeded to Portobello during the time of the fair, which beyond contradiction ought to be accounted the finest in the world. The prodigious concourse of Spanish and Peruvian merchants, of whom the one description come to buy, and the other to sell their goods, offer to the eyes a most amusing spectacle. As for me, what I found most worthy of notice, was the great number of mules which I saw arrive from Panama, loaded with bars and ingots of silver. In one hour I counted as many as two hundred, which were unloaded in the public square; making altogether some heaps of ingots extremely gratifying to the view of the parties interested.

"We did not remain long at Portobello. We again set sail for Venta de Cruzez, then Panama, whence we gained the port of the Salinas, and afterwards Carthagena. From this place we went to the town of Grenada, otherwise called Mahomet's Garden, from whence we did not long delay in proceeding to the port of Realejo on the coast of the South Sea, and a few days after we arrived at the port of the Trinity."

Here I interrupted Carambola rather bluntly: "Hollo! what the deuce," said I, "Signior Licentiate, you are making a traveller's journal. Do not name to me, I beg of you, all the places through which you passed: I acquit you of that trouble. I am only curious to hear your adventures. Be so good therefore as to make but one leap from the port of the Trinity to Saint James of Guatemala; for in all appearance this last-named town is the theatre of the principal exploits you have to relate

to me."—"Signior Bachelor," said he, smiling, "you do wrong
to complain: to avoid prolixity, and compress my story, I have
passed over the tempests and other perils which I had to go
through. I have even spared you the descriptions which I
could have given of the places, of which I have simply told you
the names, and which would perhaps be more interesting than
my own adventures. Go, you have interrupted me very
unreasonably.

"But in short," said he, "since you absolutely desire it, I
will make you a leap of five-and-twenty leagues, by conveying
you all at once to Guatemala. Permit me first to tell only one
thing of a most extraordinary nature. It is this : near the town
of Trinidad is seen, in a deep hollow rising out of the earth
without any intermission, a thick and black smoke, mixed
sometimes with sulphur and flames of fire. It is said that some
travellers, curious to discover the cause, having had the imprudence to approach it too closely, have been thrown to the
earth half dead. The people of the country assure us, that at
a certain distance they hear the cries of persons in torment,
and that these cries are accompanied by a noise of iron chains ;
which has caused the name of Hell to be given to this horrible
chasm.

"Let us now come to Guatemala," continued Father Cyril :
"I will make you languish no longer. Father Bonifacio and I
arrived there, then ; but (what was extremely laughable) we
looked for the town in the town itself. Neither walls nor gates
were to be seen at the entrance, and some thatched or tiled
houses were all that presented themselves to our view. Surprised at this sight of a town which corresponded so ill with
the idea I had formed of it, I said to my companion : 'Father,
are you not of opinion that we have done a very foolish business in quitting Cadiz, where we were so well off, to come and
preach here ? To judge of the citizens by their habitations,
we shall have nothing but a mob for our auditors. Is this the
celebrated city of Guatemala, that capital of a kingdom three
hundred leagues in extent, and where there is, we are told, a
court, independent of that of Mexico, with a first President,
who, though without the title of Viceroy, has the authority of
one ? This is what I cannot understand.'—'Nor I, neither,'
replied Father Boniface ; 'I am almost inclined to think that
they have been playing tricks with us.'

"Our astonishment, however, was of no long duration. When we had got beyond the thatched houses we found some more handsome, and, among others, two superb edifices which are in the quarter of Saint Dominic, that is to say, the Jacobins' convent, and the nunnery of the Conception. This last in particular, surrounded by high walls of an immense circumference, long attracted our attention: it appeared to us a town of itself enclosed in that of Guatemala. There are in this convent as many as a thousand females, including the nuns, boarders, and black women who are in their service.

"In proportion as we advanced into this capital, we found houses which did it more honor than the first. We at last presented ourselves at the gate of the convent of our fathers, who received us like two personages whose arrival was agreeable to them. Father Valentin Tiraquello, who was at that time prior, had no sooner read the letter which I presented him from Father Isidore, than he gave us a thousand testimonies of friendship, and to me in particular, because the letter contained a magnificent eulogium on Father Cyril. They regaled us extremely well, and left us some days to repose ourselves in.

"During this time the report ran in the town that two great preachers had just arrived from Spain. Nothing more was requisite to set all the Spanish families in motion, and, in particular, the female part of them. 'When shall we see them?' cried one. 'How impatient I am,' said another, 'to hear these new apostles!' 'Father Cyril,' said the prior to me one day, 'I can no longer hold out against the curiosity of the public: the gentry, the courtiers, the citizens—all the town ardently desire to see you in the pulpit, to judge if you answer your great name. They press me to grant them this satisfaction, and I cannot help incessantly promising them that they shall have it.'—'I will fulfil your promise, my reverend father,' said I; 'I will, if you please, preach to-morrow in our church to satisfy them.'

CHAPTER III.

" THE Prior, finding me in this mind, sent immediate notice to the principal houses, that the Reverend Father Cyril would make his first appearance on the following day at the convent of the Jacobins. This news spread so rapidly over Guatemala, that on the morrow our church was filled with all the respectable people in the town. On one hand, the congregation was honored with the venerable presence of Don Francisco de Castro, Bishop of Guatemala, and on the other, by all the officers of the Chancery, from the principal down to the registrar, without mentioning the principal ladies of the town, all dressed out with the most extraordinary magnificence. As soon as I entered the pulpit there arose a slight murmur, which appeared to me to be caused by my pigmy-like figure, for nothing escapes notice : but I had not finished my exordium before this disagreeable noise was followed by one of a more flattering nature ; and every one, forgetting in a manner that he saw me, listened to me with attention.

" If I had had the happiness of pleasing at Cadiz, I had it in a more eminent degree at Guatemala. To say all in a word, I gained the approbation of my auditors, and obtained the esteem of the bishop, who sent to me the next morning to invite me to dine, together with the Prior, at the episcopal palace.

" This good prelate, who, although a septuagenarian, had not yet an air of antiquity, overloaded me with compliments. He congratulated Father Valentin on having a person so capable

233

as I was of doing honor to the order of Saint Dominic. Judge whether his Lordship's praises failed to tickle the heart of a Biscayan. I inwardly relished them; but the more I found my vanity flattered, the more modest did I appear, like all other authors when they are praised in their own presence.

"Besides the esteem of this prelate, I attracted that of the principal courtiers, who unanimously praised me, so that it was decided that little Father Cyril was the Coryphæus of preachers in the Indies. I pleased not only people of the world; my reputation penetrated the walls of the monastery of the Conception. The nuns were desirous of hearing me, and I delighted them. Some of them wrote to me to testify in how great a degree they were satisfied with my sermon, and to invite me to go and see them at the grate; which I failed not to do when I was informed that at Guatemala, as well as at Mexico, the monks freely visit the nuns, who converse with them in the parlors, and sometimes entertain them with collations accompanied by music. This happened to myself on the very first visit I made to those ladies who had written me such obliging letters. They regaled me with confections, and made me listen to some very fine voices; among others, that of the young mother Donna Angela de Montalvan, daughter of an officer of the court, and a person, perhaps, of the greatest merit in the world.

"One sees few women, who, with great beauty, have not a defective figure, or, perhaps, a contracted mind; but it may be said that Nature, in forming Donna Angela, was desirous of effecting a work of perfection. It is most certain that this nun, who had but just entered on her fifth lustrum, was an incomparable girl. She understood music thoroughly, and joined to a ravishing voice a superior genius. She addressed me two or three times with such sprightliness and with an air so gracious, that I imagined I beheld an angel. She enchanted both my eyes and my ears.

"I left the convent of the Conception, and returned home, much taken with the politeness of the nuns, and perhaps too much with the merit of the young devotee of whom I have spoken. 'Well, Father Cyril,' said our Prior, 'are you satisfied with our neighbors?'—'I have reason to be so,' said I. 'These ladies regaled me with confections, and a concert marvellously well executed.'—'I have no doubt of it,' replied Father Valen-

tin, ' particularly if the Mother de Montalvan took a part in it.'
—' Yes, truly, did she,' said I ; ' she sang in it, and I thought
her voice admirable.'—' You must also have remarked,' replied
he, ' that this girl is possessed of an uncommon beauty.'—
' That is what I paid no attention to,' said I, with a hypocritical
air : ' I thought of nothing but listening to her.' This was not
altogether true ; for no sooner had the touching sounds of
Angela's voice reached my ears, than I looked at nothing else
but her; but I did not dare acknowledge that I had made this
observation, for fear I should appear to him to have been too
deeply interested in it.

"' I am sorry,' returned the Prior, who was a simple, natural
kind of man, ' that you did not attentively consider the Mother
de Montalvan ; you would have seen a celestial face. Signior
Don Francisco de Castro, our bishop, has a most particular
esteem for her. He goes every day to see her, and every day
sends her presents. He might be suspected of being enamoured
of her, if his consummate virtue and his great age did not put
his Excellency above such suspicion : but the world do justice
to this venerable prelate, and all the town, as well as myself,
are persuaded that he has for this lady only a pure and delicate
friendship.' If I had not known Father Valentin to be a man
incapable of slandering his neighbor, and particularly his bishop,
I should have thought that he was not speaking seriously ;
nevertheless he thought what he said, so great was his opinion
of his lordship's virtue.

"Two days after having been to visit the nuns of the Conception, a gentleman called upon me from the prelate, to say
that his Excellency desired to speak to me. I immediately
went to the palace, where Signior Don Francisco having taken
me into his closet, addressed me in the most obliging and flattering terms ; then all on a sudden changing the subject, ' Father
Cyril,' said he, ' I have need of you, to succeed in a design
which I have in contemplation. I flatter myself you will not
refuse your assistance. The nuns of the Conception, who lost
their Superior about a fortnight ago, are about to elect another.
I am desirous that their choice should fall on the Mother de
Montalvan. It will be necessary to form a vigorous faction in
her favor. I have already been able to gain over some of these
ladies : they have promised me their votes, and I am confident
of having the majority if you second me.'

" ' My lord,' replied I, ' you may dispose of your servant : lay your commands on me ; what am I to do? '—' I know,' replied he, ' that you have made acquaintance with several nuns of this monastery, and that they have conceived the highest esteem for you. I shall be much obliged by your speaking to them successively in private about the approaching election, and employing your eloquence to bring them to the way of thinking which I desire.'

" ' I do not think, my lord,' said I, ' that I shall have much trouble in succeeding in this negotiation. I am persuaded that all the nuns will readily conform to your Excellency's sentiments.'—' I doubt it,' cried he: ' let us not flatter ourselves. The extreme youth of Angela is a terrible difficulty to surmount. There are in this convent twenty nuns of high rank, who have been more than thirty years devoted to religion, and whose conduct has always been irreproachable. With what eye will these behold authority placed in the hands of a young nun? However,' added he, heaving a sigh which showed me the interest he took in the affair, ' this nun, young as she is, deserves to have the preference over all her companions.

" ' You have seen her,' he continued, ' you have seen her in the parlor; but she did no more than appear before you for an instant. You know not all her worth : you must have seen her more than once ; you must, in short, be acquainted with her to be able to estimate her, to perceive her merit in its full extent. What wit she has ! If she open her mouth to speak, it is a *bon mot* which escapes her. If a subject is to be argued, her reasons are just and solid. A girl of twenty ! how amiable is this ! But what can never be sufficiently praised, and which alone renders her worthy of being superior, is her extreme mildness: happy consequence of her temperament and her virtue ! Exempt from those sallies of humor which the most sensible persons cannot at all times restrain, she converses with a tranquillity of soul which nothing can disturb. In a word, she unites in her person every amiable and estimable quality. It is this rare merit which interests me for her ; and, between ourselves, I do not think that her youth ought to exclude her from a rank for which I consider her born.'

" I saw very plainly by this discourse that his lordship suffered himself to be rather too much swayed by his pure and delicate friendship for Angela, and his project appeared to me extravagant. Nevertheless (what I shall reproach myself for all my life), instead of combating, and representing to him the folly of it, I approved of it against my conscience, in order to pay court to the prelate and get into his good graces. It is thus that the great find almost always, among common persons, ministers ready to serve their passions. I assured his Excellency that I devoted myself entirely to him, and that I was about to do my utmost to acquit myself successfully of the commission with which he honored me. The old bishop, delighted with the zeal I evinced in his service, embraced me affectionately; and by his embraces, which flattered my vanity, put the finishing stroke to confirming me in this silly enterprise.

CHAPTER IV.

OF THE EXERTIONS WHICH FATHER CYRIL MADE TO GIVE SUCCESS
TO THE BISHOP'S FACTION—WHAT WAS THE RESULT—AN UN-
EXPECTED DISTURBANCE ARISES AT THE CONVENT GATES—CON-
SEQUENCE OF THIS EVENT.

" To show the more haste, I made but one leap from the
episcopal palace to the monastery of the Conception. I saw
there the nuns with whom I was acquainted, and conversed
separately with each of them. I found them very much
opposed to the will of the prelate; but the opposition of each
did but afford a triumph to my rhetoric. This encouraged
me. I then spoke to others of the community, and principally
to some of those who, thinking they themselves deserved the
preference, looked upon it as intolerable injustice that it should
be decided in favor of a person of two and twenty. You will
easily believe that these ancient mothers did not easily yield.
Nevertheless, shocked as they were at what I proposed, I succeeded at last in inducing them to comply with it; as if I had
had the talent of Carneades * for persuasion. In short, I succeeded so well, that in less than a week I secured the vote of
the greater part of these ladies.

" I carried these agreeable news to my lord, who received
them with inexpressible transports of joy, and gave me thanks
from the bottom of his heart. He made me, besides, a present
of a gold watch, which he obliged me to accept, and which I
received, although a Dominican. After having given me a
thousand marks of affection, he begged me to go and see the
young Mother de Montalvan, and inform her of the happy effect
of my exertions; which I readily did. I gave her an account

* Cato the Censor was for banishing the philosopher Carneades, because
by his eloquence he bewildered the mind in such a way that it was not possible to distinguish truth from falsehood.

of what I had done for her, and assured her that in all likelihood she could not fail of becoming Superior. Upon this she thanked me for my pains, and gave loose to her gratitude in terms and with an air which enchanted me. How agreeable did I find her! I admired those estimable qualities which caused his lordship so warmly to interest himself in her behalf.

" However, the day of election arrived, and we should doubtless have had a majority of votes, if all the ancient mothers of the community had not united in favor of the Mother Saint Bridget, sister of an old president of the Audience, and beyond contradiction the most worthy subject among them. This union, which we had not foreseen, and which after all we could not have prevented, disconcerted our enterprise. Discord was raised in the convent; and farther, the report having spread in the town that it was intended to elect for Superior a nun of two and twenty, several of the principal inhabitants took fire on the subject. They ran sword in hand to the monastery, threatening to force open the gates, to defend their daughters against the faction raised by the bishop in favor of the Mother de Montalvan. It was necessary, in order to appease the tumult, that the father of this lady should go to the monastery, and exert the power he had over his daughter to engage her to desist from her pretensions: this I believe she did with regret, for this little lady was as ambitious as beautiful. By this means the disorder ceased, and peace was re-established both in the town and the convent. Thus the Mother Angela was compelled to remain a simple nun, and to content herself with being the prettiest of the community, which some of her companions would have preferred to the honor of being Superior.

CHAPTER V.

" I KNOW not whether the bishop or I looked most foolish of
the two after this adventure, which made a terrible noise in the
city of Guatemala.   This prelate, whom I have never seen since
that time, was so mortified with having been foiled in a affair
of so interesting a nature, that he came to the resolution of
shutting himself up in his palace, to hide his confusion from the
malignant view of the public.   On my part, monk as I was, I
was not much less ashamed than himself.   I dared not show
myself; for, as I was known in the town for one whose fault it
was not that the Mother de Montalvan was not abbess, the
sight of me might have excited hisses.   For all the gold in the
world I would not then have preached in Guatemala, imagining
that I was no longer looked on but as the secret agent of
Signior Don Francis de Castro.   This idea gave me so much
pain, that I resolved to abandon my residence in this town,
however agreeable it was.

" I communicated my design to the prior, who, judging like
myself that after what had passed I actually had reason to wish
myself out of Guatemala, replied: 'Father Cyril, I am of your
opinion.   You will do well to disappear for some time.   Father
Boniface, next to you the best preacher of our order, will
preach here during your absence.   I have,' continued he, ' a
solid establishment to propose to you.   You know that we are
collators of almost all the cures in the environs of Guatemala.
I offer you the most considerable, which is that of Petapa, a
large market-town about six leagues from hence.   Father

Estefano, one of our monks, who has had it more than thirty years, needs repose, and demands a successor. Go to him, and act as his coadjutor until he shall abandon his place in your favor, which he will doubtless do as soon as he shall have instructed you in the language of the Indians. I promise you that you will do very well in that country, which is, besides, one of the most delicious in America.'

" I set out then from Guatemala, carrying a letter from Father Valentin to the old curate of Petapa. I was mounted on a mule from the stables of our convent, and an Indian accompanied me on foot. In order to follow exactly the instructions which the prior had given me, I stopped at Mixco, a village near Petapa, and remained there until the following day, that the Alcades and Regidors, whom I caused to be apprised of my arrival, might have time to prepare for receiving me, as they commonly receive the priests and monks who come to be their pastors; I mean with a pomp which fully marks the respect and consideration they have for them. Accordingly they preceded me on the following day for about a league with singers, trumpeters, and hautboy-players. Besides this I found, on entering the town, triumphal arches decorated with branches of trees, and the streets through which I had to pass were strewed with flowers.

" I was thus ceremoniously conducted to the Presbytery, where Father Estefano, after having read my letter of credit, gave me a reception such as might have gratified a pastor more vain than myself. This good Jacobin, though advanced in years, appeared still robust, and enjoyed an old age exempt from infirmities. With all the good sense he had had in his best days, he preserved a gaiety of humor which made him agreeable in society. ' I see very plainly,' said he, ' by this letter that Father Valentin is giving me a successor who will soon cause the loss of me to be forgotten among the inhabitants of Petapa.

" ' I am greatly rejoiced at it,' continued he, ' and I would leave this to-morrow to go and finish my holy career in some one of our cloisters, if you would not be in want of me; but I am necessary to you to teach you the Proconchi, which is the language of the Indians, and which it is absolutely necessary that a priest should be acquainted with in this town, where they scarcely speak any Spanish, the officers and the gentry being

16

almost all of Indian race. The talent which you have for preaching would be useless to you here, unless you learn the Proconchi: did not Father Valentin tell you this?'—'Pardon me,' replied I, 'truly he did represent to me the necessity of it; but he told me at the same time, that you would instruct me in it in less than three months.'—'He told you truth,' replied Father Estefano; 'I am thoroughly acquainted with this idiom. I have even composed a grammar and a dictionary in the Indian language, and these two works have had the honor of being approved of by the Academy of Petapa.'

"At this word academy I burst out laughing. 'How!' cried I, 'there is an academy in this town. There is not then a small town without one!'—'This is much celebrated,' returned Father Estefano, with a very serious air; 'by the same token that I am an old member of this respectable body, into which you will also enter shortly; for I design immediately to qualify you for preaching to the Indians in Proconchi; and when you shall be well acquainted with this language, the members of the academy will send two deputies of their company to offer you a place among them: of this I can assure you.'

"At so flattering an assurance, I manifested so much desire to learn Proconchi, that, without loss of time, he instructed me in the first principles. I profited so well by his instructions, and applied so closely to study, that in three months I became capable of composing in that tongue an exhortation which I learned by heart, and had the boldness to deliver in public; in which I was so successful, that the Indian connoisseurs looked on me from that moment as one who knocked at the door of the academy.

"If you ask me the nature of the Proconchi idiom, I will answer you that it is a tongue which has its declensions and its conjugations, and that you may learn it as easily as Greek or Latin; more easily, indeed, because it is a living tongue, which one may possess in a short time by conversing with Indian purists. For the rest, it is harmonious, and more loaded with figures and metaphors than even our own. If an Indian who prides himself on speaking Proconchi well, desire to make you a compliment, he will employ in it only fantastical singular thoughts, and labored expressions. It is an obscure inflated style, a glowing verbiage, a pompous nonsense; but this is what forms its excellence. It is the tone of the academy of Petapa.

" I had little difficulty in conforming to it, the Biscayan genius being friendly to obscurity. I made such rapid progress in the language of the Indians, that the old curate seeing me qualified worthily to replace him, put me in possession of his cure, and set out for Guatemala, there to pass the rest of his days.

" After his departure I remained master of the parsonage, where I began living in the style of one who holds a good benefice : for till that time, be it said without offence to anybody, Father Estefano, for fear no doubt of turning me from the study of the Proconchi, had taken the trouble of receiving himself the whole of the revenue of the cure, which did not amount to less than two thousand crowns of good Spanish money. This monk, with many good qualities, had one bad one ; he was avaricious. Of this he had made me perfectly sensible by the frugality which I had seen prevail in our repasts, composed almost entirely of butter, cocoa, and detestable liquors. For this reason, the first trouble I conceived I ought to despatch, was that of having a better table, and enlarging the number of my domestics. I took into my service a black whom one of our alcades gave me as a skilful cook, and with whom I was in fact well satisfied.

" This black, whose name was Zamor, had been scullion at the house of a President of the Audience of Guatemala, and had there learned the business of the kitchen. He served up to me every day some new dish which bore ample testimony to his skill and tickled my sensuality. Sometimes he gave me puddings made with Indian corn and fowl or fresh pork, seasoned with chili or long pepper, and sometimes he regaled me with a stewed hedgehog, or occasionally with a sort of lizard which they call iguana, which has black and green scales on its back, and resembles a scorpion."

Father Carambola, remarking at this passage that I was making wry faces, could not help laughing. " Signior Bachelor," said he, " it appears to me that the viands of which I am speaking do not make your mouth water."—" No, I protest to you," replied I, " they are more calculated to turn an honest man's stomach than to flatter his palate : I will never have Zamor for my cook."—" Nevertheless," replied Father Cyril, " I assure you that these ragouts are not so bad as you imagine ; and I am persuaded that if you had once come across them,

you would render them more justice. A hedgehog and an iguana well cooked and seasoned have an exquisite flavor; any one eating of either would suppose it a rabbit. The Spaniards, as well as the Indians, conform very generally to such food in the country of Guatemala. The principal officers of the Chancery prefer them to quails, partridges, or pheasants."
—"It is all very well," returned I; "there is good reason for saying that one must not argue upon tastes."

"God be praised !" cried the friar, as if he had not already sufficiently extolled his hedgehogs and lizards; "I protest to you that I found these viands delicious. I also ate with pleasure both land and sea turtles; and it was to me a feast of the gods, when with this ambrosia I drank nectar, that is to say, a drink called by the Indians Chicha, composed of water and the juice of the sugar-cane, with a little honey. Nevertheless, excellent as was this beverage, I became disgusted with it when I found that, in order to give it strength, they throw into the vessel in which it is made some leaves of tobacco, and sometimes a live toad, and that it often causes the death of people who have drunk too freely of it. I therefore renounced Chicha as soon as I found in what manner it was made, and stuck to other drinks, which it must be acknowledged were not equal to the wines which are drunk in Europe; but thanks be to Heaven, one gets accustomed to everything.

"With my cook Zamor, I had besides four other domestics: one who waited at table, and did my errands to the town; another whose employment was to go out to collect my tithes, which consisted in eggs, poultry, and a certain sum of money which was regularly paid me every month by the regidors; a gardener, with a valet and a groom; for I kept a mule to carry me when I went to preach in a little village about three leagues from Petapa. This little village, which was called Mixco, produced me a great revenue. I went there often, and never without bringing home half a dozen fowls at least, with cocoa to make my chocolate, without counting the money given me for my mass and my sermons: for, notwithstanding I had to do with auditors very little capable of deriving advantage from my exhortations, I did not fail always to mount the pulpit and preach to some purpose; so that my presbytery was well furnished with provisions.

"As each village is dedicated to some saint, whose festival

the inhabitants celebrate during eight days, the patron of Mixco is highly honored during his octave, and the curate has every reason to be satisfied with the offerings he receives. The brethren of St. Hyacinth rejoice in a manner which, in my opinion, deserves to be succinctly detailed to you. On the first day, the men, with the prettiest girls in the village, dress themselves out in fine silks or linen stuffs, ornament themselves with feathers and ribbons, and join together in well-concerted dances, which they execute to perfection. But, what I by no means approve, and can only be pardoned in Indians who are still in idolatry, is that they begin dancing in the church, and continue it in the churchyard. After this, the rest of the eight days are passed in banquet, prodigally supplied with Chicha, of which all the guests drink till they are ready to burst.

CHAPTER VI.

FATHER CYRIL MAKES HIMSELF BELOVED AND ESTEEMED BY THE INDIANS—INTERESTING HISTORY OF TWO BROTHERS AND A SISTER—HE PREACHES IN PROCONCHI, AND BY THE BEAUTY OF HIS SERMONS OBTAINS A PLACE IN THE ACADEMY OF PETAPA.

" I FEATHERED my nest then pretty well, both at Mixco and Petapa. Though I was obliged to send three hundred crowns a year to our house at Guatemala, there still remained with me money enough not to allow me cause for envying the happiness of the monks of Peru, who hold benefices in the Indian villages, and keep all they can get. I was neither less rich nor less happy. Besides that I could have paid my convent five, instead of three hundred crowns, I began to carry on a little underhand traffic in merchandise, a thing which I confess was a little against my vow of poverty; but what would you have? I imitated other monks, who had good cures like myself. Such is the effect of bad example.

" The Indians of the environs of Guatemala are a mild, gentle kind of people : all they desire is to live in peace. They would love even the Spaniards themselves, if these would treat them with humanity. We must, however, except a species of black slaves who live in the Indigo farms. These are ferocious and formidable fellows. Though they have no other weapon than a small lance, they have the boldness to face a wild bull in the height of his fury, and to attack crocodiles in the river, which they do not quit till they have killed them : such slaves sometimes make their masters tremble. As for the Indians of Petapa, I pronounce them the best in America : as polished as the others are clownish, they form together a mild society, in which reigns a spirit of concord and fraternal amity. But what

246

is the most to be admired, is their good faith and integrity. Of this I will recount to you an instance.

"A noble and rich Indian of Petapa died, and left a tolerably large succession to his daughter and two sons. The eldest of the two brothers undertook to divide it into three equal portions. When he had done so, he desired his brother and sister to take their choice. 'You are our elder,' answered they; 'it is for you to choose.'—'No,' replied he, 'since I have made the lots, it is right that you should take which of them you please.' The younger brother and the sister each chose a lot, and the third remained to the elder. There was in this latter a heavy coffer, in which had been contrived a secret drawer, where he discovered by chance a thousand pieces of gold. Having made this discovery, he invited his brother and sister to a repast, towards the end of which he served them up all the money in a dish, saying, 'Here is what I found hid unknown to me in a coffer, which fell to my lot; we must share it—justice demands it.'

"I lived in the most perfect union with these Indians, who loved me, Spaniard though I was. I amused myself with them every day. I conversed freely, and played at cards with their wives, of whom they are not jealous, and who for the most part are so sprightly, that it is a pleasure to hear them speak Proconchi. The members of the Academy of Petapa consult them too very often; and when in the conferences of these gentlemen their opinions are divided upon any word, they say, 'We must consult the women on the subject.' This proves that the Academy are very gallant.

"The Indian ladies, then, decide, and their decisions are respected, sometimes even in contempt of the grammar of Father Estefano. I knew, among others, a lady at whose house the choice spirits of the town assembled, and whom they listened to as an oracle: she expressed herself with wonderful elegance, and decided so judiciously on all works of taste, that she never found any to contradict her. This lady was widow of a noble Indian, who had left her wealth enough to live in a manner suitable to her quality. I went often to see her, and met at her house, almost every day, members of the Academy, whose conversation I turned to account. I retained everything remarkable which I heard them say. I took notice of their turns, of their expressions; and I remarked that these

men had a mode of thinking superior to that of ordinary persons.   In fine, by listening to them I finished learning all the
delicacies of the Proconchi language.

"When I thought I possessed the spirit and the refinements
of it, I was bold enough to wish to preach before the whole
body of the Academy.   But, in order to be sure of pleasing
these masters of the Indian language, I bethought myself of
an expedient which crowned my boldness with success.   Among
the books which Father Estefano, on returning to Guatemala,
had left to render me perfect in Proconchi, I found besides
his dictionary and grammar, a collection of discourses recently
pronounced at the Academy of Petapa : I turned it over ; and
fishing, as one may say, in troubled waters, extracted the most
brilliant phrases, the newest modes of speaking, and composed
from them a sermon which struck the members of the Academy
with wonder.   'There was something very fine in it,' said they
one to the other ; 'this Jacobin says some very good things,
and in a style marked with our stamp.'

"What shall I say?   These gentlemen were so satisfied
with my diction, or, if you will, with their own, that at their
first meeting they resolved to associate me in their glorious
labors.   They sent to announce to me this honor by two of
their deputies.   I had again recourse to my collection in order
to compose a discourse, and the day of my reception being
arrived, I returned my acknowledgments to my new brethren,
delivering myself with effrontery to their very beards in their
own phrases."

CHAPTER VII.

FATHER CYRIL was about to continue his narration, but I
first asked him a question. "You have," said I, "been just
extolling the minds of the Indians of Petapa, without saying
anything of their beauty. This does not prepossess me in
favor of their charms."—"They are not less handsome than
those of Mexico," replied he, "nor less neatly dressed, but
their habiliments are of a different kind.

"They wear instead of a shift, a species of surplice, which
they call guiapil, which descends from the shoulders below the
waist, with very large sleeves, so short that they do not cover
more than half the arms. This guiapil is ornamented on the
stomach with some work of feathers or of cotton, which rather
serves to set off the bosom than to hide it. With that they
have bracelets and earrings, but no covering on the head; their
hair is only turned up with silken fillets. They go with the
legs bare, and wear shoes fastened with a large ribbon.

"I speak to you only of rich women or those of quality, for
the others go barefoot, and have but a simple mantle of wool,
which they wrap round them; a thing which at first view does
not dazzle the eyes. Nevertheless, though these have not a
seducing appearance at the first glance, they do not fail to
make their conquests. There are some noble Indians and
Spaniards of capricious taste who court them : they go secretly
to see them in their thatched cabins, where all the dwelling
consists in one low room, in the middle of which these Indians
make a fire for dressing their food: and as there is no vent

in the roof of the cabin, the smoke necessarily fills the whole room in such a manner, that it may be said of these gallants, that being there as in an oven, they are smothered with love and smoke.

" Let us return to the wives of the principal Indians.   These inhabit houses better built and better furnished.   When they go to church or on a visit, they wear a veil of Holland, Spanish or Chinese linen, which covers the head, and descends to the ground ; but when they return home, they let down the upper part of the guiapil so effectually as to leave the neck and shoulders bare.   It is true that, either through decency or affectation, they speedily replace the guiapil if a man come to visit them.   I say from affectation, for they are not naturally either cruel or hypocritical.   Far from arming themselves against the young men who court them, they usually give them fair play.   In short, they are gallant like the other Indians ; but at the same time very superstitious.   Whatever inclination they may feel for a man who courts them, they will not yield to his love until they have consulted the flight and the song of birds, or made observations on the meeting of animals who are passing along the roads.   If from these they draw a favorable omen, the gallant has everything to hope for, instead of which, if they conceive from them an unfavorable presage, he has only to seek his fortune elsewhere.

" Some of these Indians carry superstition farther, and resort to magic to secure the success of their enterprises.   I remember that one of them, wishing to inspire with love an Indian girl, whose heart he knew to be otherwise engaged, composed an amorous philter which rendered her unfaithful."

" What is it you are saying, Father Cyril ? " interrupted I, laughing.   " You are using the traveller's license ; you are re- lating fables."—" There is no disputing facts," said he, " and what I relate to you is one of which I was myself a witness.   I can tell you, moreover, that the philter was composed of the powder of the colibri.   The colibri," added he, " is a bird of brilliant plumage, and nearly about the size of a starling. They put it to dry in the sun, then pulverize it ; and this fatal powder, mixed in wine or any other liquor, conveys the poison of love into the heart of the person whom it is desired to in- flame, according to the intentions of him who performs the charm.   Do not give faith, unless you please, to what I have told you; but it is certain that several Indians have assured me of having seen this powder used with success. The woman who employed it so efficaciously, herself avowed it to me."

In vain the monk would have had me seem persuaded of this, in vain he protested that nothing was more true; I could not believe him. Nevertheless, it will be seen in the event, by an adventure which happened to myself, that the story of the Indian lover detached from his mistress by sorcery, might probably not be a fable.

"To finish describing to you the Indians of Petapa," pursued Father Cyril, "I must tell you that they profess the Catholic religion only to outward view. What passes their comprehension meets in them with nothing but incredulity. My efforts to convert them were useless, though I employed for that purpose the most energetic expressions in the Proconchi language. These intractable and superstitious spirits adore in secret their idols of stone and wood. They preserve in their houses with religious care a toad or some similar animal, to the life of which they firmly believe that their own is attached.

"When I say they adore their idols in secret, it is to be understood that they would not dare to offer them public worship. The Spaniards prevent this, and treat their false divinities very roughly when they have the misfortune to fall into their hands. But of this these idolaters take particular care. They generally hide them in some cavern, of which they close up the mouth, and in which they assemble at night, as in a pagod, to adore them. If, unfortunately for them, their pastors be informed of these nocturnal meetings, it is for him to put them in order; which he can do by demanding assistance from the alcades and regidors, who, to show themselves zealous Catholics, fail not to supply him with Spanish soldiers to escort him and demolish their idols. But expeditions of this kind are not without danger to an ecclesiastic, who by means of them puts himself in the way of obtaining the crown of martyrdom by having the Indians tear him to pieces.

"So glorious an end is not to the taste of all pastors. Father Estefano had always taken care to avoid it. He contented himself with preaching the word of God to his parishioners, without going to destroy their idols; and I believe I should have done very well following his example, instead of

yielding to the temptation which one day assailed me of deserving a place in the martyrology. Having learned that at
the foot of a mountain between Mixco and Petapa, there was a
cavern which concealed an idol, and in which were frequently
held secret meetings, I gave information of it to the alcades,
bravely offering myself to destroy the idol. These officers
praised my zeal and courage, and furnished me with an escort
of twenty well-armed Spaniards, at the head of whom I marched
proudly towards the cavern in the middle of the night.

"We found it lighted up with a prodigious quantity of wax
candles, and saw about five hundred Indians, men and women,
some of whom were offering incense to the idol, whilst others
danced, singing praises to it. This idol was nothing more
than a large painted dragon, elevated on an altar of stone.
Our arrival disturbed the festival; and the appearance of my
soldiers, who had all their swords in their hands, terrified the
idolaters so much, that, far from putting themselves in a posture
for defending their divinity, they thought of nothing but making their escape.

"I ordered that they should not be opposed in their flight,
and that no harm should be done them. I gave over the
dragon to my escort, who broke it into a thousand pieces.
After this I returned in triumph to Petapa, looking on this fine
exploit as a very important service rendered to the church."

CHAPTER VIII.

CONSEQUENCES OF THIS GLORIOUS EXPEDITION—OF THE DANGER
IN WHICH FATHER CYRIL FOUND HIMSELF, AND OF THE PRU-
DENT COURSE HE TOOK TO EXTRICATE HIMSELF FROM IT—HE
RETIRES TO HIS MONASTERY—HE RECEIVES AN ORDER FROM
HIS PROVINCIAL TO GO AND PREACH AT MEXICO.

"So vigorous an execution made a great noise in the country. Those of the Indians who were really converted did not disapprove of it ; but the others, by far the more numerous, viewing it as a sacrilege which they ought not to leave unpunished, held a council together, in which it was decreed that I should, one fine night, be assassinated in my house.

"All their measures were taken for striking this blow, and my ruin was inevitable, had not Heaven interposed. But the objects which it had in view for me engaged its bounty not to abandon me, and permitted that on the day before that appointed for the execution of the project, I should receive an anonymous letter, apprising me of my danger. This charitable information came to me from an Indian woman, to whom one of the conspirators had revealed the business, and who, though an idolatress, had preferred the life of an honest man to the revenge of her idol.

"On the receipt of this letter, which appeared to me deserving of attention, I made up my bundle, composed of all my money ; and without saying a single word to my servants which could cause them to suspect my design, I mounted my mule, and took the road to Guatemala, without choosing to be accompanied but by my guardian angel, who, if he saved me from the danger which threatened me, did not preserve me from fear. I looked a thousand times behind me to see if any were following, and I was finally fortunate enough to arrive safe and sound at our monastery.

"I related to our prior my holy prowess, which he praised less than my flight. 'Father Cyril,' said he, 'to console you for having lost the crown of martyrdom which the Indians designed you, I have an agreeable piece of news to announce to you. There is wanting in Mexico a monk of our order who has a talent for preaching: the Jesuits and Cordeliers at the present moment take the lead of us in that city. We have need of some powerful person to maintain the balance, and we have cast our eyes on you. Our provincial, on the report which I have made him of the applause which your sermons received at Guatemala, is desirous of sending you to Mexico. I was on the point of writing to you by his orders, to recall you from Petapa: you could not have come more critically in time.'

"This news gave me so much the more pleasure, as I wished to see Mexico; and Father Cyril found his vanity not a little flattered by the choice which had been made of him, to go and dispute the honor of the pulpit in this fine city against such formidable rivals. I therefore prepared myself for obeying the orders of the father provincial, who, in a conversation we had together before my departure, particularly recommended that I should labor to sustain by my sermons the good name which the preachers of our order have always had in the Indies. His reverence then assured me that my toils should be, one day, well recompensed ; and joining to this assurance a letter which he wrote in my favor to the father prior of our convent at Mexico, he gave me his benediction, with which I took the road to this great town. I had for my guide an Indian who was perfectly acquainted with the road, and who had the address to enable me to avoid the negroes, who inhabit the mountains and murder travellers. Without him these honest folks would perhaps have carried off my tithes and Signior Don Francisco de Castro's gold watch: at the same time I had to pay him very handsomely for his trouble.

"Having arrived at Mexico, I went to wait upon the prior, who is called Father Athanasio, and delivered him my provincial's letter. Before he unsealed it he very respectfully kissed it. He read it to himself with attention, and I observed that while reading it he appeared surprised and satisfied. 'Father Cyril,' said he, after having finished it, 'even though this letter were not from our reverend father provincial, it contains so handsome an eulogium on your merit, that I could not omit receiving you as a man sent by Heaven to preserve the glory of our order. We cannot sufficiently rejoice at your arrival: for in fact,' pursued he, 'the Jesuits have taken the wall in Mexico: that is certain. But I trust they will soon yield it to us: if this letter may be believed, you are about to deprive them of the prize of preaching.'

"I returned to this compliment a reply as modest as that was flattering; and after a rather long conversation, in which the prior evinced a very great impatience to hear me preach, I prepared to comply with his desires. I mounted the pulpit after a week, and from my very first sermon made a noise in the town. What shall I say to you? This noise is daily augmenting, in spite of those who are jealous of it, and I have become the fashionable preacher of the day."

CHAPTER IX.

WHAT DON CHERUBIN AND FATHER CYRIL DID AFTER HAVING MUTUALLY RECOUNTED THEIR ADVENTURES—DESCRIPTION WHICH THE LATTER GAVE OF HIS PRIOR—DON CHERUBIN IS RECEIVED WITH PLEASURE—WHAT TOOK PLACE AT THIS VISIT.

WHEN Father Cyril had finished his relation, I expressed the joy I felt at finding him, after so long an absence, so honored and esteemed in the capital of Mexico. I congratulated him on the success of his sermons without telling him what I thought of them, or rather by telling him what I did not think ; for I praised him even so highly as to call him Cicero's orator, a thing for which some reader may reproach me. "Signior Bachelor," he may say, "we ought to flatter no one, and particularly our friends." Agreed : but I reply that it is not necessary to be unseasonably sincere and that it is better to approve of the praises which one's friend receives, than to tell him brutally that he does not deserve them. Besides, Father Cyril had taken his mould, and my candor would not have been less useless than indiscreet if I had undertaken to give him advice.

When I had complimented him on his reputation of being a great preacher, I asked him if he was content with his prior's behavior to him. "Is he properly sensible," said I, "of his happiness in having you? How does he act towards you?"—"The best in the world," replied the Biscayan. "I have every reason to praise Father Athanasio : he honors me with his confidence ; he consults me, and causes me to enter into a thousand little details which prove he has a friendship for me. Moreover, he never invites any party in which I am not included. If he regale seculars in his apartment, he sends for me to help him to do the honors of the table with my conversation, which, without vanity, is not of the dullest. If we go to visit the nuns, I am his companion. In a word, I partake of all his pleasures."

"As far as I see," replied I, "this Father Athanasio appears a virtuoso."—"Without doubt," replied Carambola. "To give you a portrait of him, I will first tell you that he is not yet two and forty years of age. For his person, he is one of those portly friars whom one cannot see passing along the street without admiring their good mien. The ladies of Mexico are delighted when he visits them. Besides that he has a most amusing wit, he may be said to be one who sings well, and is thoroughly acquainted with music. Moreover, he has a talent for poetry which ought not to pass for nothing. I must," continued he, "make his reverence known to you."—"You will do me pleasure," said I: "such a monk appears to me to be a very desirable acquaintance."—"Very well," said he, "I will do it for you immediately." At the same time he took me by the hand, and conducted me to the apartment of Father Athanasio. While going there, I said to myself: "Let us now see whether the prior of the Jacobins of Mexico be as well off for furniture as the guardian of the Cordeliers of Xalapa. I ought not to doubt it: Saint Dominic is richer than Saint Francis."

In effect, Father Athanasio had a floor of eight or nine rooms, all ornamented with pictures and magnificently furnished. The most beautiful ornaments of Mechoacan feathers shone on all sides. There were seen tables covered with silk, and buffets ornamented with vases of the finest porcelain of China or Japan. In short, my eyes were dazzled by the beauty of all that struck them, and which would have certainly done honor to the palace of a cardinal. We found the prior amusing himself with singing and touching the strings of a lute. "My reverend father," said my conductor, "your reverence will allow me to introduce to you one of my best friends, Don Cherubin de la Ronda, the illustrious governor of the young Count de Gelves, son of the Viceroy." Father Athanasio, on my friend Carambola's account, showed me all imaginable politeness. He even regaled me with a collation, during which he talked of nothing but music and concerts.

This friar gave me by these means to understand which was his accessible side; and making my attack accordingly, "Reverend father," said I, "my friend has praised your voice to me in such terms as have inspired me with a violent desire

17

to hear you sing : I can hardly believe that he has not overdone his praise."—" You shall judge for yourself," replied the prior modestly. " You have reason to mistrust Father Cyril : besides that he has a great friendship for me, he is not very sensible to harmony." At these words he rose to take his lute, and without ceremony began playing, singing at the same time a song of which he had himself, he informed us, composed the air and the words. In this song a lover was complaining of a cruel mistress, and essaying to soften her by touching expressions. It was amusing to see how the friar entered into the spirit of the song, and vented the most tender sounds, rolling his eyes at the same time with the languor of a lover, making a most singular contrast with his religious habiliments and emblems of mortification.

" Signior Don Cherubin," said Father Cyril, when the prior had done singing, " you see what are the innocent recreations of his reverence. What do you think of his voice ? Do you not perceive in it an infinite softness, and would it not be a murder not to exercise it ? " I took care not to tell him, in reply, that the voice of priest and monk ought to be devoted to the praises of the Almighty, because persons who preach to others are not fond of having sermons addressed to themselves ; on the contrary, I approved very highly of the prior's amusements. I made him repeat his song, telling him that I was charmed with his voice, his music, and his poetry. I did not, however, fail to impart to Father Cyril, in private, my opinion on this subject. He took the part of his prior, and to make the apology of the American monks in two words, said : " If the monks of this country have not faces which speak of mortification, be not therefore prejudiced against them : they are not the less virtuous because they have not an air of hypocrisy."

After spending the rest of the day with these two friars, I left them with a promise of returning occasionally to see them, and begging them to honor me with their visits when their affairs should call them to Mexico.

WE FOUND THE PRIOR AMUSING HIMSELF WITH SINGING
AND TOUCHING THE STRINGS OF A LUTE.

CHAPTER X.

DON CHERUBIN GOES TO SEE THE PENITENTS OF THE DESERT,
AND RECOGNIZES AMONG THEM DON GABRIEL MONCHIQUE, THE
SEDUCER OF DONNA PAULA—OF THE CONVERSATION WHICH
THESE TWO CAVALIERS HAD TOGETHER, AND HOW THEY SEPA-
RATED—IMPRESSION MADE ON DON CHERUBIN'S MIND BY THE
RECITAL OF THE MANNER IN WHICH HIS WIFE HAD BEEN CAR-
RIED OFF.

ONE evening, being in a company where the conversation
turned upon the beauty of the environs of Mexico, it was stated,
and every one agreed in the opinion, that the most agreeable
of all was that which is called the Solitude of the Desert. As
I had never yet been there, though I had frequently heard the
place highly praised, I resolved to go thither the following day
along with Toston, who was no less curious than myself to see
this spot. We accordingly repaired to it, mounted on two
mules from the stables of the Viceroy. In a very short time
we had completed the three leagues, the distance between the
town and this solitary abode, which well deserves to be described. It is a mountain environed with rocks, and on which
there is a convent built by the Barefooted Carmelites, to retire
to as to a hermitage.

There are at the base, and all around this mountain, a number of chapels, all of which have gardens filled with flowers
and fruits. There even run from the rock in many places,
fountains, which, together with the shade of palm-trees, render
this solitude delightful. The interior of each of these chapels
is ornamented with paintings in fresco, which represent the
different kinds of torments suffered by martyrs; and, as if it
were not enough to expose to the view of the world scourges,
hair shirts, and other instruments of mortification, to intimate
the life of penance led in this desert, there are also to be seen

259

in each of the chapels a kind of hermits, who are employed in lacerating their skin with rods of iron wire; a great attraction to the people of Mexico, who are as fond of horrid spectacles as the English themselves.

These self-scourged penitents pass for saints. I considered them with admiration; and, having observed that several of the spectators gave them money in order to be remembered in their prayers, I was desirous of imitating them, and with this intention approached a chapel to present a pistole to the holy personage who was there flagellating himself with great severity; but imagine what was my astonishment at recognizing in this miserable hermit, all disfigured as he was, Don Gabriel de Monchique, the seducer of Donna Paula. I doubted at first the evidence of my eyes, and said to Toston: " Examine that penitent attentively; do you not recognize in him the features of the perfidious Don Gabriel? Is it an illusion?"—" No, sir," replied he, " you do not deceive yourself; it is indeed your enemy. I cannot mistake, though he is so covered with blood as to make the recognition barely possible."

While I ran my eyes over this miserable wretch, the sight of whom, while it awaked my vengeance, forbade me to gratify it, he placed himself by my side. As soon as he knew me, he threw to the ground the scourge with which his cruel hand was armed against himself; and presenting me his breast all covered with blood: " Don Cherubin," said he, " strike; revenge the outrage which I have committed on you: far from wishing to screen myself from your blows, I entreat them as a favor; by piercing my heart, you will deliver me from the remorse with which I am eternally tortured, or rather from the furies which for the last two years have incessantly pursued me."— " What have you done with my wife?" cried I, hastily interrupting him; " what has become of her? Speak, wretch, inform me of her situation."—" Donna Paula is no more," replied he; " a month after our flight she was snatched from me by death. Scarcely had I tasted the fruit of my crime, ere Heaven punished me for it. If you would know more," added he, " enter my chapel, and I will inform you of all you can desire to learn: it is also due to justice that I should vindicate Donna Paula, who was not culpable." Thus addressing us, he drew Toston and myself into the chapel, and continued in the following terms:

"Listen to me, Don Cherubin; I am about to make you a faithful recital of the seduction and rape of your wife. When I had formed the design of winning her, I gained over, by means of presents, her old attendant, Antonia, who informed me that Donna Paula loved you too sincerely to become unfaithful to you. On this, instead of renouncing my silly love, as I ought to have done, I abandoned myself to it in such a degree that I do not hesitate to avail myself of an amorous philter which was made known to me by an old apothecary of Alcaraz, and which was, he informed me, composed of the powder of a certain bird whose species exists in some part of America. As I put no faith in such things, which I treated as mere chimeras, I doubted very much of its success; yet no sooner had Antonia administered some of this powder to her mistress in a cup of chocolate, than the charm operated.

"As soon as I was apprised of this, I took my time and arranged my measures so well, that at the beginning of a very dark night I left Alcaraz with Donna Paula and her servant, unseen by any person about the place. We arrived before day at the village of Villa Verde, distant about two leagues, where we concealed ourselves in the castle of a gentleman with whom I had contracted an acquaintance, who was a relation of Don Ambrosio de Lorca, and, consequently, an enemy to Don Manoel and yourself. This gentleman pleased himself with the idea of lending us an asylum, and of favoring an action which would dishonor you both. We remained about a fortnight in our retreat, without entertaining any apprehension from your prequisitions, since we were with a cavalier whose domestics were all discreet and faithful. After this, taking the road to the coast near Carthagena by night, we arrived at a small port, and embarked on board a vessel which I had freighted for Genoa, my own country, where I proposed to conceal my prey; but Heaven, tired with the profligacy of my life, would not permit the accomplishment of my design : Donna Paula fell ill and died on the passage, in spite of all that could be done to save her.

"This melancholy event," continued Monchique, "induced me to look into myself. I reproached myself with my crime, of which I now saw all the enormity, and took a resolution to expiate it, if possible, by devoting the remainder of my days to the rudest penance. Arrived at Genoa, I sold with this design

all my effects, and this is the use I made of the money I by
that means obtained : I gave a part of it to old Antonia, to
enable her to go and mourn in an establishment of female penitents the part she had acted in the seduction of her mistress ; I
paid and dismissed my servants, and after having distributed the
the rest of my property to the poor, I set out from Genoa in the
habit of a hermit, determined to stop in the first wood or place
which might appear to me adapted for the residence of an
anchorite ; and that I speedily found.

"But, Don Cherubin," continued he, "I believe it is not
necessary to tell you more, nor to relate to you by what means
I was brought from Italy to Mexico ; in that you can have no
interest : enough that I have revealed that which is connected
with your own affairs ; and I think I have said sufficient to excite your vengeance. Plunge, then," added he, presenting me
his breast, "plunge your sword into the heart of a miserable
wretch, who can only appear a very monster in your eyes."—
"No, no," replied I, "whatever injury you have done me, I
cannot resolve to revenge myself by assassination. I choose
rather to leave you in this desert, that by long and rigorous
penance you may obtain the mercy of Heaven."

So saying, I left the chapel and resumed the road to Mexico,
my mind filled with the most serious reflections upon this adventure. They were of a melancholy kind when I considered
that Donna Paula had not swerved from her duty but through the
means of a most detestable artifice, and was therefore excusable
in what had happened. Nevertheless, there arose in my mind
a secret joy when I remembered that by her death I was placed
in a situation to aspire to the possession of Donna Blanca. As
for Toston, who found in this adventure nothing but what was
calculated to inspire joy, his ideas were all of a pleasing kind.
When he saw me lamenting over the fate of Donna Paula, he
talked to me of Salzedo's daughter : and, all things considered
both on the part of joy and grief, the former preponderated.

CHAPTER XI.

I was returning with my valet from the desert, and had my
mind still full of what I had been told by Don Gabriel de
Monchique, when I had a rather singular rencounter, which dissipated for a time the melancholy in which I was plunged anew,
on reflecting on the tragical end of my unfortunate wife, whom
I pitied from the bottom of my heart. Stopping in a village, or
rather in a small town, to rest the horses, I was surprised by
the sight of a great number of persons assembled round the
door of the parsonage, so I judged the house to be, as it immediately joined the church. I desired Toston to go and inquire into the cause of the tumult. He accordingly went, and
returned in a moment after, crying out like a madman: "Oh,
sir, a most laughable adventure has just taken place: the
curate of this parish has recognized his wife in the habit of a
pilgrim to whom he was giving alms, and these people are waiting to see her come out."

My valet again burst into laughter about this event, and
begged me to stay like the rest, to see what would be the
result. I, however, ordered him to be silent, not choosing that
he should make a fool of himself in a village where it was probable I might be known. I fell into reflection on this subject.
What a difference, thought I, is there between this man's fortune and my own. I have lost a wife, without the slightest
hope of ever seeing her again, while the priest had met with his

at a moment when he had not the slightest expectation of it. Curious to be informed of this history more in detail, I made my way through the crowd and desired to speak with the curate. They at first made some difficulty about admitting me, but my dress and equipage catching the attention of those who came to open the door, my request was ultimately complied with. On entering, I saw in a rather large-sized saloon all the principal people of the village assembled round a venerable pastor, whom they were endeavoring to persuade that the pilgrim was not his wife; and that she even did not know, and had never seen him.

I approached the pastor, who was in absolute despair that the pilgrim would not acknowledge him. He rose as I advanced, and, finding no doubt my countenance prepossessing, entreated me to listen to him; and this I readily assented to, addressing to him at the same time some few words of consolation, calculated to inspire him with hope. He received my compliments with his eyes full of tears, and replied : " My misfortune, sir, is this. It is now about fifteen years since, travelling with my wife, whom you see here surrounded by my friends, and who now disowns me, we encountered a dreadful storm. Our vessel was shattered into a thousand pieces, and I should have fallen a victim to the fury of the winds and waves, but for the peculiar interposition of Providence. After having been long tossed about the surge, which one moment gave me to see the very depths of the ocean, and at another raised me to the skies, I had the good fortune to discover an empty boat, which, like myself, was driving at the mercy of the storm. I got into it. Although all was dark, I by accident discovered a pair of oars, which I immediately seized, returning thanks to Heaven ; and, without an idea of which way I was going, continued rowing for two or three hours, until I at last perceived that the sea had grown more calm, and that my boat was aground. While awaiting the day, I put up a thousand prayers to Heaven for the safety of my wife and two children who had embarked with me. Scarcely had the morning dawned, ere my surprise was excited at finding myself in a harbor filled with numerous vessels. Doubtless Providence had conducted my boat, and watched over my days. Some sailors who perceived me from afar came to my assistance. They were much astonished at seeing me escape from such a furious tempest. They pitied my situation, and lent me some articles of dress, for which I gladly exchanged the wet clothes I wore.

" Saved from this frightful peril, I entered the church, and offered up my heart to God. I was firmly resolved never more to embark on board a ship. I deeply regretted, however, the loss I had sustained of a wife who was so dear to me, and of two children whom I tenderly loved. After inquiring of a number of travellers whether there were any news of the vessel called the Shepherd's Star, and having heard that all had perished, and that I was the only person who had escaped from this cruel wreck, I travelled from port to port, with money which I made of some jewels which remained in my possession, and two rings which I had upon my fingers. Hearing no intelligence whatever of my wife, I came to the resolution of devoting my life to the service of God, since I could never be sufficiently grateful to Him for the mercy He had shown me. I resumed my studies, which I had not yet forgotten, and sometime after entered into a seminary. In about four years I entered into holy orders, perfectly to my satisfaction, and after having some time served this parish, was appointed its pastor. I have now been here six years, and this morning, while giving alms to this pilgrim, I thought that in her features I could recollect those of my wife. The surprise I felt at the moment caused me to utter a cry which brought all my people around me. The pilgrim, terrified at this accident, not knowing to what cause to attribute it, came herself to my assistance. Recovering my senses, and looking more closely at this woman, I caused all the rest to retire, and when alone with her, asked if she were not the daughter of Don Bardo de Mendoza. She admitted that she was, and inquired in her turn how it happened that I knew anything about her. I embraced her, and told her that in me she beheld her unfortunate husband, Don Raxas, escaped by the mercy of God from the fury of the waves. But judge of my astonishment, when, withdrawing herself from my arms, she told me that I was mad, and that she had never been married. She would then have gone out, but I stopped her, and her cries have been the means of attracting the people of the village to my door. Am I not most unhappy," continued the good priest, " not to be recognized by one who was dearer to me than the world ? Gentlemen, I appeal to your judgment."

Curious to see the end of this adventure, I told the curate

that prudence should forbid him to divulge this matter out of
respect to his own character, and that it was requisite to act
with caution under such circumstances; that, if he would permit
me, I would go and speak to this pilgrim in private, and might
by that means discover who she was: to this he consented, and
desired that we should be left together.   I accordingly approached the woman : but what was my astonishment at recognizing, in a pilgrim's dress, Nise, my earliest love.   She was no
less troubled at the sight of me, and inquiring by what chance
I came there, I told her what had been said about her, and that
curiosity had induced me to enter the curate's house.   I exhorted her to tell me the truth.   She replied that it was true
she had never been married, and that she was the daughter of
Don Bardo de Mendoza.   I asked what was her Christian
name.   She told me it was Theresa Nise, and that finding herself unable to continue at service in consequence of a malady
with which she had some time been afflicted, she had taken the
resolution of asking charity in the habit of a pilgrim ; that she
had made up her mind to that course, and that it had afforded
her subsistence.   " But had you not a sister ? " asked I.
" Alas ! yes," said she : " but having been separated from her
in my earliest infancy, at which time she was married, I am
ignorant in what part she is, or whether she be still alive."   I
asked her sister's name.   " Francisca," replied she.   " That is
enough," said I, leaving her.   I then returned to the curate,
who, as soon as he saw me, demanded if this woman were
really his wife ?   I answered that I did not believe she was, and
that her resemblance to his wife had surprised him, and struck
upon his imagination.   " What," I asked, " was the name of
your wife ? "—" Donna Francisca," replied he.   " Well then,"
said I, taking him by the hand, " Come hither, and in this pilgrim embrace your sister-in-law, Donna Theresa Nise."—" My
sister-in-law !   Is it possible," cried the priest, rushing towards
her, " that you should be Nise, of whom my wife has so
frequently spoken ? "   The pilgrim assured him it was so, and
I confirmed her story, stating that I had formerly known her.
To this effect I related to them where I had seen her, saying
nothing, however, of the share which she had had in my affections.   But what was most convincing of all, was that our pilgrim drew forth a register of her baptism from a small box
which she had by her side, and showed it to the priest, who

could now no longer entertain the slightest doubt of the truth, and once more embraced her as his sister-in-law. After being apprised of her circumstances, he told her that they should in future live together, and be only separated by the tomb. The news immediately spread in the village that the pilgrim was the priest's sister-in-law, and that her great resemblance to her sister had been the cause of the mistake.

This adventure appeared to me too singular not to afford it a detail among my memoirs, and I think that my readers will not be displeased with me for having inserted it. I took my leave of the priest, who would not allow me to set out before I had partaken of a frugal collation to which he invited me ; by which means I had an opportunity of witnessing his excessive joy at seeing a sister who had been hitherto unknown to him. His eyes were full of tears, and when he looked at Nise he could not help sighing incessantly at the recollection of his wife. I was much moved with this spectacle, and if I were delighted at see-ing the turn which the affair had taken, I was still more so at the generosity of the worthy pastor. How many are there far more rich than he (his revenue amounting to less than two hundred crowns per annum) who leave their relations in the extreme of indigence, while they have it in their power to relieve them by taking them to their homes, or at least by aiding them to subsist.

The priest, curious to learn to whom he had been speaking, asked who I was. I did not conceal my quality from him, and he consequently evinced the greatest respect for me. He begged me to permit him to come and see me, to which I readily consented. His conduct in taking his sister-in-law into his house appeared so praiseworthy in my eyes, that some time after I procured for him, through the medium of Don Juan de Salzedo, a rich benefice a few leagues from Mexico, in the direction of Petapa, worth two thousand crowns a year.

The curate never ceased to thank me, and manifest his grati-tude for the favor. I have mentioned here the end of this story, because it will not be again adverted to in the course of these memoirs. When I left him I perceived that the good curate's housekeeper looked with an evil eye upon her new hostess : she was the only person who appeared chagrined at the event. I returned with Toston to Mexico ; and had my brain so occupied with this adventure, that I related it immediately on my arrival to Don Juan Salzedo, and totally forgot to mention that in which I was infinitely more interested, and which I afterwards resolved not to omit acquainting him with the next morning.

END OF THE FIFTH PART.

PART THE SIXTH.

CHAPTER I.

DON CHERUBIN, ON HIS RETURN TO MEXICO, GIVES DON JUAN
SALZEDO AN ACCOUNT OF HIS JOURNEY—OF THE JOY WHICH
THE SECRETARY FELT AT FINDING HIM IN A SITUATION TO BE-
COME HIS SON-IN-LAW—OF THE NEW EMPLOYMENT WHICH HE
OBTAINED FOR HIM, AND THE GOOD ADVICE WHICH HE GAVE
HIM.

I WENT in haste to Salzedo, to inform him of the unexpected
rencounter which I had had, and which I had forgotten to give
him an account of on the evening before. I accosted him with
an agitation which gave him to see beforehand that I had some
interesting news to announce to him. "What is the matter,
Don Cherubin," said he, "that you are so agitated? Has anything extraordinary happened to you?"—"Yes, Signior," replied I, "and you have little notion of the astonishing recital I
am about to make you." At the same time I gave him a detail
of what had passed in the desert between Monchique and
myself.

Don Juan heard me without interruption; after which, embracing me with transport, "How agreeable to me is this
news!" cried he. "The obstacle which opposed the repose of
my life is then removed. Nothing can now prevent us from
joining the ties of blood to those of friendship. I am at the
height of my wishes. In talking to you thus, I suppose that
for my daughter, *tuum semper sauciat pectus amor :* for if, since
you have refrained from seeing her, your heart has become
engaged elsewhere, it would be melancholy for her to have a
husband whose affections she would not possess."

I protested to Salzedo that I had not changed my sentiments, and hereupon he again promised me the hand of Donna Blanca. I returned him, as may be supposed, the thanks which I owed to a man who, while he had in his power to marry his daughter to some lord of the court, or to some contador mayor, did not disdain my alliance, or rather sought it with as much ardor as if he would have derived considerable advantage from it.

I expressed my gratitude to him in terms which gave him to understand that I was still more touched by the affection he evinced for me than by Blanca's dowry, great as it was. " I am persuaded," replied he, " of the sincerity of your sentiments ; and if I only consult my own desires, you should be in less than a week the husband of my daughter ; but a reason which I will state to you obliges me to defer this marriage for some months. Don Alexis will soon put on the virile robe, I mean that he will no longer have a governor. I wait for that time in order to procure you a more important post than that which you now hold, and, permit me to say, more worthy of a cavalier who is to be my son-in-law.

" In the meantime," added he, " I permit you again to see my daughter as before, and to hold with her such conversation as is consistent for two persons who are on the point of binding themselves together by everlasting bonds." I did not neglect this permission. I revisited Blanca, who, receiving me as a lover who had the consent of her father, conceived a little affection for me, at the same time that she inspired me with a great deal for her.

I was anxious to know what new place my destined father-in-law wished I should possess, in order to render me worthy of the honor he was desirous of doing me ; when he, one morning, entered my room with an air of gaiety. " My son," said he (for he no longer called me by any other appellation), " *albo dies notanda lapillo!* You are no longer governor of Don Alexis. This young lord is now master of his actions, and you are my colleague. The Viceroy, to recompense the care you have taken of his son's education, consents that you should take a part in my labors, and share with me the title of principal secretary to the Viceroyalty. It is a favor which I have asked him, and have just obtained. Do not tell me that, not feeling competent to acquit yourself well of the employment, you have a repugnance to accepting it. Let not my functions frighten you: there is no black art in the case. To fill my place, regularity and good sense alone are requisite. Be under no uneasiness on that subject: I will soon qualify you for the most difficult duties."

Upon this assurance, I lost all at once the aversion I hitherto entertained for offices, and told Salzedo that truly my incapacity frightened me, but, since he was not alarmed, I would do what he desired, assured that he would assist me with his advice, or, to speak more justly, that he would guide me by leading strings. As soon as he found me determined on doing as he desired, he conducted me to the Viceroy, to whom he presented me as his colleague and son-in-law. His Excellency approved his design of associating me in the ministry, and of giving me his daughter Blanca in marriage, " not thinking," said this nobleman, in a very obliging way, "that he could find any person more proper than myself to become his son-in-law and his substitute." After this flattering discourse, the Count told me that he exhorted me to take my father-in-law for a model; a thing which he might very well have dispensed with recommending to me, as he knew that I was well acquainted with Salzedo's merits.

" My lord needed not to have persuaded me to walk in your footsteps," said I to the Secretary, when we had quitted the Viceroy. " Who but you could I have proposed to imitate? What guide could, better than yourself, conduct me in the path which you have opened to me, and on which I do not enter without trembling? Alas! I fear that I have a capacity too narrow to admit of my fulfilling your design."—" I repeat to you again," replied Don Juan, "the matter is much easier than you imagine. I have only one advice of the last importance to give you. Be accessible, obliging, and give every one a good reception. An air of gravity does indeed become a person at the head of an office, but there should be in it nothing of pride. ' Gravity and foolish pride,' says a Castilian author, ' are two sisters who very much resemble each other, and who may notwithstanding be distinguished: the one repays the politeness which is shown her; the other is rendered by it only the more insolent.' "

CHAPTER II.

DON CHERUBIN DE LA RONDA SHARES THE FUNCTIONS OF SAL-
ZEDO, AND ACQUITS HIMSELF PERFECTLY WELL—HE MARRIES
DONNA BLANCA—TRAGICAL HISTORY OF THREE INDIAN
BROTHERS.

As soon as I was declared colleague of Don Juan de Salzedo,
the clerks of all the offices of the Viceroyalty came in haste to
pay their respects to their superior; and I received abundance
of visits, the greater part of the gentlemen and principal citizens of Mexico having come to see and form an acquaintance
with a man whom they knew to be the most particular friend of
Salzedo, and designed to be his son-in-law.

In the commencement I went on only step by step, and did
nothing without having first consulted my oracle, that is to say
my senior, who taking a pleasure in instructing me, with which
I was enchanted, daily increased my taste for business. I applied myself to it with so much ardor, that I had soon no need
of a guide. After three months' practice it would have been
said that I had all my life applied to nothing else but what I
was then engaged in. It is true that I devoted my whole attention to copying my model; and I succeeded so well, that
I was called in the town, by way of excellence, Salzedo's ape. I
know not whether I did not surpass my original in the art of
receiving with politeness those persons who had recourse to our
ministry. It is at least certain that Don Juan had nothing to
reproach me with on this score. On the contrary, he said to
me one day, having seen the politeness which I used to a simple
citizen: "Very well, my son; very well: that is the reception
to be given to all who apply to us. Whether their requests be
granted or refused, we ought always to send them away
satisfied with our manners."

I was then without the fault which is often the property of

principal secretaries, and sometimes even of the lowest clerks ; I did not act the petty minister. I will say more; I joined to my mild and civil demeanor, an obliging heart. I did all the services I could, and principally to unfortunate persons, who came to implore my support. By this I acquired the reputation of an honest man, and gained the esteem and friendship of the whole town.

My colleague applauded himself for his work. He was delighted to see me so well justify his choice; and the time at which he proposed to give me his daughter having arrived, he caused me solemnly to espouse her in the cathedral of Mexico, in presence of the Count and Countess de Gelves, and all the officers of the Chancery. The principal gentlemen of the town were also present at this ceremony, and among others, my friend Don Andre Alvarade, and Don Josef de Sandoval, both of them descended in a direct line from those brave captains of Cortez who rendered their names so celebrated. There was also Don Christoval, the grandson of the famous Garcias Holquin, who seized the canoe and person of King Cuahutimoc, successor of Montezuma. In a word, the most distinguished cavaliers were at our nuptials ; forming a brilliant assembly. Blanca and I, after having received the nuptial benediction from the hand of the Archbishop, returned to the palace, and our wedding was celebrated with splendor during three days: feasts, balls, concerts and plays, everything was resorted to to render it magnificent.

When the rejoicings were concluded, I applied myself to business still more closely than before, and my lord soon became so well pleased with me, that he made scarcely any difference between the father and the son-in-law. He consulted us both on the important orders he received from court, and sometimes it happened that my opinion prevailed over that of Don Juan, who, far from showing himself jealous, appeared delighted at it.

The Count placed great reliance in our advice, but he did not always follow it ; and when he had taken a thing into his head, neither one nor the other of us could turn him from his design. I must relate an instance of his obstinacy, from which may be seen what kind of man this nobleman was. He learned one day that in the province of Mechoacan there were three Indian gentlemen, brothers, who dwelt on the borders of a river,

18

in some parts of which gold was found, not unknown to them, since it was ascertained that they had trafficked in gold dust with a merchant of Seville.   The Count de Gelves, prompt to seize the opportunity of augmenting his riches, sent some Spanish soldiers into the country of Mechoacan, with an order to carry off the three brothers, and bring them to Mexico; which was executed with as much exactness as diligence.   The Indians were put into the prison of the palace.   The Viceroy interrogated them himself.   They denied that they had any knowledge of the parts of the river where it was pretended there was gold.   To engage them to the discovery, they at first used mildness and fine promises, afterwards threats, and even torments.   All was useless ; they could not obtain their secret.

If his Excellency would have been prevailed on by Salzedo and myself, he would there have stopped.   He would have sent these unfortunate men back to their country, and contented himself with having used them ill.   Such was our advice, which notwithstanding, judicious as it was, was not followed.   The Viceroy, unable to forego the hope of obtaining gold from these prisoners, took the resolution of writing to the Court to inform the prime minister of what had passed, and to ask him what should be done with the three Indian gentlemen.   The Duke de Olivarez, thinking he had already twenty tons of gold dust, returned a speedy answer to the Count de Gelves, and ordered him without ceremony to have the three brothers beheaded if they persisted in keeping silence.

Although this order appeared cruel to the Viceroy, he did not fail to prepare for the bloody execution, notwithstanding all that my colleague and I could say to him, to prevent him from staining himself with the blood of three men who only persisted in silence because, perhaps, they had nothing to reveal.   He opposed us by two arguments to which we were obliged to yield.   In the first place, he knew the character of the Count Duke, a proud minister, and one who wished to be obeyed without remonstrance : then he was working upon him, to continue him in his post some years beyond the term of his commission, which was near expiring ; for he had now been four years governing Mexico, the Viceroyalty of which is but for five years, but is sometimes prolonged to ten by means of presents which the Viceroy sends to Spain, both to the prime minister and the members of the Indian Council.

When I saw the three unfortunate victims of the Count Duke's and the Viceroy's avarice menaced with a speedy death, I had compassion on them. "My lord," said I to his Excellency, "before the blood of these unfortunate Indians be shed, let us put address in practice, since the torture has been unavailing. I know a Jacobin who is very eloquent, and who speaks the Indian language very well; I think if he were to see the prisoners and to have some interviews with them, he would succeed in getting them to discover what they now conceal with so much obstinacy." "I approve of your idea," said the Count, "and nothing ought to prevent us from following it. Go instantly in search of this monk, and bring him to me: if he can succeed in this business, he has only to be assured that I will get him a bishopric." I immediately got into my carriage and proceeded to the convent of the Jacobins, saying to myself as I went along: "God be praised! if my friend Carambola could become a bishop, it would be laughable enough."

"What brings you here?" said Father Cyril, as soon as he saw me appear. "Is anything here for your service?"—"The business is rather connected with yours," replied I, "since it concerns a mitre which it is desired should be placed on your head."—"I hope you will explain yourself," said he, "for I do not understand you. I do not think myself of the wood from which bishops are made, although persons of our order are every day raised to the episcopal dignity." I made known to the monk the motive of my visit, and on what condition it was promised that he should become a prince of the church. "Oh, I have not got the mitre yet," said he, shaking his head: "what is expected from me is not easy to be performed."— "You deceive yourself, Signior Carneades," replied I, laughing: "you who possess the happy talent of persuading, you who speak so well the Proconchi language; you fear to be unable to induce these prisoners to comply with the intentions of the Court to save their lives!"—"Yes," replied Father Cyril, "I fear that I shall not be able to accomplish it: you do not know the Indians. There are some of them so firm in the resolutions they have taken, that the most cruel execution cannot frighten them. If these have agreed among themselves to die rather than discover what they desire to conceal, it is in vain to indulge the hope of forcing them to it. I will, nevertheless," added he, "make the proof to content the Viceroy; but I much doubt of his Excellency being well satisfied with the event."

I conducted the Jacobin to the palace, and presented him to the Viceroy, who said to him: "Father, you understand the nature of the business. Don Cherubin has, of course, fully acquainted you with it; and as he has very much praised your eloquence to me, I have every reason to flatter myself that you will induce these three Indians to break the silence which they are so obstinate in maintaining, and which will prove fatal to them if they do not attend to your remonstrances. See them, I entreat you; converse with them in their own language; and proceed, if possible, so that they may obey the orders of the king in pointing out the parts of the river in which there is gold. Represent to them that without this indication their ruin is certain; instead of which, if they make it with a good grace, I shall be grateful to them for it, and will confer on them great favors. As to yourself, Father," added he, " be assured that if you succeed, the Court will be mindful of your services."—" My lord," replied Father Cyril, "I am disposed to second your zeal for the king's service, and I will spare nothing to satisfy your Excellency; but I have already told Don Cherubin I know not if my exhortations will have the effect you promise yourself."

At the same time our Jacobin, to show that he desired nothing more than to contribute to the accomplishment of the Count's desire, or rather to a bishop, had himself conducted to the prison where the three Indians were shut up, and re- mained with them four hours. His lordship and myself both drew a favorable omen from so long a visit, and we could not imagine that the Indians would be mad enough to prefer death to life. However, we deceived ourselves. The member of the Petapa Academy returned to us with a mortified air. " These unhappy men," said he, "are not capable of hearing reason, in the despair which possesses them. I have in vain exhorted them to comply with the will of the Court; my dis- course only served to irritate their fury. They persist in maintaining that they are ignorant whether there be gold in this river in which it is pretended that it is found, and they add that if they did know it, they would not acknowledge it, to punish the avidity of the Court and the Viceroy."—" Very well," said his Excellency, irritated at the firmness of the prisoners, "they shall perish, since they desire to appropriate to themselves the riches which belong to the king."

These words of the Count's were followed by a sentence of death which he pronounced against them, in conformity to the sanguinary order of the Court, and that without opposition from the judges of the Chancery, though these officers are entitled to oppose the unjust designs of the Viceroy; a circumstance which is doubtless to be attributed to their fear of displeasing the minister, with whose vindictive spirit they were acquainted.

A scaffold was therefore set up in the market-place, on which the eldest of the three brothers was first made to mount. They were accompanied by Father Cyril, who exhorted them in Proconchi to satisfy the Viceroy, while the executioner stood by with a large cutlass in his hand, of which he studied to make the steel sparkle in the eyes of the unfortunate men whom he menaced: but the Indian, viewing with an eye of firmness the preparations for his execution, and more fatigued than moved by the exhortation of the monk, hastened to offer his throat to the executioner, who inflicted on him the mortal blow.

The second was immediately brought forward, whom the monk would have persuaded that he ought not to follow the example of his elder. " Useless talk ! " said the Indian, who spoke a little Spanish. " My friend," pursued he, addressing the executioner, " do thy duty quickly; consummate the unjust and barbarous work of thy superiors." At these words he laid his head on the block, and the executioner severed it from his body.

There remained to be executed only the youngest of the three brothers. He had no sooner appeared on the scaffold, than there arose a murmur among those who were present, who were very numerous; and this murmur was the effect of the general compassion which the sight of him excited. It is certain that it was impossible to contemplate him without pitying his misfortune. He was a youth of about twenty at most, well made and of good mien. The ladies, who are naturally compassionate, pitied his youth, and wished that he might not imitate his brothers. All the spectators put up prayers for him to Heaven. For my part, I expected, and my lord flattered himself with the hope, that this young Indian would lose his firmness on seeing the steel raised over his head, and the bodies of his brothers extended on the scaffold. Even Father Cyril, in spite of the knowledge which he had of the resolution of the Indians, did not despair of snatching this one from his fate; and to this end, redoubling his efforts, he exhausted the most eloquent discourses with which his book of academical collections supplied him : but he was not more fortunate in this enterprise than he had been at Guatemala in the affair of the Abbess's election; for when the young Indian saw on the ground the heads of his two brothers separated from their bodies, he gathered them up in a transport of rage, and kissing one after the other, " Wait," cried he, in his own language, " wait, my dear brothers; I am about to follow you. Death has nothing but charms for me, since it is about to reunite me to you." The Jacobin, judging by these words that this furious man was determined to perish, ceased to exhort him to live, and abandoned him to the executioner, who struck off his head.

The market-place immediately re-echoed with a cry of horror. The populace burst out in confused murmurs. They pity these three Indians, and their judges are accused of injustice. It is certain that this event did little honor to the Count de Gelves and the prime minister; but I believe that these two noblemen were less mortified at having unjustly caused the death of three gentlemen, than at having committed a bad action to no purpose. As for Don Juan Salzedo and myself, we were really afflicted at it, as was also little Father Cyril, who returned to his monastery as one who had lost a bishopric.

CHAPTER III.

BY WHAT ACCIDENT TOSTON ALL AT ONCE MADE HIS FORTUNE, AND
OF THE LAUDABLE RESOLUTION WHICH HE TOOK SHORTLY AFTER
—DON ALEXIS PARTS WITHOUT REGRET FROM HIS CREOLE,
TOSTON'S WIFE.

ON the day after this tragical event, one of a more joyful
nature happened in the palace. Blandina finding that Don
Alexis had abused her weakness for him, confided in Toston
the secret of her situation, and that domestic immediately
informed the Vice-Queen.

This lady appeared as much astonished as if she ought not
to have foreseen the accident. "Ah, my friend!" cried she,
"what is it thou tellest me? This news pierces my heart. I
should never have thought Blandina capable of forgetting herself so far."—"Madam," replied Toston, "you know that a
tender engagement goes farther than is calculated on. When
the mistress is softened and the lover very warm, reason and
virtue easily lose their influence over them."

"Ah, feeble Blandina!" resumed the Countess, "what hast
thou done? Oughtest thou to have allowed my son liberties
which are only permitted to husbands? But why reproach
thee with it? It is to my imprudence alone that thy misfortune
must be attributed. Alas! it is I who have ruined thee in
exposing thee to the evil under which thou hast fallen. After
this tirade of dolorous exclamations, I should be inconsolable,"
pursued she, "if there were no remedy for this evil. Happily
there is one: yes, doubtless, it is a certain mode of saving
Blandina's honor. We have but to marry her quickly to some
honest man, to thyself, for instance: thou appearest to me to
be suitable for her."—"Madam," replied Toston, "I thank
you for the preference."

"Thou hast reason to thank me," cried the Vice-Queen;

279

" learn, my friend, that thou wilt be doing no bad business in uniting thyself with Blandina.   In the first place, this Creole is very pretty, and I will give her a large dowry ; with that I promise thee a considerable employment, and, what ought not to pass for nothing, my protection."—" Candidly, madam," said Toston with much vivacity, " you dazzle me : I must be an enemy to my fortune if I were to refuse a similar establishment.   The business is done ; I am ready to preserve the honor of Blandina at the expense of my own."

The Vice-Queen, charmed to see the young man in these sentiments, made haste to get him united to the Creole, whose honor, in consequence of this marriage, received no taint, for no one was astonished to see a *valet-de-chambre* to Don Alexis marry an attendant of the Countess.   The best thing for the husband in this precipitate match was that he touched a thousand Spanish pistoles, which the Vice-Queen caused to be told out to him.   Add to this three thousand crowns, which he received from me for services he had rendered me.

When this domestic saw himself so well supplied with money, he took an inclination to return to his own country, and carry thither his wife, of whom he had long been enamoured, and more beloved by her than Don Alexis ; so that he might flatter himself, as well as the young lord, with being in reality the father of Blandina's child.   He communicated his design to me.   " Sir," said he, " though the residence of Mexico is perhaps the most beautiful on the habitable globe, I have resolved to leave it, to go and see once more my country and my parents. My father, who as you know was a schoolmaster in the village of Alcaraz, is still alive, as well as my mother ; if, at least, death has not carried them both off since our separation.   They are not rich, and you will of course judge that the return of a generous son who has made his fortune will be very agreeable to them.

" Besides the pleasure which I propose to myself," continued he, " in rendering their circumstances more easy, I feel that I shall not have less in carrying news of you to Signior Don Manoel de Pedrilla, your brother-in-law and friend, who must be in mortal impatience to hear something of you."—" It is not to be doubted," replied I ; " Don Manoel loves me too well not to be in pain about me ; and, on my side, I should be unworthy of his friendship if I were longer to delay informing him of the happy situation in which I am. It is accordingly my design to make him acquainted with it as early as possible, by a letter which shall contain an ample detail."

"No, no, sir," interrupted Toston; "that is a charge which I take upon myself. I shall better inform them by word of mouth than you can by a letter, of all that has happened to you since your departure from Alcaraz. Besides, I shall be able to reply to the questions which they may desire to ask, and you need not doubt they will ask me an infinite number."—"It is certain," replied I, "that a report from you will be preferable to the longest despatch; but I fear one thing: Don Alexis will not consent to the departure of Blandina."—"Oh yes," returned Toston, "this nobleman's love has considerably relaxed; he begins to detach himself from the Creole; and, walking in his father's steps, in spite of all we have been able to do, he is taken with the sight of an Indian coquette, whose acquaintance one of his pages has procured him. I am delighted that he is grown inconstant, for, without vanity, Blandina has a greater liking for me than for him. She will readily abandon Mexico to follow me to my own country, where we shall live at our ease, bringing up the little family which her fecundity promises."

In reality, Don Alexis, very far from wishing to retain his Creole, received her adieux with an unmoistened eye; but in default of the grief which the young ingrate ought to have had at losing a person who had had so much kindness for him, he made her a present of some jewellery. After this Toston having taken charge of the despatches which I gave him for Don Manoel and my sister, set out with Blandina for Vera Cruz by the muleteer's road.

CHAPTER IV.

OF THE CONFIDENCE WHICH DON JUAN SALZEDO REPOSED IN HIS
SON-IN-LAW, OF A PROJECT FORMED BY THE VICEROY—WHAT
THIS PROJECT WAS, AND HOW IT WAS EXECUTED—THE ARCH-
BISHOP OF MEXICO TAKES THE PART OF THE PEOPLE, AND EX-
COMMUNICATES DON PEDRO AND THE VICEROY—VIOLENCE
WHICH THIS LAST RESORTED TO, IN HAVING HIM CONDUCTED
TO VERA CRUZ.

HAD my father-in-law been ever so little inclined to jealousy,
he could not without pain have seen the gentlemen press as
they did for my friendship in preference to his own; but he
was a man who took pleasure in seeing me esteemed and
honored by every one. Perhaps, also, in attributing to the
consideration they had for him that which they manifested to
me, his vanity might find its account. However this be, he
loved me as if I had been his own son. He had no secrets
with me, and sometimes he confided to me matters of great
importance. This is one of which he one day informed me.

"The Count de Gelves," said he, "begins to lose the hope
of getting his government prolonged. One of his friends, a
courtier, well informed of the measures which several noblemen
are taking at Court to obtain the Viceroyalty of Mexico, informs him that the Count Duke de Olivarez has directed the
king's choice to the Marquis de Serralvo. Another, less avaricious than the Count de Gelves," continued he, "would console
himself, and return satisfied to Madrid with the fish he has
caught: but he cannot moderate his views; he is desirous of
making one good cast of his net. He expects by raising the
price of salt that he shall gain immense sums; and, in order to
throw on another the public odium which this monopoly must
excite, he has in hand a man born for executing such enter-

282

prises : this is Don Pedro Mexio, one of the richest gentlemen in Mexico, and perhaps the most audacious of mortals.

" I esteem his lordship," pursued Don Juan, "and cherish his glory and honor too much to applaud his design when he communicated it to me. I combated it, like a sincere friend and zealous servitor; but although the Count commonly listens to me and follows my advice, I can tell you there are occasions like this on which he will not be contradicted ; he is determined on executing his project, whatever may be the consequence of it." Thus spoke my father-in-law, and then asked what I said to this project. " I say," replied I, " that it makes me tremble, and that it may have consequences very disagreeable for his Excellency and for us."—" That is what I feared," replied he, " and I am much mortified that I cannot prevent them." Salzedo and I, then, disapproved of this enterprise, and we were in despair when we beheld preparations making for executing it. I will detail in what manner the undertakers of it commenced this work of iniquity. The reader will see by the event the truth of the proverb, *la codicia quebra el saco.**

Don Pedro Mexio, according to the agreement made between the Count and him, bought up all the salt he could find for sale in the country, and filled the stores which he had hired with that intention. By this means salt grew scarce, and became every day dearer. Don Pedro then beginning to sell his own, daily augmented the price, so that the poor began to complain and the rich to murmur ; and so much the more, as both classes knew what to think of this dearness. They did not confine themselves to plaints and murmurs. A petition was presented, in the name of the people in general, to the judges of the Chancery, demanding that salt should be reduced to its former price : but the Viceroy, who was at the head of these judges, of whom the greater part dared not be of an opinion different from his, gave them to understand that this dearness would not last long, and that they must have patience. Thus, no one having the boldness to oppose his avarice, Mexio was suffered to continue his plunder at his ease.

At last the people, tired at seeing no end to the monopoly, implored the assistance of the Archbishop, setting forth in a memorial to his lordship, that he ought to interpose his pastoral

---

* Covetousness bursts the bag.

authority to preserve his flock from the tyranny of Don Pedro. The pastor, touched with their distress, or to speak more justly, urged by a secret hatred to the Viceroy, seized this opportunity for mortifying him, under the specious pretext of solacing the people. He resolved to employ the censures of the Church against Mexio, knowing that this would be indirectly attacking the Count. This violent prelate was named Don Alonzo de Zerna. He was the son of a hidalgo of New Castile. He had obtained, I know not how, the archbishopric of Mexico, which is worth sixty thousand crowns of rent; and, proud of the possession of so rich a benefice, he thought himself at least equal to the Viceroy.

Don Alonzo, to vex his enemy, excommunicated Don Pedro, and fixed his excommunication on the doors of all the churches, that no one might be ignorant of it. Mexio only laughed when he was informed of it. He derided the Archbishop, and to let him see how little value he set upon his excommunication, he continued to sell his salt, and even raised the price. This boldness did not fail to irritate the impetuous prelate, who, on his side, listening to and following nothing but his own boiling humor, pushed his resentment so far as to interdict divine service.

Nothing is more considerable in New Spain than this interdiction. It is, as one may say, to sound the tocsin to apprise the people that the house of the Lord is on fire: for, from the moment it is published, the doors of the churches are closed; no more masses, no more prayers are said in them; it is a general suspension of all the ecclesiastical functions. Rightly to conceive the importance of this formidable censure, it must be known that there are more than a thousand priests in Mexico, both regular and secular, who subsist only on masses, which they say at a dollar apiece, which daily amounts to more than a thousand crowns; and this the excommunicated person has to pay.

Don Pedro, rightly judging that the Archbishop wished to ruin him, by rendering him odious to the people, and perceiving besides that they began to insult him in the streets, lost part of his firmness, and retired to the palace to entreat the Viceroy to protect him, since after all he had only complied with his orders. On this the Count de Gelves sent the greater part of his servants to tear down from the doors of the churches the excommunication and interdiction papers, which were there put up. He then caused the superiors of convents to be told that he ordered them to open their churches and perform masses, under penalty for disobedience. But the monks replied, that on this occasion it appeared to them they ought rather to obey their pastor than the Viceroy. On their refusal, his Excellency called me and said: "Don Cherubin, go immediately to the Archbishop, and tell him from me that I order him to revoke his censures."

I repaired in haste to the archiepiscopal palace, and made known my commission to the prelate, who told me bluntly, that he could not do what the Count commanded until Mexio, the disturber of the public peace, should have previously submitted to the Church, and reimbursed the priests in the sums which he had been the cause of their losing. I wished to represent to his irritated lordship that he did not reflect it was disobeying the king to refuse submission to your orders; but the furious Don Alonzo haughtily interrupted me. "Hold your tongue, my friend," said he; "I have no need of your remonstrances. I know what I owe to a Viceroy who makes so bad a use of his power, and who would deserve to be treated like Don Pedro." I did not deem it seasonable to reply, whatever mind I had to do so, and retired for fear of being myself excommunicated.

The Viceroy, who was scarcely less violent than the Archbishop, was transported with rage when I informed him what the prelate had said to me; and, giving way to his first impulse, called the captain of his guards. "Tirol," said he, "I order you to go and seize the person of the Archbishop, in whatever place he may be, the immunity of the Church itself not being worthy of respect on this occasion. Conduct this priest to Vera Cruz, and place him under the castle guard, until he can be embarked for Spain."

Whilst Tirol was assembling his people to execute the order of his Excellency, the Archbishop was apprised of it. He immediately left the town, and took refuge in the suburb of Guadaloupe, accompanied by several ecclesiastics. He there made out himself an excommunication, which he charged one of his priests to have stuck up on the door of the cathedral. Then, having learned that he was pursued, he took refuge in a church, where he had the candles lighted on the altar, and dressed himself in his pontifical robes, too fully persuaded that in this state no man would dare to lay his hand on him.   But he was soon undeceived.   Tirol, at the head of his people, entered the church ; and having respectfully approached the prelate, begged him to hear read the king's order, of which he was the bearer, and to submit to it quietly, to avoid scandal. Upon this our Archbishop began crying out that the privilege of the church was violated, and took all his priests to witness the outrage that was done him.   Nevertheless, after having stoutly declaimed against the Viceroy, he took off his habiliments, and gave himself up to Tirol, who immediately conducted him to Vera Cruz.

CHAPTER V.

OF THE MELANCHOLY CONSEQUENCES WHICH AROSE FROM CARRY-
ING OFF THE ARCHBISHOP OF MEXICO—THE VICEROY IS OBLIGED
TO RETIRE TO THE MONASTERY OF THE CORDELIERS—DON
CHERUBIN, HIS WIFE, AND HIS FATHER-IN-LAW RETIRE THERE
ALSO—DON CHERUBIN SETS OUT FROM MEXICO.

DON JUAN and I were afflicted at this seizure of the Archbishop, foreseeing that it would have disastrous consequences.
We had spies about, who rendered us an exact account of all
that was said in the town, and we had reason to judge by their
reports that the inhabitants did not approve of the conduct
which the Count had pursued, and even that they pronounced
him in the wrong.

We soon learned that the ecclesiastics, above all, were animated against his Excellency; that they diffused among the
people a spirit of revolt, and excited the Creoles, the Indians,
and the Mulattoes, the secret enemies of the government, to
begin the sedition. Insensibly the number of the malcontents
increased to such a pitch, that it seemed the whole town had
taken part against the Viceroy. His servants could not appear
without exposing themselves to insult. Even Salzedo and myself had our share in the hatred of the people, who imagined,
doubtless, that we had a part in the monopoly of salt. In
short, everything announced approaching sedition, which the
return of Tirol to Mexico caused to burst forth. The first who
raised the buckler was a priest, who, seeing this captain passing
on horseback through the market-place, took it into his head to
cry out, "There goes the man who dared to lay his impious
hand on the minister of the Lord."

At the voice of this priest, the populace were roused. They
assembled and pursued Tirol with stones as far as the palace,
where he, fearing a general insurrection, ordered the gates to be

287

closed. The precaution was not unnecessary, for the affair became serious. In less than a quarter of an hour there were in the square more than six thousand persons of all conditions, who, loading Tirol with abuse, began crying, as in emulation of each other, that he ought to be exterminated.

Hitherto the seditious had only made a noise; and the Viceroy believing that to appease them he had only to send and request them to retire to their houses, assuring them that Tirol had escaped from the palace by a back gate, charged me with this commission, the honor of which I would willingly have yielded to another, and of which I, notwithstanding, acquitted myself boldly enough for a man who exposes himself to be stoned, which I expected to happen to me; for, having shown myself at a balcony, for the purpose of addressing the mutineers, I saw a shower of missiles fall around me, of which happily none took effect. As nothing but blows were to be gained by preaching reason to these madmen, I wisely retired, and, by my abrupt retreat, avoided the fate of the Emperor Montezuma.*

Things did not rest here. Some priests having joined the party, irritated the fury of the malcontents, some of whom being armed with fusees, began firing at the windows, and made the balls whistle about the palace, whilst others with levers began battering down the wall to gain admittance. During five or six hours which this tumult lasted, a page and two of the Count's guards who appeared at the balconies with their carbines to return the fire of those without, had the misfortune to perish, after having themselves brought down some of the seditious. We should have made a great carnage among them if we had had some pieces of cannon; but there were none, either in the palace or the town, the Spaniards having no apprehension of being attacked by foreign nations.

In default of cannon, the Count de Gelves ordered the royal standard to be displayed on the balconies, and the trumpet sounded to call the inhabitants to the succor of the king, of whom he was the representative. This was unavailing, since no one of his friends or the officers of the Chancery came to his assistance. However, the night approached, and the mal-

---

* This prince was killed by the blow of a stone, as he was addressing his subjects from a balcony to induce them to lay down their arms.

contents awaited it with impatience to increase the disorder. As they had observed that the gate of the prison could easily be forced, they burst it open, or rather the jailer opened it to them. They set the prisoners at liberty, who joining them, assisted them to set fire to the prison, and burn a part of the palace. Then the principal inhabitants, fearing that the town would be reduced to ashes, came out of their houses, and, for their own interest, appeased the populace. They got them to extinguish the fire; and but for that, Mexico would have had the same fate as the city of Troy.

But if they had authority enough to prevent the mob from burning the palace of the Viceroy, they had not the power of preserving from pillage all that nobleman's effects. A part of his furniture was carried off, and, to secure the safety of his person, he was himself obliged to take refuge with his wife and son in the monastery of the Cordeliers, who were the only monks not among the number of his enemies. These fathers assigned him a commodious lodging enough in their convent, which is of vast extent. This consisted of the apartments belonging to the provincial of the order, who was not at that time in Mexico. It was a large *corps de logis*, which contained several suites of apartments very small and very plainly furnished, excepting where his reverence slept. For this last it was composed of five or six rooms, and it may be said of it that nothing was there seen which spoke of religious poverty.

Salzedo, Blanca, and I joined the Count in the convent the same night. His lordship's principal domestics and our own also came there; and, in short, we were all provided with lodging, some well, some ill. On the morrow, at the break of day, my lord sent for my father-in-law and myself to deliberate with us on what was to be done in this melancholy conjuncture. " There is no other course to take," said Don Juan, "than promptly to send a man of spirit and confidence to the Duke de Olivarez to inform him of this revolt; and I do not think you can make choice of a person better calculated for executing this commission than Don Cherubin."—" I am of your opinion, Salzedo," said the Count: " Don Cherubin must immediately set out for Madrid: it is impossible to use too much haste."

The Viceroy employed the whole of the day in preparing despatches for the Court, and giving me instructions; and on the morrow I took the route to Vera Cruz, with a *valet-de-*

19

chambre and a lackey. I left his Excellency, the Countess, Don Juan, and my wife in the convent of the Cordeliers at Mexico; and making all possible haste, arrived at Vera Cruz, where I learned that the Archbishop Don Alonzo de Zerna had sailed for Spain two days before. As there is always in the harbor of this town a vessel prepared for the service of the Viceroy, I embarked on board it without loss of time, and set sail for Cadiz, where I arrived after a short and successful passage.

CHAPTER VI.

I HAD no sooner set my foot on shore in Cadiz, than hastening to traverse Andalusia and New Castile, I was speedily at
Madrid. I flew immediately to the prime minister, who gave
me audience the moment my arrival was announced to him. I
delivered to him the despatches with which I was charged. He
read them with the attention which they deserved, and seeing
the Count de Gelves stated that I could instruct him in all the
circumstances of the revolt, he failed not to demand from me
an ample detail. I obeyed him, like one who was well prepared
with his story. I will in good faith confess, that in my relation
I did as much disservice as I could to the Archbishop Don
Alonzo. I painted him in the blackest colors, and finished by
throwing on the arrogance of this prelate all the blame of this
fatal event.

The Duke de Olivarez read in full Council the despatch of
the Count de Gelves, and all considered the affair important.
It was judged absolutely necessary to punish the most guilty of
the rioters, in order to confirm in their duty the other provinces
of America, the which, seeing themselves with regret under the
yoke of Spain, might be tempted to follow the bad example of
the Mexicans. It was decreed in Council that Don Martin de
Carillo, a priest and inquisitor of Valladolid, should be sent to
Mexico in quality of commissioner, to take the necessary infor-

mations, with power rigidly to punish some of the principal in-habitants, for not having pressed forward at the sound of the trumpet to range themselves under the royal standard. They resolved also to change the officers of the Chancery, for having seen the Viceroy in danger without taking the slightest step to bring him out of it.

With regard to the Archbishop Don Alonzo, it was in vain for him to solicit at Court : not one of the Council would under-take his defence, so much did they consider his conduct deserv-ing of censure. They even deprived him of his rich benefice to make him Bishop of Zamora, a small diocese of four thou-sand crowns a year. It was in a manner from a bishop be-coming a miller; but it was still thought that the Court showed sufficient consideration for the house of Zerna.

The prime minister, who was troubled at the sedition of the Mexicans, did not retain me long at Madrid. He speedily sent me back with a despatch for the Viceroy. I returned to Mexico with Don Martin de Carillo, whose arrival spread terror through that city. The citizens, feeling themselves for the most part culpable, were in dread of punishment. Everybody judged that the Court would make an example, and every one was trem-bling for himself or for his friends. But they were quit for their fear : Don Martin reassured them by declaring to them, on the part of the King, that his Majesty, choosing rather to listen to his clemency than his justice, accorded them a general amnesty.

This declaration produced an admirable effect. The people, who everywhere change like the wind, were touched with the kindness of their sovereign, and cried : " Long live our good King Philip! long live the Count de Gelves, his minister !" There might be seen those same rioters, who would have mas-sacred this nobleman, running in crowds to fetch him from the monastery of the Cordeliers, and conduct him to his palace with acclamations and excessive demonstrations of joy.

The Viceroy, who hitherto had not left the convent since the time he had taken refuge in it, seeing he could now with im-punity show himself in public, returned home, where (what afforded him an agreeable surprise) he found everything in the same order he had left it when he went to the monks; for, by the greatest good fortune in the world, the gentlemen who had had power enough over the populace to calm their fury and make them extinguish the fire, had, at the same time, had the precaution of having the palace doors guarded by the mutineers themselves, forbidding them to plunder, lest there should come orders from the Court which might make them repent it.

I forgot to say, that when, on my return from Spain, I was giving an account of my journey to my lord, he asked me one question. " How did the Duke de Olivarez receive you ? " said he ; " how do you consider him disposed towards me ? " —" He gave me a most gracious reception," replied I ; " and as far as one can guess the mind of this minister, he appears full of esteem and friendship for you. Moreover, I can tell you that I heard him pronounce your eulogium in terms "—— — " So much the worse," interrupted the Viceroy with precipita- tion ; " that makes me suspect him, as does also the letter you have brought me from him. This letter is too flattering not to alarm me. I do not know, but I have an idea that he wishes to put the Count de Serralvo in my place, and I do not think I am influenced by a false presentiment."—" You deceive yourself, perhaps," said I ; " and the Duke rather thinks of prolonging your government."—" I dare not," said he with a sigh, " I dare not flatter myself with such a hope. I expect no other than orders to recall me to Court."

In effect, three months after, there arrived from Madrid a courier, who placed in the Count's hand a packet from the Duke de Olivarez. The prime minister informed him that his Majesty, wishing to have him near his person, appointed him to one of the principal employments in his household, and had just named the Marquis de Serralvo for the Viceroyalty of New Spain. The Count de Gelves, then losing the hope of being continued in his post, took his part with a good grace. He now thought only of returning to Madrid with all his wealth, and of making preparations for his departure. On our part, Don Salzedo and I prepared to follow him with our small effects, which amounted to the worth of two hundred thousand crowns. By this it may be judged how much his Excellency carried off. Finally, we set out from Mexico ; and it may be said that the day of our departure we presented a spectacle to the Americans, which gave ample scope for their curses. The wags, at seeing two hundred mules loaded with bales of goods, made themselves a little merry at our expense, and we repaired with their money to Vera Cruz.

We now awaited in this town the arrival of the new Viceroy,

to embark on board the vessel in which he should arrive. As soon as he disembarked, the Count and he had a conversation together. During two days they held repeated conferences on the affairs of New Spain ; after which they separated with more politeness than friendship, one of them proceeding, meagre enough, to Mexico, and the other returning well fattened to Madrid.

CHAPTER VII.

IN WHAT MANNER THE COUNT DE GELVES WAS RECEIVED AT
COURT—HIS VISIT TO THE PRIME MINISTER—THE DUKE DE
OLIVAREZ MAKES HIM GRAND EQUERRY—OF THE COURSE TAKEN
BY SALZEDO AND DON CHERUBIN—ONE BECOMES STEWARD AND
THE OTHER SECRETARY TO THE DUKE DE GELVES.

WE now set sail for Cadiz, and if we had met on our way
some large vessel from Algiers or Salee, as occasionally happens, the rencounter would have been fortunate for its crew;
but we had the happiness of completing our voyage without
meeting any ship of unfavorable omen. Arrived at Cadiz, we
remained there no longer than was necessary to put ourselves
in a state for proceeding to Madrid, to which we proceeded by
easy journeys. We alighted at the Hotel de Gelves, in the
Square of Servada, near the Church of Our Lady of the Peace.
It is not the best in the town, but it is commodious, and we
found ourselves more comfortably lodged there than we had
been with the Cordeliers in Mexico.

On the morrow after our arrival, the Count went to wait on
the prime minister, by whom he was received with distinction.
He took him into his closet, and embracing him in a manner
which displayed esteem and friendship, " You doubtless," said
he, "think that it is I who desired to put the Marquis de Serralvo in your place; but learn that you are mistaken. If you
have not been continued in your post, you have nobody to
blame but yourself; it is your own fault. All the Council were
no less unanimous in blaming your conduct than that of the
Archbishop; and as that prelate had been punished, they have
deemed it necessary to punish you also, in order to satisfy the
Mexicans, who have the affair of the salt at heart.

" I dared not," pursued the duke, " undertake your defence;
far from doing so successfully, I should but have incensed the

Council against you.   But if I have not been able to get your government prolonged, I have at least obtained the King's consent to your filling the place of Grand Equerry, and this ought to console you for the loss of a place which has not been unproductive to you during five good years." The Count de Gelves, mistrustful as he naturally was, took the minister's word; and imagining that he owed him nothing but thanks, vowed an eternal attachment to him, and became one of his best friends.

The Duke then conducted him to the King, to whom he said, on presenting him: "Sire, I bring you one of the most zealous of your servants, and of all Viceroys him who has perhaps best known how to make your royal authority respected in the Indies.   He comes to thank your Majesty for having honored him with the office of Grand Equerry, with which he is so much the more pleased, as it will procure him every day the happiness of seeing his master." The young monarch gave the Count de Gelves a reception of the most flattering kind; and, as he was very curious, did not fail to ask him a number of questions about the Mexicans, and, among others, the following.   "Count," said he, "is it possible that among the Indian women, there are any sufficiently attractive to merit the notice of Europeans?" Our Viceroy reddened at this question, imagining that his Majesty asked it with a malicious motive; and to reproach him for his taste for the blacks. "Sire," replied he, a little agitated, "there are some among them who may be looked upon without horror; but after all, the prettiest of them ceases not to be a disagreeable object to eyes accustomed to the beauties of Madrid." If the Countess de Gelves had heard her spouse talk thus, I believe she would not have answered for his sincerity.

The Count de Gelves having entered upon his office of Grand Equerry, augmented his household by the addition of several officers, though he had before a number sufficiently large, and spared nothing to make a figure at Court becoming his rank.   As for Don Juan Salzedo and myself, we begged that we might be allowed to quit him, and establish ourselves as private gentlemen in Madrid, having, thanks to his bounties, enough to support us honorably; but this nobleman refused his consent to our wishes.   "My friends," said he, "let us not separate.   I have too much accustomed myself to the pleasure of being in your society, to consent to your leaving me. Condescend, I entreat you both, to take a part in my affairs. Let one take upon himself the administration of my rents, and the other be my secretary."

It was impossible to refuse, and we accordingly yielded to his solicitations, and accepted the offices for which he had designed us. Rich as I was, I would willingly have foregone this secretaryship; but I accepted it out of compliance to Salzedo, who, being too much attached to this nobleman to refuse his request, was very glad at the same time to retain near him his daughter and his son-in-law.

CHAPTER VIII.

I HAD another reason also for acting as I did : Blanca had
paid her court so well to the Countess de Gelves, that she had
become her favorite. The Vice-Queen would have been in
despair at losing her ; and my wife on her side, delighted with
this lady's attention to her, repaid her with the most lively
and sincere attachment. This was the principal reason which
induced me to sacrifice to the Count the pleasure of being
master of my time.

As my employment did not occupy me much, I led an agreeable life enough. I went almost every morning to the King's
levee, to see the concourse of noblemen who came to pay their
court to the monarch ; and in the evenings, in St. Jerom's
Meadows, I had the pleasure of contemplating the ladies,
among whom I found many who appeared to me fully equal to
those of Mexico. One day, as I was just going out to this
promenade, I was not a little surprised at meeting Toston in
the street. " How ! " said I, " is it thou ? what art thou doing
in Madrid ? I thought thee in Alcaraz."—" My dear master,"
replied he, " you know that our projects do not always succeed.
I had proposed to return to my own county, there to pass with
Blandina the rest of my days ; but Heaven has not thought
fit to allow me that satisfaction. I happened to meet at Cadiz
a Gabriel Monchique, who carried off my wife, without my
having it in my power to oppose him."

" Is it possible," cried I, " that this misfortune has happened
to you ? Recount to me, I entreat you, in what way it occurred."
—" It is a recital," replied Toston, " which I shall make you
in a few words. On disembarking at Cadiz, it happened to

me for my sins, that I went to lodge in St. Francis Street, at
the sign of the Pelican. There was in this inn a young English
captain, whose ship was at anchor in the bay. As soon as
this rogue saw my wife, he was taken with her; and forming
the design of robbing me of her, it was thus he executed his
intentions: he took good care not to betray his passion, lest I
should suspect and disappoint him by changing my lodging,
which I should not have failed immediately to do; and he
affected so sober a demeanor that I was astonished at it. 'Is
it possible,' said I to myself, that a naval officer of that nation
should be so mild and polished in his behavior?' This captain, whose name was Cope, offered me a thousand little civilities, without appearing to take the least pleasure in seeing
Blandina, and, in fact, scarcely looking at her at all. I was
the dupe of this manœuvre. I treated him with corresponding
politeness, and we supped together the first day, as familiarly
as if we had been the best friends in the world.

"Cope, while at supper, asked me from what part of Spain
I came? 'From the village of Alcaraz,' replied I, 'near the
province of Murcia.'—'That is fortunate,' replied the Captain.
'I am to sail in two days from Cadiz for Alicant. I will land
you, if you please, at Vera, which I believe is not far from your
home.' I accepted this offer with joy, imagining that I could
not do a better thing, and returning thanks to Heaven for having afforded me so fine an opportunity of speedily returning to
my own country. I therefore carried Blandina two days after
on board Cope's vessel, and he received us with manners so
open, that I congratulated myself on having made such a good
acquaintance. 'Come,' said he, when we were fairly out at
sea, 'let us live well. I have an ample supply of all kinds of
eatables, and some excellent wines. Let us be always at table:
that is the way to prevent the voyage from growing tedious.'

"You know my weakness," continued Toston; "I love a
sprightly life. Captain Cope had no difficulty in persuading
me to drink, and I got as drunk as a German. While I was
in this pretty state, he had me carried on shore by his sailors,
who left me on the ground extended at my length. There I
lay in a profound sleep; from which awakening about sunrise,
and seeing nothing of a vessel, I had abundance of leisure to
reflect upon the politeness of the Englishman, whom I cursed
with so much the more reason, as he had in his power, together

with my wife, the coffer in which was all my money, and I was left with only twelve pistoles, which I had in my pocket. I thought myself still fortunate that the sailors had not robbed me even of this sum, to repay themselves for the trouble of bringing me on shore, and abandoning me to Providence.

"Not knowing where I was, nor in what direction to turn my steps, I followed at hazard a path which conducted me to the village of Alzira near Gibraltar, from whence I proceeded to the city of Ronda. I here reposed myself two or three days: then, instead of going to my parents, to whom I was no longer in a state to be useful, I took the route to Seville on a hired mule, with a resolution to go again to service, if I could meet with a master who would suit me. I did not find one, and judging that it was at Madrid I must seek him, I took the road to this town, where I have again become a lackey, after having been *valet de-chambre* to the son of a Viceroy."

"I am sorry for you, my friend," said I, when Toston had finished his recital, " and I am still more concerned for the misfortune of Blandina. What an unhappy adventure for her! I can conceive the grief with which she must have been seized when sensible of the treason of the perfidious Cope. Perhaps she actually died of regret."—"No, no," replied Toston, "Blandina is not a woman to imitate those heroines of romance, who, when they find themselves in the clutches of corsairs, choose rather to die than yield to their desires. I know very little of the Creole, or Cope had not much trouble in prevailing on her; and I do not believe, between ourselves, that he wanted any Colibri powder to triumph over her virtue."

"What is it you tell me?" cried I. "By this account it appears that Blandina is a jilt."—"Past a doubt," replied Toston. "I suspected it at Mexico; but she converted my suspicions into certainty on our voyage to Cadiz. There was among the passengers a young cavalier, who amused himself with ogling her; and I remarked more than once that she replied to his advances with glances of invitation. In a words she is a little personage, the care of whom would have given me abundance of trouble at Alcaraz, where the young cavalier, are distinguished for sprightliness and gallantry. In fact, I can console myself for the loss of her. I would only that Captain Cope had made a fair division with me—that he had returned me my coffer and kept my wife."

"I am very glad, my child," said I, "that you are not more afflicted at this loss of your wife ; and, in reality, you have not much cause to be so, if Blandina be such a character as you have described. As to my part, you may be assured that I shall refuse nothing which may contribute to replace you in a state for performing your journey to Alcaraz, in a manner agreeable with your wishes. I am also persuaded that Don Alexis will not fail to pity your misfortune. He may probably take you back into his service ; but perhaps you may be too much attached to your present master to be desirous of leaving him."—"Oh, as to that, indeed I am not," cried he, laughing. "My master," who is called Don Tomas Trasgo, is an original without a copy : he is a visionary who is possessed with a most laughable kind of fantasy. He says, and actually believes, that he has, like Socrates, a familiar spirit. 'My friend,' said he, when he engaged me in his service, 'know that a geni has taken a liking to me, and instructs me in all I am desirous of knowing. I have an interview with him every morning, and I warn you to retire when you hear us in conversation with each other ; for he chooses to speak to me without witnesses.'

"In reality, one morning when Don Tomas was in his closet, I heard him talking aloud, and imagined that he had some person with him. Not at all ; he was entirely alone. He was speaking to and answering himself, conceiving that the geni was actually present." I burst out laughing at this most extraordinary portrait, and finally quitted Toston, after desiring him to come to me on the following day ; which he failed not to do, perfectly persuaded that he would be retained in the family. He first caused himself to be announced to the Countess, who did not refuse to see him. He related to her his misfortune, and she appeared to pity him, though in reality she cared very little about the matter. "My friend," said she, "we will do something for you. It is enough that you have eaten our bread, for us not to abandon you in your distress. Go and see my son : I doubt not that he is well disposed to serve you."

Don Alexis, to whom I had already spoken of him, and whom I had engaged to take him back into his service on the same footing as before, received him very well. "Welcome back, Signior Toston," said he, with an air of raillery, "how do you get on with Captain Cope? He played you, I think, rather an ugly prank, but have patience; perhaps he may send you back both your wife and money. Perhaps he has only served you so for a joke, and to try how you would bear it. Tell me the whole; I like to hear you tell comic stories; you acquit yourself admirably."

" And why, sir," said Toston, " would you have me relate a story which you are already acquainted with, and which I cannot recollect without renewing my grief? "—" Never mind," said Don Alexis, " you must absolutely tell it me; the detail from your own mouth will amuse me exceedingly." Toston, to satisfy him, complied with his wish, to the infinite diversion of the young lord, who interrupted him more than once to give way to the most immoderate laughter, as if the adventure had been the most pleasant in the world.

When Don Alexis was tired of diverting himself at Toston's expense, he resumed his gravity, and said: " Well, my friend, to console you for the loss which has happened to you, come and resume the employment about my person which you had before your marriage. Be again my principal valet, and the depository of my secrets. I shall soon give you something to do," added he. " I have a conquest in view, and I have need of your advice to enable me to complete it." This speech highly rejoiced Toston, who that very day quitted Don Tomas and his geni, to reside in the Hotel de Gelves.

CHAPTER IX.

BY WHAT ACCIDENT TOSTON MET WITH HIS WIFE, WHEN HE HAD
ENTIRELY FORGOTTEN HER—ACCOUNT WHICH SHE GIVES OF
THE CIRCUMSTANCES ATTENDING THEIR SEPARATION—HER
JUSTIFICATION—FRESH CHANGE WHICH THIS RECITAL PRODUCED
IN HIS HEART—HIS AFFAIRS ASSUME A BETTER ASPECT.

DON ALEXIS, as soon as he rose the following morning, said
to Toston: "You must know, my friend, that I have been
making a very interesting acquaintance. I will tell you how.
One morning when I was walking all alone on the Prado, I
saw coming out of a house a lady covered with a veil, whose
noble and majestic air prepossessed me in favor of her quality.
She took two or three turns in the walk ; and, perceiving that
I was advancing towards her for the purpose of surveying her
more conveniently, retired towards the garden to disappoint my
curiosity ; but, whether my haste prevented her, or whether she
was desirous of giving me time to join her, I was at the garden
gate before her.

"'Madam,' said I, saluting her with respectful politeness,
'I must be extremely deficient in gallantry, if, meeting a person so charming as yourself, I omitted to testify to her the
pleasure which the sight of her affords me.'—'Signior Cavalier,'
replied the lady, 'you are extremely liberal with your soft say-
ings. Far from refusing adoration to those ladies who are
worthy of it, you have very much the air of one who offers it
to those who do not deserve it.' Upon this I answered, the
lady retorted, and we separated after a tolerably long conversation."

"Have you ever seen her since that time?" asked Toston.
"No," replied the young Count, "I have not, although I go
almost every day to the Prado. If she have not come out of
the garden since that day, it is in all probability because she

is desirous of proving me, for, without vanity, I think she is
satisfied with me."—" I cannot doubt it," said Toston; " a
cavalier of your figure is sure to please. What is her name?"
—" That I do not yet know," said Don Alexis. " She forbid
me to inquire who she was; and, for fear of displeasing her, I
dared not take any measures to obtain that information."—
" The devil!" cried Toston, " you are a rigid observer of ladies'
commands; but you must know that they sometimes find it
convenient to be disobeyed. Faith, sir," continued he, " you
are still far enough out of your reckoning. I see very well that
I must have a hand in this business, or it will turn out badly
for you. Let us go directly to the Prado, and show me the
garden from which you saw your princess come out: I require
nothing more. Don Alexis took him at his word, and led him
immediately to the garden gate.

When they had got there, Toston said to the young Count:
" Leave me here, and return home; I will speedily rejoin you,
and be assured that I will inform you who are the inhabitants
of this house: we will then take our measures." Upon this
assurance Don Alexis returned to the Hotel de Gelves, and his
confidant seated himself near the garden gate, waiting until
perhaps some servant might come out, from whom something
might probably be learned.

He had been there more than an hour, when all at once the
gate opened, and presented to his astonished eyes a young
person whom he took for Blandina; as, in effect, she it was
who appeared before him. She immediately recollected him,
and running to him transported with joy, threw herself into his
arms and fainted. The bad opinion which he then had of the
virtue of his wife prevented him from sharing in the delight
which she experienced at this meeting. He thought that it was
a pretence, and that the hussy was perhaps rather sorry than
pleased at having found him. He did not, however, neglect
the necessary assistance, and when she had recovered the use
of her senses, " Is it you, my dear husband," cried she, " is it
you whom I behold? you whom I thought at the bottom of the
sea? you whom I believed to be numbered with the dead?"
So saying, she embraced her husband with manifestations of
affection with which he would have been most sensibly touched,
if he could have believed them to be sincere; but instead of
yielding to this with a good grace, he gently repulsed his wife,

saying, in a serious tone : " No tricks, Blandina. Wherefore all these transports of joy, or rather all these false demonstrations of affection ? Are you not about to tell me a finely invented tale, to make me believe that Cope foolishly relinquished his prey ? No, no, do not believe that I am credulous enough to place confidence in your assertion. Either you yielded to the solicitations of this captain, or were at least forced to submit to his violence."

" Toston," replied the Creole, " listen to me without interruption ; I may appear before you without a blush. If my honor was exposed to imminent peril, know that it was proof against it. I will give you a faithful account of what took place between Cope and me, and you shall see that instead of betraying you, I carried my love of virtue even farther than Lucretia herself.

" You recollect," continued she, " that perfidious supper which the Englishman gave us on board his ship. While you were drinking with him I retired to a small cabin, which he told me had been prepared for you and me, and slept there tranquilly till the morning. When I awoke, and found that you were not by my side, I arose to seek you. At this moment Cope entered my cabin, affecting an air of the most excessive sorrow. ' Madam,' said he, ' you behold me in despair ; an accident has this night happened for which I shall never be able to console myself. Signior Toston, your husband, while leaning over the side in his drunken state, fell into the sea and was drowned. I shall never get over this fatal accident.'

" At this melancholy intelligence I made the vessel resound with my piercing shrieks. I tore my hair, I was like one mad. In the meantime our captain, acting the part of a man in deep affliction, sighed, groaned, and seemed desirous of giving encouragement to my grief. He had during two entire days the patience to hear me utter my complaints and witness the flowing of my tears, without venturing to say anything to me in the way of consolation. On the contrary, the traitor irritated my affliction by the regret he manifested at having taken you on board his vessel. He bitterly accused himself of having been the cause of your death, with which he was incessantly reproaching himself.

" But on the third day he deemed it time to throw off the mask ; and assuming a different character, ' Beautiful Blandina,'

20

said he, ' it is no doubt melancholy to lose a person whom one loves; nevertheless, whatever reason we may have to mourn such a loss, it is better to listen to the voice of consolation than obstinately to persist in grief.   After all, at your age the death of a husband ought not to give you so much uneasiness. Young and handsome as you are, you cannot long be in want of a new one: I am even sensible of having one to propose to you; it is myself.   If you have no aversion to my person, I am a candidate for the preference.'   I thanked Cope for the honor he intended me, and rejected without hesitation his proposal. Besides that he was not at all to my liking, I was at that moment in a disposition very unfavorable for a lover.

" The Englishman employed five or six days in making love to me very politely; but judging that by so doing he was taking the longest method of arriving at his object, he changed his courteous manners for the rough deportment of a sailor; and I confess I then had need of all the resolution with which Heaven inspired me, to be able to resist him.   Fortunately for me, my opposition, instead of increasing his violence, caused it to relax.   He suddenly passed from love to contempt.   He ceased to torment me, and, viewing me with a disdainful air, ' For a servant maid,' said he, ' methinks you are extremely inexorable.   Recover yourself, my love; I will not be indebted to violence for a victory which I despise.'   At the same time he caused me to be taken on shore by two of his sailors, whom he ordered to convey me to the nearest village, and there leave me.   The men did not fulfil with perfect honor the commands of their captain.   They did indeed conduct me to the village, and then abandoned me; but, considering that I was a woman whom, in all probability, they would never see again, they carried off with them the trunk in which our money was deposited.

" I had happily about thirty pistoles in my purse, and a large diamond on my finger.   With such recommendations, assistance may be found in any place inhabited by man.   The master and mistress of the village inn to which I had gone, took an interest in my misfortunes.   I had no sooner related to them my story, than they pitied and offered me their services, with abundance of execrations on the captain and his sailors.   I inquired in what part of Spain I was.   ' You are in the village of Molina,' replied my host, ' on the coast of Grenada, between Marbellin and Malaga, about twelve leagues from the city of Antequerra, to which I will, if you please, myself conduct you.'—'You will oblige me,' replied I, ' my design being to go again to service in the family of some person of quality, if I can there meet with any such who will engage me.'—'You need not doubt it,' replied he; 'Antequerra is a populous town, in which there are resident a great number of nobility. I have acquaintance there,' added he; 'I know, among others, a good lady who was formerly duenna in a house where I was servant: I will take you to her, and I am sure she will very soon obtain you a place.'

" I accordingly set out with my host for Antequerra, and as soon as we arrived there, he went to see the old governante. He told her my unhappy story, at which she was so much affected that she said to him : ' Bring this unfortunate woman hither; I offer her bed and board; I espouse her interest; I take her under my protection.' To suppress superfluous circumstances, this lady placed me with Donna Leonora de Pedrera, daughter of a gentleman of Antequerra, with whom, after the death of her father, I came to Madrid, to the house of Donna Helena de Toralva, her aunt, whose sole heiress she is.

" I have nothing more to tell you," continued Blandina. " I have given you an account of my conduct, and I think you ought to be satisfied with your wife."—" I am perfectly so," said Toston, " and things being as you have related, it would be unjust in me not to be so. I will confess to you (excuse my candor) that I should not have expected so much resistance on your part; but, between ourselves, the delicacy of Cope astonishes me greatly; and it must be confessed, that if your tale be truth, it does not look very much like it."—" I am perfectly of your opinion," said she ; " my escape was a narrow one."— " That I am sure of," returned the husband ; " I was seized during your recital with a cold sweat, from which I have not yet recovered. Independent of the risk you ran from this captain, you were scarcely exposed to less danger from the two rogues of sailors who conducted you to Molina. You were very lucky that they only robbed you of your money.

" Come, then, my dear wife," continued he, " let us say no more about it. We at last have met together again, with the exception of property, much in the same state as on our departure from Cadiz. God be praised for it. What ought to

console us, my child, is, that we are about to make a new
fortune. The Count de Gelves has returned from the Indies
with immense riches, and has been made Grand Equerry.
Don Cherubin de la Ronda, my old master, is his secretary,
and I am once more *valet-de-chambre* to Don Alexis. As this
young nobleman advances in age, he is furnished with more
money for his pleasures ; and as I have become administrator
of his money, my place will be every day growing better."

"Is Don Alexis still gallant ? " inquired Blandina. "More
than ever," replied Toston : "he is at present enamoured of a
lady whom he saw come out of this garden a few days ago, and
this lady may very probably be Donna Leonora, your mistress."
—"It is she herself," said the Creole ; "for she told me that
one morning a cavalier accosted her in the walk, and that she
had a long conversation with him."—"And how," asked Toston, "did she appear to be affected by the said interview ? "—
"Not unfavorably," replied the attendant. "I assure you that
if he had another, he might succeed in obtaining her affections.
Moreover, I can tell you, I do not know whether my mistress
be not afraid of again seeing this cavalier ; she has not gone
out of the garden since the day she spoke to him, most likely
lest she should meet with him."

"Fine news for my master," cried Toston ; "I will carry
them to him forthwith. I bid you not adieu, my dear Blandina,
my faithful love; we shall see each other again. Remain
with Donna Leonora ; the interest of Don Alexis requires it.
Second with your good offices the endeavors we are about in
order to win her." After this conversation this couple separated, protesting on both sides that they pardoned fortune the
trick she had played them, in consideration of the pleasure they
experienced in meeting each other again.

CHAPTER X.

Toston, before he returned to Don Alexis, came to inform
me that he had found Blandina; and after relating to me all
the conversation he had with her, " Well, sir," said he, " what
do you think of that ? Do you think that all she told me about
Captain Cope is to be taken literally ? As for me, I tell you
candidly, I do not believe it at all."

" It is true," replied I, " that one may doubt it without being
thought particularly incredulous ; however, the best thing a
husband can do in such a case, is to persuade himself that his
wife has told him the truth : that is what I would do to rid myself of all uneasiness. But, my friend," said I, " you made no
mention in your story of the child which Blandina must have
brought into the world since she quitted Mexico."—" Ah, truly,
you bring it to my recollection," cried Toston ; " my wife forgot to tell me, and I to ask anything about it. When I see her
again I will not fail to inquire about this child, though nature
does but half speak to me in his favor."

Toston here took leave of me, saying : " Will you allow me,
sir, to leave you now, in order to wait on Don Alexis, who
doubtless is expecting me with impatience ? I shall delight
him with the information I got from Blandina about his mistress."—" Go, run, my lad," said I ; " when agreeable news are
to be carried to a lover, one cannot make too much haste. I
doubt not but Don Alexis will speedily place Donna Leonora
de Pedrera among his conquests, since he has the advantage of
your assistance and your wife."

As soon as Don Alexis saw his confidant, he hastily advanced towards him. "Well," said he, "have you discovered who are the inhabitants of the house from which I saw my divinity come out?"—"I have done more than that," replied the valet; "I have learned the name and quality of your goddess. She is called Donna Leonora de Pedrera, the daughter of a gentleman of Antequerra, after whose death she came to Madrid, and is now living at the house you saw with Donna Helena de Toralva, whose niece and sole heiress she is."—"You have become very well informed in a short time," said the Count. "And I have not yet told you all," returned Toston; "I know, from good authority, that she has taken a liking for you."

"Hey! how the deuce," cried Don Alexis, "have you been able to discover even the sentiments of this lady? who could have given you the information?"—"Chance," replied Toston; "that served me much better than my own ingenuity, if indeed it may be called a service, to have brought my wife unexpectedly to my eyes."—"What say you?" cried the young lord in surprise; "have you found Blandina?"—"Yes, sir; Heaven had the kindness to restore her to me, without my having asked the favor," replied the confidant, "and, what is very fortunate for you, she is waiting-maid to Donna Leonora."—"You enchant me," cried Don Alexis, in transport, "by informing me that Blandina is in the way to serve me. I am sure she will not refuse to carry a note from me to Leonora."—"No, I will answer for that," said the valet; "and you may assure yourself of all the services which depend upon her interference."

The young Count de Gelves, profiting by the opportunity which thus presented itself of declaring his love to Leonora, wrote a letter which he charged Toston to get delivered to the lady. The confidant went accordingly on the following morning to the Prado, and there found his wife awaiting him at the garden gate. He accosted her with a gallant and affectionate air. "My dear Blandina," said he, "before we enter upon my master's affairs, permit me to converse with you a moment about my own. Yesterday, if you remember, you did not say the least word about the child with which you were pregnant when fortune separated us near Gibraltar."—"Alas!" replied she, "my poor girl died almost in the moment of her birth, a short time after I had entered into the service of Donna Leonora, and her death would have been infallibly succeeded by my own, had not the most particular care been taken of me; but my mistress, who had conceived an esteem for me, omitted nothing for my preservation. I owe my life to her; and, out of gratitude, have vowed eternal fidelity to her."

" You have done very properly," replied Toston; " such a mistress well deserves your love. Does she know that you have met with your husband? "—" I have informed her," replied Blandina, " and she has permitted me to introduce you to her, which I will do immediately: follow me." So saying, she ushered him into the garden, and pointing to two ladies who were walking there, " These," said she, " are Donna Leonora and her aunt. Let us join them, and give them to see that I have not married a man ill made or destitute of merit."

Thus saying, she took him by the hand and conducted him to the ladies, and accosted them jocularly. " Ladies," said she, " here is the husband whom I thought dead, and for whom I shed so many tears. Look at him, and tell me if you do not think he was worthy of them."—" Assuredly," replied Donna Helena ; " husbands less agreeable are often deeply lamented." Here Toston made a profound reverence to the lady who had spoken, and cast his eyes towards the ground in respectful silence. " They are both well matched," said Leonora, " and I am very happy that Heaven has again brought them together."

Donna Helena, desirous of making Toston talk, said : " You are, then, with the Count de Gelves? "—" Yes, madam," replied Toston ; " I have the honor to be principal *valet-de-chambre* to Don Alexis, his only son."—" And you are apparently satisfied with your situation ? " said she. " Very much so, madam," replied he ; " my master is a perfect cavalier : I know no fault he has. Although he is young, he possesses consummate prudence ; he is wise without assuming the air of a Cato, and sprightly without being a coxcomb ; he is a model of a young nobleman.

" Besides a thousand good qualities," he continued, " with which Don Alexis is endowed, he will one day be possessed of considerable wealth; the Count, his father, having amassed great riches in the government of New Spain. Happy the high-born maiden for whom his hand is destined."

Thus pronouncing his master's eulogium, Toston, the adroit Toston, carefully examined Leonora, and conceived that she took pleasure in listening to him, although she affected to hear him with an air of indifference. This observation encouraging him to go on in praise of Don Alexis, he drew so flattering a picture of him, that Donna Helena could not help saying: " But, my friend, you go beyond bounds, you exaggerate. It is not possible that the young Count de Gelves should have all the merit you ascribe to him."—" Pardon me, madam," replied he with great effrontery, " he is a most accomplished person, an epitome of all that is amiable."

At this part of the conversation they were interrupted by a page, who came to deliver a billet to Donna Helena. She read it, and, as it demanded an immediate answer, she went into the house in order to prepare it. Leonora followed her, leaving her attendant with her husband in the garden. This couple finding themselves alone, gave way to the laughter which they could no longer repress. " It must be confessed," said Blandina, " that you are admirably expert in drawing handsome portraits; but, between ourselves, they are not exactly likenesses."—" I confess," replied he, " that I have flattered Don Alexis a little, but I do not think that that has done much harm. I am sure that your mistress is enamoured of my master already ; for, though she did not tell me so, I dare be sworn you have told her that Don Alexis is the cavalier with whom she con- versed one morning on the Prado."—" It is true I did so," said Blandina, " and I will again privately speak to her about him. I will ascertain her mind, and inform you of it to-morrow."— " Very well," said Toston ; " and if by chance you find the lady disposed to receive a letter from Don Alexis, here is one containing a most elegantly conceived declaration of his love, and in which I have myself had a hand." Blandina took charge of the letter, telling her husband that he might assure his master of all the good offices she could render him with Leonora. Hereupon they separated, with a promise of meet- ing again on the same spot the following morning.

They did not fail in their appointment. " Victory ! " cried the Creole, " victory ! I have spoken with my mistress about Don Alexis, and given her much about the same description of him as you did yesterday. She at first dissembled; but I at- tacked her in so many ways, that she could not help discover- ing her sentiments. 'Yes, my dear Blandina,' said she, 'I love Don Alexis; I have thought of nothing but him since the day I saw him at the garden gate; and all the good I hear of him serves to complete his conquest.'

" Let us come to my master's letter," interrupted Toston;
" did Leonora read it ? "—" With avidity," replied the attendant, " and we both admired it. You had reason to say that
you had put your hand to it: I very plainly perceived it. This
letter has made an impression on my mistress."—" Bravo ! "
cried the enraptured *valet-de-chambre*, " nothing could go better.
Let us go forward with this business ; let us contrive a nocturnal meeting between these two lovers. They want nothing more
to make them irretrievably in love with each other. Get Donna
Leonora to walk to-night in the garden, and I will bring Don
Alexis thither : they will have a long interview, after which they
will breathe of nothing but marriage."

CHAPTER XI.

BLANDINA approved of the design, which was accordingly
executed. The young Count de Gelves, accompanied by his
confidant, arrived between eleven and twelve o'clock at the
garden gate, and was presently admitted by Leonora and her
servant, who were awaiting their arrival impatiently. Don
Alexis respectfully accosted the lady. She received him in the
same way; and, after some compliments of pure politeness on
both sides, they began to assume the tone of love. Toston and
his Creole seeing them about to enter upon a tender conversation, retired to talk in private of their own affairs.

Love, which renders hours so long to lovers when separated
from the objects of their affection, by way of equivalent, causes
them to pass with rapidity enough when they are together. It
was already day ere Don Alexis and his mistress thought of
separating. It was necessary for the confidants to remind them
of it; a charge which was willingly undertaken by Toston, to
whom the night had not appeared so short as to his master.
The two lovers parted at last, with a promise of meeting again
on the following night.

This interview, just as the husband of the Creole had pre-
dicted, increased their passion. As soon as Don Alexis was
out of the garden, he began to extol the charms of Leonora,
particularly her wit; and did nothing but repeat the same thing
all the morning. His mind was occupied the whole day with
the pleasure he was to derive from his assignation in the even-

314

ing, but, before he could enjoy the promised happy interview, he was constrained to go through one of a less agreeable nature. The Count, his father, taking him after supper into his closet, addressed him thus : " My son, I have an affair of the greatest importance to communicate to you. The prime minister, in proof of the sincere friendship he entertains for me, has told me that he wishes to have you married, and give you a wife from his own hand."

Don Alexis, at these words, was much embarrassed, and remained unable to speak. " How then l " said his father; " does matrimony frighten you ? Ah l when you shall know the person whom the minister proposes for you, you will feel no repugnance to fulfilling his wishes." The young Count, a little recovered from his embarrassment, replied : " My lord, I shall implicitly obey you in all things ; but deign to allow me to represent to you that I feel an aversion to marriage "——

" You are deceiving me," interrupted his Excellency, " you dissemble. I see well whence proceeds this dislike to the match proposed; your heart is otherwise engaged. Formally entrapped by some she-adventurer, you would make a point of honor of remaining faithful to her."

" No, my lord," replied Don Alexis, " I burn not with an unworthy flame. I love, it is true, and I seek not to subdue my love; but the object of my affections is not of a rank to make me blush for the sentiments she has inspired. If you will, I will inform you of her family "—— —" I dispense with the information," again interrupted the father ; " I have no curiosity to know the lady. I order you to renounce her. I will have no other daughter-in-law than her the minister has offered me ; and know that she is a person who joins to extreme youth and beauty a noble origin and large estate. Go," added he, " go and consult Don Cherubin de la Ronda, your governor, on the subject : I am persuaded that his advice will be conformable to my intentions."

The young lord immediately left the closet without making any answer, but instead of coming to me, he thought it more to his purpose to go and consult with Toston. He informed him of the violence which his father wished to do to his feelings ; and, after having complained of this tyranny, " My friend," said he, " what must I do to preserve my faith to Leonora ? how am I to rid myself of this embarrassment ? "—" Sir," replied

Toston, " the thing is not easy. My lord, your father, as you
know, is confoundedly obstinate : he has resolved that you
shall espouse the person proposed by the minister, and he will
not be turned from his purpose. But it is not yet time to
despair. Let us first exert our ingenuity. Dissemble ; affect
to consent to this marriage, while I invent some expedient to
break it off."—" Ah, Toston," cried Don Alexis at these words,
which appeared in some sort to flatter his love with a dawn of
hope, " if you can accomplish that object, there is nothing
which you may not expect from my gratitude. Haste," added
he, " let us fly to the rendezvous ; I will inform Leonora of the
misfortune which threatens us, will assure her of using every
exertion to avert it, and renew the oath I have made never to
be united to any one but her."

They both returned to the garden, where Leonora and her
attendant amused themselves, while awaiting their arrival, with
conversing on the good qualities of Don Alexis. Blandina,
who knew him best, was praising him to the skies. The lovers
gained the verdant enclosure in which they had passed the
former night, and the married pair retired to another spot,
where Toston thus addressed Blandina : " My child, life is a continued succession of good and evil, of joy and of grief. Yesterday, for instance, we came here gay as larks, and now we arrive
as melancholy as owls."—" Hey ! what cause for grief can there
be ? " said his wife ; " have you heard any bad news ? "—" The
most distressing possible," replied he ; " they want to separate
Don Alexis and Donna Leonora." At the same time he gave
her an account of what had passed between the Count de
Gelves and his son.

Blandina was penetrated with grief at this recital. " You
have cause," said she to her husband, " you have cause to distress yourself ; nothing can be more mortifying than what you
tell me. Unhappy Leonora," continued she, apostrophizing her
mistress, " what a clap of thunder will this be to you ! But is
it then impossible to avert this evil ? Will Toston, who possesses wit and ingenuity, make no exertions to preserve the
lovers from the frightful destiny which is preparing for them ? "
—" Pardon me," said he, " I am beating my brains for some
expedient to prevent it, but I will confess to you that I can
think of nothing with which I am satisfied."—" An idea this
moment presents itself to me," said the Creole, " and I think

it ought not to be rejected : you are not ignorant that the Countess loves her son most affectionately; do you think that nothing may be done in that quarter? "—" Quite the contrary," replied Toston; " I embrace the idea. I will go to-morrow to the Countess's levee, and request a private interview with her: I will give her a pathetic description of the situation in which Don Alexis is placed, and may perhaps be able to soften her, so that she may interest herself in favor of him and Leonora."

While this conversation passed between the confidants, the two lovers were promising, swearing to each other an affection which should be proof against every obstacle that fortune could place in their way. In these sentiments they parted. The young nobleman proceeded with Toston, who on the way informed him of his design to try if, by his eloquence, he could prevail on the Countess, his mother, to protect his love. " I approve of your project," said Don Alexis, " and to render it the more efficacious, I will myself accompany you. I will throw myself at the feet of my mother, and embrace her knees, while you shall plead for me : I am sure that we shall gain our point."

In this opinion, they determined on having recourse to the measure proposed ; and this is the detail of their success. They found the Countess de Gelves at her toilet. As soon as she saw her son and his confidant, she sent all her women out of the room, and first addressing herself to Toston, " My friend," said she, " in what disposition has my son come hither ? has he still any repugnance to linking his destiny with that of an amiable person offered him by the prime minister of the kingdom ? "—" Madam," said Toston, " my master has vowed implicit obedience to your will; he is ready to do whatever you order him : but if you oblige him to marry the lady you propose, you may calculate on losing your only son."—" Yes, mother," said Don Alexis, throwing himself at her feet and kissing one of her hands. " Toston has told you the truth : if you force this wife on me against my inclination, you will kill me."— " This is a strange thing," cried the Countess. " Is it possible to become prejudiced in so high a degree, against a person one has never seen? Wait till you have been introduced to the lady in question, and then, if you find her disagreeable, I have enough of a mother's fondness to oppose a union which must destroy your happiness, although in marriages among persons of our rank, the want of beauty is not thought a matter of much importance. But," added she, "if I may believe the description I have heard of this lady, she is extremely handsome."—"Though she were more lovely than Venus," said Toston, " let us, if you please, madam, say no more about her. Love has been beforehand with the minister, by presenting to us a kind of divinity with whom we are enchanted."

"She must, indeed," said the Countess, "be possessed of a most uncommon beauty to have made so strong an impression. Does her birth correspond with her charms? I fear that on that side she has reason to complain."—"Oh, no, madam," returned Toston, " she is a young lady of quality. Leonora de Pedrera owes her birth to a gentleman of Antequerra, and is, besides, niece to Donna Helena de Toralva."

The Countess no sooner heard these last words, than she burst into so violent a fit of laughter as completely disconcerted Toston and her son. "Madam," said the astonished young lord, "pray be kind enough to acquaint me with the cause of this extraordinary merriment; do you suspect us of wishing to impose on you with regard to Leonora's quality?"—"Let me laugh without interruption," cried she, and redoubled her mirth, while the master and the valet, not knowing what construction to put on such behavior, stared at her in stupid silence.

At length it pleased Heaven that her laughter should have an end; and when she had resumed her gravity, "Don Alexis," said she, " do not alarm yourself any more: you will not be obliged to renounce your beloved Leonora, for it is she herself whom the prime minister has destined for your wife. Donna Helena de Toralva is related to the Duchess de Olivarez, and it is these two ladies who have caused this match to be proposed to the Count de Gelves by the Count Duke. Had I not cause to laugh?" pursued she. "Do you not think this a very droll adventure?" She then again burst into laughter, while her son and Toston now followed her example. The young lord and his confidant then returned transported with joy, and proceeded immediately to Donna Helena's, where they found everybody in a good humor, the report of the approaching marriage of Donna Leonora and Don Alexis having already transpired there. To sum up all in a few words, the nuptials were solemnized a few days after, with abundance of demonstrations of joy, both at the Hotels de Gelves and de Toralva.

CHAPTER XII.

OF WHAT TOOK PLACE AFTER THE MARRIAGE OF DON ALEXIS DE
GELVES—TOSTON'S JOURNEY TO ALCARAZ, AND HIS RETURN TO
MADRID—DON CHERUBIN HAS THE SATISFACTION OF HEARING
GOOD NEWS OF DON MANOEL AND HIS FAMILY.

DONNA HELENA, at whose house the wedding took place, loved her niece as much as if she were an only daughter; and, wishing not to part with her, this kind aunt gave up the half of her mansion for her accommodation. The first care of Don Alexis was to reward Toston for having contributed to his happiness. Not satisfied with making him a present of three hundred pistoles, he appointed him his steward, a post less considerable from what it was worth at that time, than from what it was likely to be at a future day. Leonora was not less generous to Blandina, who, more sensible to her mistress's friendship than to her own interest, was attached to her from heart and inclination, an extraordinary thing in a waiting-woman.

One morning Toston, coming to me, said: "Signior Don Cherubin, I am going to take leave of you, and receive your commands. I shall set out in two days for Alcaraz, to gratify my desire of again beholding the authors of my existence. Don Alexis, my master, has allowed me to take this journey, on condition that I return in two months."—"My child," said I, "the desire by which you are actuated is laudable, and it is right that you should be gratified; but when you shall have passed a few days with persons so dear to you, return quickly to Madrid. You know the inconstancy of men of high rank; you may lose your place, which is one that cannot fail to conduct you to a considerable fortune."—"Oh, never fear," said he, "that I shall be much diverted by the company of my old friends. I have already imbibed the spirit of the Court; I could not live in the country."—"And by what conveyance,"

said I, " do you design going ? "—" On one of the best horses
in our stables," replied he ; " and followed by a lackey from
the house, who will be dressed in the livery of Gelves, and as
well mounted as myself. The steward of a great house must
not travel like a beggar." In effect two days after, Toston set
out upon an elegant horse, followed by a lackey in brilliant
livery, and charged with despatches from me to my brothers-in-
law.

During his absence, some changes took place favorable for
the house of Gelves. Don Alexis, having paid assiduous court
to the Count Duke de Olivarez, was fortunate enough to please
him so much, that that minister got him appointed Gentleman
of the King's bedchamber ; which was the most sincere testimony of regard which he could possibly give him, it being the
disposition of his Excellency to place no one near the person of
the monarch but such as he could repose confidence in himself.
This was not all : Donna Leonora became at the same time
maid of honor to the Queen, through the interest of the Lady
Olivarez, who was *camarera mayor ;* * so that Toston, at his
return, found his master and mistress holding a rank at Court
higher than when he left them.

The impatience of this new steward to give me an account
of his journey would not permit him to visit his wife, nor even
to wait on Don Alexis before he had come to me, with a haste
expressive of his regard. It was not without emotion that I
saw him enter my room ; and, not knowing what he might have
to tell me, I asked him tremblingly if his news were calculated
to please or distress me. " I bring you," replied he, " no news
but what are good : Don Manoel and Don Gregorio are in the
most perfect health, as are also their wives. These ladies, who
are still very lovely, have enlarged the family : your sister, besides Francillo and the two daughters she had, she has now
another son, who is at nurse ; and her friend, besides the boy
she had immediately after her marriage, has brought Don
Manoel two sons in less than twenty months. All these children," added he, " both male and female, are in wonderful good
health, and are extremely genteel. Your daughter, among the
rest, is as beautiful as the day."

" All this gives me pleasure, my friend," replied I ; " but tell

* Principal Lady of the Bedchamber.

me, I entreat you, how my sister and my brothers-in-law listened
to the recital which you, of course, gave them of my adventures.
Did they appear to be much interested in my fortune ? "—
" Assuredly," replied Toston : "they asked me a thousand
questions, and I found it no easy matter to answer all their
questions, each of them interrogating me in turn, and sometimes
all together. But when I related to them the meeting with
Monchique, and the manner in which he told us he had seduced Donna Paula, my auditors began to shed tears, particularly the ladies, who, seeing your wife fully justified, bitterly
deplored her misfortune. They then questioned me about
Donna Blanca: they asked me what was her character ; and
they had room to judge from my replies, that of all the favors
Don Juan de Salzedo has conferred on you, that of giving you
his daughter was not the least.

" I have now no more to do," added Toston, " than to deliver
to you the despatches of which I am the bearer, from your
family ; and then allow me to quit you in order to wait upon
my master. I shall see whether my absence has injured me in
his esteem."—" No, my child," replied I, " you will find Don
Alexis just such as you left him. I took care, during your
absence, to preserve you in his good graces. I have also some
good news to announce to you ; the King has honored this
young nobleman with the post of Gentleman of the Bedchamber, a thing which will be to the advantage of your steward-
ship."

I also informed the steward that Donna Leonora was in attendance on the Queen. " Good ! " cried he, full of joy ; " my
wife is then at Court : that will fix me in Madrid."—" I hope so,"
said I, " and that you will never again be troubled by the desire
of seeing your own country."—" Oh, sir," said he, " that is all
over, I have bid it an eternal adieu. I went there, as you
know, only to see my father and mother ; I found them both
dead and buried. I have shed over their graves the tears
which were due to them, and now I am entirely detached
from the place of my birth." So saying, he delivered me his
despatches and left me.

CHAPTER XIII.

ALTHOUGH the Count de Gelves had, as has been stated, brought immense wealth from the Indies, he had affected, through avarice and policy, not to imitate other viceroys on their return from their governments. He appeared in the streets with but few attendants, and paid his visits, it may be said, without noise, and in a manner too modest for a governor of Mexico. With regard to the presents he had made both to the King and the infants Don Fernando and Don Carlos, they are not worth speaking of, as they consisted only in some orna- ments of feathers, and such like trifles. For this reason, the public, who sometimes censure without cause, did not applaud his magnificent humor.

This nobleman was not ignorant of what was said of him in the world, and said to me one day: " I had rather pass for a miser than expose myself to ruin by a display which would only serve to excite envy. The example of the Duke de Os- suna, who had just died in prison, ought to afford instruction to viceroys. This great man would probably still have been alive, if he had not had the imprudence to make his entry into Madrid with a pomp more suitable to a sovereign than to a governor who is recalled in order that he may give an account of his administration ; if he had not made such rich presents to the Court, and if, in fine, he had not exposed his wealth to the eyes of his enemies, and those who were envious of him. Perhaps you never heard of this pompous entry. I must give you a detail of it, less to excite your admiration at its magnificence, than to show you the ostentation of the Viceroy of Sicily and Naples.

" Four trumpeters, with twelve Neapolitan and twelve Sicilian guards, began the march. The maitre d'hotel on horseback, and twenty-four mules with gold embroidered housings, conducted by twenty grooms, preceding three litters and three superb carriages belonging to the Duchess de Ossuna, which the maitres d'hotel of herself and her son followed, with twenty horses led by as many grooms. After these came the major-domo of the Duke, accompanied by twelve pages on horseback dressed in the Spanish, and twelve halberdiers in the Sicilian costume. Then Don Juan Telles, at the head of thirty Spanish, Neapolitan, and Sicilian gentlemen, all richly dressed in the Hungarian fashion, and mounted upon valuable horses. Afterwards the Duke, in the same costume, appeared in a most magnificent carriage with Donna Isabella de Sandoval, his daughter-in-law, having four tall footmen at each door, and twenty halberdiers' followed by thirty carriages full of relations and friends, without counting six other in reserve. Finally, this indiscreet and silly procession was concluded by a crowd of officers, pages, and Turkish slaves.

" It was thus," continued the Count de Gelves, "that the Duke de Ossuna entered Madrid, amid the acclamations of an immense concourse of spectators attracted from all parts by the sight. You may well conceive that such an entry did not diminish the number of his secret enemies; and, to add to his indiscretion, he exposed during three days at his house, to the curiosity of the public, the riches he had brought from Italy, taking a foolish pleasure in showing them to the Spaniards as spoils taken from the Turks, and glorious monuments of the victories he had obtained over those infidels. I have not, therefore, done ill," added the Grand Equerry, " in pursuing a conduct the reverse of his, especially as I have come from a government in which all the world suspects me of having acquired immense wealth. By my modest entry, I have disappointed the envy which I should not have failed to excite by an air of greater opulence.

CHAPTER XIV.

OF DON MANOEL'S ARRIVAL AT MADRID—THE EXTREME JOY
WHICH THAT CAVALIER AND DON CHERUBIN FELT AT AGAIN
MEETING AFTER SO LONG A SEPARATION, AND OF THE AR-
RANGEMENTS WHICH THEY MADE NOT TO PART AGAIN.

Toston had not been a week returned to Madrid, when one
morning, while I was writing in my closet, I was informed that
Don Manoel de Pedrilla had arrived. I immediately started
up to receive a man who was so dear to me. We held each
other long in a mutual embrace, and both testified by tears
rather than by words the joy we felt at meeting. The remem-
brance of Donna Paula affected us at first, and we could not
refuse our tears to the memory of that innocent adulteress, in
spite of the grief which she had caused us both; but we
speedily passed from grief to joy, and began to converse about
our family. "We have some lovely children," said Don Manoel.
"If Toston has given you a faithful description, he must
have told you that Donna Teresa, your daughter, is excessively
pleasing, and that my son, Don Ignacio, is a pretty boy. As
for your nephew, Francillo, who is now called Don Francisco
de Clevillente, he is no longer a child; he is a well-grown
cavalier, and fit to serve the King.

"Having spoken of the children," continued Don Manoel,
"let us now speak of their mothers. Ismenia and Donna
Francisca are still pretty women. I am more fond than ever of
one, and Don Gregorio has for the other an attachment, the
warmth of which seems daily to augment."—"You delight me,
my friend," interrupted I, "by informing me that you all four
live in such a perfect union. Why can I not go and partake
the sweets of your society?"—"Why, what hinders you?" said
Don Manoel; "are you not master of your actions?"—"No,"
replied I, "the Count de Gelves will not allow my father-in-law

to leave him ; and he, a slave to that nobleman's desires, has the complaisance to sacrifice to him the inclination he has to repose himself after his long labors. On my part, gratitude and friendship bind me so strongly to Don Juan, that I make it a point of duty not to abandon him."—" In these sentiments," said Don Manoel, " I recognize my friend. So then, it seems, our ladies and myself must be disappointed in the hope we had formed of having your company and your wife's."—" I should ask nothing better," replied I, "than to pass with them and you the rest of my days; but you see what obstacles are opposed to such a desire."—" Well," said Don Manoel, after having reflected some minutes, " since we cannot engage you to leave Madrid, I must prevail on our ladies to come and settle here : this is what I shall propose to them, and I think they will readily comply with my suggestion."

" I applaud the idea," said I, " and hope that they may be pleased with the project. If you be eloquent enough to persuade them to that, I will undertake to hire a house sufficiently large to contain our whole family : I am in a situation to do so, and even to defray all the expenses of living in it. Return, then, as speedily as possible to Alcaraz ; persuade, if you can, the ladies to come and live in Madrid, and bring them hither with you. We shall lead a delicious life together. In our house will be seen only joy, and there the best of company will be met with."

Don Manoel, impatient for the arrival of so happy a period, hastened home ; but, before his departure, I introduced him to Salzedo, who received him in a manner that enchanted him. Nor was he less satisfied with the civilities he received from my wife, who, looking upon him as my best friend, thought she could never treat him with sufficient attention. When we parted, he said to me : " Don Cherubin, I admire your happiness. You have entered into a most amiable family. You have a wife worthy of your tenderness, and a father-in-law who merits all your devotion to him. I shall describe these two in such terms to Clevillente and our ladies, as will contribute no little towards the success of my design."

CHAPTER XV.

I HOPED, or rather I entertained no doubt, that Pedrilla would be able to prevail on the ladies, and was already employed in looking out for a house; but it was an unnecessary trouble, as I shall presently explain. One day after the Count de Gelves had been with the prime minister, he closeted himself with Salzedo, and addressed him thus: " Don Juan, you will be surprised at what I am about to say to you. I have just been with the Count Duke, with whom I had a conversation which turned upon yourself. ' Count,' said he, ' you have about you a man who is not agreeable to me; it is Don Juan de Salzedo. He was secretary to the Duke de Lerma, and afterwards to the Duke de Uzeda; in a word, he is a creature of the house of Sandoval. I think this is saying enough to induce you to get rid of him. However, as I know that you esteem him, and that he deserves to be recompensed for the services which he has done the state, the King appoints him Corregidor of the city of Alcaraz, in New Castile.'

" You know this minister," continued the Grand Equerry. " You know that he is full of whims, and that he is absolute in anything which he commands. If, consulting only my own friendship for you, I were to refuse compliance on this occasion, I must make up my mind to break with him forever; a thing which might be disastrous to me in its consequences, as it is dangerous to have for an enemy a minister who governs both the monarchy and the monarch.

" I am sorry to lose you," continued he, " but we must separate. You see plainly it is a matter of necessity."—" My lord," replied Salzedo, " to that I have nothing to reply. It

326

would not be right that you should quarrel for such a trifle with a man who has everything in his power. With regard to the place with which it is intended to honor me, I could well do without it, being, thanks to your bounty, in a situation which leaves me nothing to wish for. Nevertheless, I have reasons for not refusing it. Alcaraz is a city well known to my son-in-law, and there reside his family and friends, who will do everything to make me happy. Since I must depart from your Excellency and from Madrid, it is a consolation to be sent to the very place in Spain which I would choose in preference to any other."—" I am glad it is so," said the Count; " if I regret parting with you, at least I shall have the satisfaction of believing that you are comfortable."

After this interview, Don Juan came to me. " Here are some great news," said he, recounting to me at the same time what had been just said to him by the Grand Equerry. He then asked me what I thought of it ? " It appears to me," replied I, " that the Count is terribly afraid of losing the good graces of the minister, and that he seems well disposed to sacrifice everything to his fear. As to the rest, we ought to rejoice at this event. We have been a long while attached by complaisance alone to this nobleman ; and since he himself affords us the opportunity of quitting him with honor, let us avail ourselves of it without ceremony. Let us go and join my brothers-in-law. They will be delighted, as will likewise their wives, at seeing their society increased by three persons whose company will be so far from tiresome. I will, if you think fit, send this day an express to Don Manoel, to apprise him that, having been gratified by the King with the post of Corregidor of Alcaraz, you are going to set out in order to take possession of it. He will be charmed with this intelligence ; for I am sure he would rather bid us welcome in Alcaraz, than come to us in Madrid."

My father-in-law had no sooner informed me that he was ready to follow me, than I despatched a courier to Pedrilla, to inform him of our design ; and, in the letter which I sent him, I pointed out that we should pass near Cuença.

CHAPTER XVI.

Don Juan de Salzedo, after having returned thanks to the
prime minister, and taken before the King the necessary oaths,
set about the preparations for his journey, which were speedily
finished. Our departure from Madrid was not quite so splendid
as the entry of the Duke de Ossuna; but it had, notwithstanding, an air of opulence that did us honor. Three litters, one
of which was filled with the Corregidor, *plena ipso*, the other
with my wife and myself, and the third with two waiting-women,
followed twelve mules laden with our effects, and ornamented
with fine sounding bells. Add to this five or six servants
mounted on very handsome horses, of which the Grand Equerry
had made us a present. Indeed, our equipage somewhat
resembled that of a Viceroy who is going to take possession
of his government.

We proceeded by short stages to Cuença, where we found
Don Manoel, who had been awaiting our arrival two days.
After a thousand embraces on both sides, this cavalier informed
us that the moment he received my letter he had set out to
Cuença, whence he proposed to conduct us to the village of
Bonillo, to a farm which belonged to him there, and in which
he had left his wife, with my sister and Don Gregorio. The
more speedily to reach this farm, we hastened to resume our
journey; and there, in effect, we met Clevillente and the two
ladies, who were no less anxious to see me than I to embrace
them. Here were embraces and compliments in abundance.
" Signior Don Juan," said my sister to Salzedo, " what pleasure

328

is it to me to see a gentleman to whom my brother has so many
obligations! But of all the good you have bestowed on him,
that which I most value is having united his destiny to that of
this amiable child." At these words, she threw her arms round
the neck of Blanca, whom she had already more than once
embraced. Ismenia was equally lavish of her caresses to my
wife, who, not to be behindhand with these ladies, returned
them kiss for kiss.

On the other hand, Don Manoel, Salzedo, Gregorio, and
myself were acting nearly the same scene. We had all four,
for about an hour, nothing but a confused conversation inter-
mingled with embraces.

After this we resumed our gravity, and the new Corregidor
had every reason to be satisfied with the obliging discourse
which was addressed to him both by ladies and gentlemen.
He told me two or three times in private that he was charmed
with my brothers-in-law, and still more with their wives, who
appeared to him, he said, to have the manners of princesses.
I was inwardly amused with this idea, for I thought at the
moment of the source whence they derived these airs of grandeur.
We rested some days at the farm, where, by Don Manoel's precaution, nothing was wanting; and at length repaired to Alcaraz,
which is only about five or six leagues distant.

Our equipage dazzled the eyes of the citizens of Alcaraz.
"This is not," said one, "our poor defunct Corregidor, whose
whole equipage consisted in two old mules."—"No, faith,"
said another, "it is not an ordinary Corregidor, but a Viceroy
who is sent us." The populace, who had placed themselves
under arms, the more honorably to receive their new magistrate,
now gave a triple discharge of musketry. We alighted at the
Hotel de Pedrilla, where we had no sooner entered, than all
the Superiors of the religious orders came to harangue my
father-in-law in Latin; who, in order to let them see whom they
addressed, replied to each in the same language, and thus gave
his visitors a favorable opinion of him. After the monks, the
nobility came with their compliments, and he replied in the
tone of a courtier.

To say the rest in a few words, he took possession of his
charge; and soon, by his vigilance, his integrity, his equitable
judgments, and his extensive information, he made the inhabitants of Alcaraz sensible that they had for Corregidor a man

capable of governing a kingdom. As he joined to his merit as a judge all the qualities of an elegant man, he gained, without difficulty, the esteem and friendship of everybody.

With such a father-in-law have I now the happiness of living, sometimes at Alcaraz, at Don Manoel's, sometimes at the castle of Elche, which is but three small leagues distant, and which we purchased with some of the Mexicans' money, or at the castle of Don Gregorio de Clevillente, whose wife agrees wonderfully well with my own, although they are sisters-in-law.

THE END.

www.ingramcontent.com/pod-product-compliance
Lightning Source LLC
Chambersburg PA
CBHW021215090426
42740CB00006B/230